MW00987638

PASSPORT

— to —

HEAVEN

PASSPORT
— *to* —
HEAVEN

———

Micah Wilder

HARVEST HOUSE PUBLISHERS
EUGENE, OREGON

Unless otherwise indicated, all Scripture quotations are taken from The ESV® Bible (The Holy Bible, English Standard Version®), copyright © 2001 by Crossway, a publishing ministry of Good News Publishers. Used by permission. All rights reserved.

Verses marked KJV are taken from the King James Version of the Bible.

Cover design by Faceout Studio

Cover photo © fotoslaz / Shutterstock; Leah Flores / Stocksy

Photo of Micah Wilder provided by Micah Wilder

Interior photos used by permission

Interior design by KUHN Design Group

For bulk, special sales, or ministry purchases, please call 1-800-547-8979. Email: Customerservice@ hhpbooks.com

Some of the names of individuals mentioned in this book have been changed to protect their annonymity.

The conversations in this book were reconstructed from the author's memory and diligently kept journals at the time the events occured.

M is a federally registered trademark of the Hawkins Children's LLC. Harvest House Publishers, Inc., is the exclusive licensee of the trademark.

Passport to Heaven
Copyright © 2021 by Micah Wilder
Published by Harvest House Publishers
Eugene, Oregon 97408
www.harvesthousepublishers.com
ISBN 978-0-7369-8287-0 (pbk.)
ISBN 978-0-7369-8288-7 (eBook)
ISBN 978-0-7369-8551-2 (eAudio)
Library of Congress CIP data can be found on p. 346.

All rights reserved. No part of this publication may be reproduced, stored in a retrieval system, or transmitted in any form or by any means—electronic, mechanical, digital, photocopy, recording, or any other—except for brief quotations in printed reviews, without the prior permission of the publisher.

Printed in the United States of America
21 22 23 24 25 26 27 28 29 / KP / 10 9 8 7 6 5 4 3 2 1

A testimony of the gospel of the grace of God,
to the eternal glory of Christ Jesus the Savior.

CONTENTS

PART 3: A GREAT REVELATION

PART 4: SET FREE

FOREWORD

SEAN MCDOWELL

I *love* this book. It has all the elements that make a great story, including conflict, drama, and courage. But there are three aspects, in particular, that set *Passport to Heaven* apart. These are the reasons I believe you will love this book too.

First, it is *enjoyable* to read. Having not read anything by Micah Wilder before, I didn't know what to expect. But I was pleasantly surprised! Micah is a wonderful writer. While this book includes theological reflections, they are presented through the lens of Micah's life story. He recounts conversations and experiences with remarkable detail and shares them with intrigue. If you enjoy a good story, this book is for you.

Second, it is *inspiring* to read. While I was familiar with Micah's story, I had no idea about all the costly challenges he had faced along the way. From the first moment he began to question the faith of his childhood, Micah endured some considerable trials from which he could have taken the easy way out. He could have folded. He could have chosen the safe route. He could have gone with the script that other people had for his life. But he didn't. And along the way, he offers some lessons that inspired me to think about *my* willingness to follow truth even when it is costly to do so. I am confident these lessons will do the same for you.

Third, it is *charitable*. We live in polarized times. Sadly, there is often minimal kindness toward people who see the world differently. And yet this book is different. Micah engages some ideas that are deeply held by people. These ideas shape the direction of people's lives. And while Micah states his beliefs with conviction, he always exudes love and kindness toward others. He doesn't set up strawman arguments, nor does he cast others in an unnecessarily negative light. Rather, he engages both people and ideas with charity. This is refreshing.

A ton more could be said about why I love *Passport to Heaven*. As I was reading it, I frequently shared some of the stories and insights with my family. Having grown up in a religious home, I could personally relate to so many of Micah's stories. And yet, whether you grew up in a religious home or no, you will relate deeply to his story as well. You are going to thoroughly enjoy it.

Because I am a professor, blogger, and podcaster, I read somewhere between 100-150 books each year. But this is a book I am going to remember and recommend for a long time.

As I said at the beginning, I love this book. I am grateful for all the effort Micah invested in writing it, and I appreciate the humility with which he shares what he has to say.

I am confident you will too.

Sean McDowell
Author, speaker, associate professor

PART 1

THE
SEEDS

CHAPTER 1

REFUGE

Beverly Hills, Florida | January 20, 2006

Though muffled and almost inaudible, Lucas' soft-spoken voice crept its way to my ears from the other side of the door: "You have a call, Elder Wilder."

Bemused by his uncharacteristic boldness, I slid back the shower curtain just enough to stick my head out and away from the droning pitter-patter of the freezing cold water. I listened intently for a moment, hoping he would tell whoever was on the phone that I was temporarily indisposed. But I could see from the shadow fretfully shifting under the door that he was still there.

After a few seconds of painful shivering calm, I surrendered to the fate that I was about to be seriously inconvenienced.

"What...a call?" I exclaimed through the rumbling of the shower. "Okay, just a minute!"

Since I had known Lucas, my timid mission companion had never even been brave enough to answer the phone, let alone appeal through a closed door. What luck that he had waited until I was fully compromised to seize an interest in whatever foolishness was taking place in the world.

I couldn't be frustrated with him, though, because Lucas was—by any metric—no ordinary missionary. My slightly stout, blond-haired, teddy-bear of a roommate was the most childlike and innocent adult I had ever come to know. In our short three weeks together, I had grown accustomed to his many eccentricities that pervaded our daily missionary life. His antics—slightly embarrassing to me at times—tested my patience and yet simultaneously grew my love for him.

Although Lucas loathed getting out of bed at daybreak (due to his affinity for staying up until ungodly hours of the night doing puzzles in his cartoon pajamas), mornings for me had always been anticipated with eagerness. I thrived on arising early and going through my morning rituals while relishing the only moments of true privacy that I was offered in life. It was during these times that, as I robotically prepared for the day, I could legitimately be lost in my own private thoughts.

In my youth, I would often enter the dense forest along the river near my boyhood home as the sun pierced the seemingly impenetrable darkness of night. Climbing my favorite tree, I would survey the land and reflect on the events of my uncomplicated life, talking to God as one would a friend. Although a far cry from the river hideaway that had become my personal sanctuary as a child, the stillness of the approaching dawn here in Beverly Hills, Florida, had afforded me much-needed time for daily intimacy with God and His Word.

Now that my life was infinitely more complex, I once again found myself perched on a precipice—no longer overlooking a forest canopy, but emotionally surveying the final days of my unprecedented mission. After twenty-three-and-a-half months, the dawn habits were second nature and had molded themselves seamlessly into the military-like routine that was quite appropriate to the ethos of our religious crusade. Feeling seasoned by now, most of my tasks were set on autopilot and had become a predictable routine.

This morning, however, I varied our tedious schedule by allowing Lucas to shower first—a concession I now sorely regretted. Because he had taken more than two hours, I not only found myself tremendously tardy, but I was also enduring the punishment for my generosity as glacial-cold water poured over my constricting back muscles. Lucas' lack of discipline had robbed me of every drop of hot water and set the entire day off kilter.

Regardless, I was looking forward to a new day of dragging my affable yet slightly narcoleptic comrade to a couple of engagements (even if it did require the aid of a few motivational tricks and treats).

"Wilder, telephone," he gently implored one more time while adding a light tap on the door.

Stepping out of the shower with my eyes stinging from soap, I reached for the phone and placed it on my shoulder. As I groped for a towel, I began speaking before the receiver was even tight to my ear.

"Good morning, this is Elder Wilder!" I said, calling upon every ounce of false enthusiasm I could muster, trying to hide the fact that I was standing there very naked and equally wet. The first words I heard sounded as if they were from a cheap radio.

"Well, good morning, Elder Wilder."

I knew that voice. I knew it *all* too well. I was hit so hard that a shock wave cascaded down my spine. Sorensen! It was my mission president[1]— my spiritual leader and the individual with the God-given authority to judge me righteously. Lucas had just coldcocked me!

"G…good morning, President," I stammered. Why on earth was he calling me? Worse, I felt as though his all-seeing eye was able to perceive my nakedness, forcing me to flush with embarrassment so deep that it must have evaporated every drop of water from my body.

Before I could recover from feeling as though I had been caught in dereliction of duty, President spoke up.

"Elder Wilder, I was wondering if you could meet with me at the Leesburg Stake Center[2] today at twelve o'clock."

As President's unexpected request sunk in, I panicked.

"Okay, President," I responded, my voice trembling, "I'll meet you then."

"I will see you at noon, Elder Wilder."

I stood in dumbfounded silence for a few moments, feeling as though the room was spinning. In an effort to relieve the nausea developing inside of me, I turned on the faucet and splashed a handful of cold water over my face. Staring at myself in the slightly foggy mirror, I tried to calm my anxiety, but couldn't help but wonder what would transpire. My eyes slowly filled with tears as I was temporarily left to the devices of my imagination and all sorts of cruel scenarios were free to play out in my mind. How had my life come to this?

"God, what's going to happen?" I pleaded. "Please, Father, don't leave me alone. Give strength to Your beloved and rescue me. What do I do?"

The Love Epidemic

As I viewed myself in the mirror with bewilderment, it was clear that I was not the same person who began this journey two years ago, and the evidence of my transformation had become more apparent than I wanted to admit. My faith was no longer rooted in this religion I still represented; rather, it was found in the fullness of God's superlative love, which I had received through His Son Jesus Christ—a love that was profoundly unveiled to me when I least expected it.

Certainly, from President's point of view, I had been infected with a frightening disease that consumed my life, thoughts, and actions. Over time, this plague had manifested itself into a dangerous threat by spreading to half of the other missionaries. In a desperate effort to combat the ever-growing epidemic, President implemented the only logical recourse he could—he quarantined me to the outer reaches of the mission boundaries less than three months ago.

Without ever being accused of any crime—or even told that I had done anything wrong—I had been demoted, dishonored, and finally exiled. Although it took time to bury the pain of my relegation, I eventually accepted my humbling fate. I was confident that the worst of my reprimands had played out already. What more could President do to me now?

Before the initial shock of my predicament had time to wear off, I paged my most trusted friend, Erik. From the time I had been caught in the devastating bowels of Hurricane Jeanne—the third of four fateful hurricanes that seemingly blew my life off its previous course—Erik had become the first person I went to when in need. Like David's faithful companion in the Bible, Jonathan, Erik was knit to my very soul in the love of Christ. He had gently and lovingly guided me to God's Word at key points during my time in Florida. He would know what to do. I was confident of that.

As I waited for my friend to return my call, I turned off the faucet. I grabbed a towel and wiped a small section of the clouded-up mirror and leaned over the sink, trying to calm my panic. I carefully approached the pitiful creature staring back at me, a pathetic doppelganger who looked confused and insecure. The fear within me was growing, and I longed for an escape as I gazed at my reflection.

Soon my mind was transported to the tranquil landscape of my youth—the thick woodlands of rural Indiana. It was there in my sanctuary on the banks of the White River that my intimacy with God was born and cultivated, and within that fertile land, I found my place of solitude from the troubles of the world. Whenever I perceived myself to be in hopeless despair or facing some imminent peril, I would run to my river hideaway—all the while pleading with God, knowing that He would be my refuge from whatever storm was threatening me. Upon arrival, I would spend countless hours on the eroding embankment and stare at my reflection in the dark and turbulent water until I felt His peace.

Now fast approaching my twenty-first birthday and no longer a child, I knew I was facing possibly the greatest plight I had ever experienced, and more than ever I needed a refuge from the oncoming tempest. Thankfully, over the past year and a half, I had rediscovered my safe harbor—not on a riverbank in central Indiana, but rather, alongside a river of living water within the Word of God.

In the last moments of my time of reflection, I pondered the comforting words of Psalm 91:1-2:

> He who dwells in the shelter of the Most High
> will abide in the shadow of the Almighty.
> I will say to the LORD, "My refuge and my fortress,
> my God, in whom I trust."

CHAPTER 2

THE CROSS

The ring of the phone snapped me out of my daydream. Hoping it was my friend, I quickly pulled on my pants as I hopped to the phone on one foot.

"Hello?" I blurted awkwardly. I had expended so many emergency reserves lately that my ability to breathe was compromised. I took in a loud gulp.

"Hey, Kid." Erik had always called me Kid from the first day I met him.

"Well, I just got off the phone with President. He wants to meet with me today at noon."

"Did he say why?" Erik asked.

"He didn't say. But it must be something serious."

Erik pointed out that in less than three weeks, my two years of service to the Church would be complete. Meeting with me now was no insignificant demand—the timing of the request was peculiar.

"Do you think somebody told him about everything that's been going on?" I questioned, pacing around the room. I couldn't seem to stay still. "What should I say, Erik? What do you think he wants?"

In an attempt to calm myself, I sat on my bed and ran my hands through my hair. Out of the corner of my eye I spotted the source of the miraculous transformation that had set my life on a new trajectory: The

Bible, God's very Word, and my most valuable earthly treasure. Peace swept over me and everything seemed to change in that moment. For the first time, I resigned myself to submit to my dilemma.

Adjacent to my Bible was a letter Erik had given to me sixteen months earlier during the height of a devastating hurricane. He had made me vow to not open it until my mission was completed. I had kept that promise and realized the day I could break its seal was fast approaching. I had been tempted many times to breach my oath, but much more so right now because perhaps therein lay the answer to my quandary. But I resisted.

The seconds ticked by as Erik and I found ourselves in an eerie silence. Then, in an apparently sudden epiphany, he spoke.

"I think this is the end," he said softly.

"The end of what?" I asked.

"The end of your mission, Micah. I was afraid this was going to happen. I didn't want you to have to go through this, but I believe there is no other way." He paused for a second. "If you are who I believe you are—and who you know you are—then you must endure this trial."

Just as I was about to respond, my mind recalled an unusual comment Erik made to my mother more than a year ago: "I don't believe your son is going to finish his mission." Naturally, my mom didn't know what to make of this declaration, but for me, the pieces of an intricate puzzle seemed to be coming together and a picture was starting to formulate in my mind.

Initially when Erik made his mysterious pronouncement, I had assumed that—if what he said were to come true—he was referring to sickness, or injury; something related to my well-being. After all, I had been plagued by unexpected health problems from the very beginning of my mission experience. However, I had never considered that the ramifications of my rebirth in Christ—which had slowly enveloped me over the course of two years until it culminated in outright astounding events over the past four days—would lead to the termination of my missionary service. I knew this radical change had set me apart from the other missionaries, but surely that wasn't grounds for sending me home...or was it?

"I had a strange feeling when you paged me that something was going to happen, and I was afraid it would affect whether you finished your mission," Erik said. "I even tried calling your parents to tell them, but no one answered. Now I understand why. This was always meant to happen."

As the overwhelming reality of my predicament was setting in, I remembered an email Erik had written me just days earlier. The contents were so puzzling that I had printed it out and placed it on my nightstand. In light of my situation, its words now took on new meaning:

> Sometimes we have to have something happen in our lives that shakes up our world for us to see what truly is important. With only three weeks left in your mission, I know that the trials will come at an even faster pace than before. It is at this time that we have to hold fast to the Lord. It is at this time that He shows Himself to us in so many different ways. Know that He will hold you up when others try to knock you down. Remember what Jesus said and store up for yourself treasure in heaven, where no man can take it from you. Your friend and brother, Erik[3]

Although I didn't want to accept the certainty of what was facing me, I vocally relented to the inevitable.

"I have a feeling after this interview everything is going to change. I don't think I'm going to be a missionary after today."

"Micah, what was that scripture I gave you to read the other day?" Erik asked.

"I can't remember. Let me go look."

I slowly stood up and walked over to my desk, my knees nearly buckling with each step. I grabbed my notebook (a rare, private niche where I had recorded—daily—nearly everything I had experienced over the course of my two-year mission) and sat down. Eventually I found where I had noted the scripture: Luke 21:12-19.

About a week earlier, Erik had called me and said that during prayer, he was inspired by the Holy Spirit to have me read that specific passage. After hanging up the phone, he sent me the rather cryptic email as a sort of afterthought. I had read the scripture, but at the moment it didn't seem pertinent to anything that was taking place in my life, so I entered it into my journal and had forgotten about it. Maybe today's activities would reveal its purpose.

"Did you find it?" he asked.

"Yeah," I said, skimming over the words.

"Well, read it to me," he insisted.

"They will lay their hands on you and persecute you, delivering you up to the synagogues and prisons, and you will be brought before kings and governors for my name's sake. This will be your opportunity to bear witness."[4]

Immediately after the words left my lips, I found myself speechless. I was beginning to perceive what might be transpiring, so I took a deep breath and kept reading with trepidation: "Settle it therefore in your mind not to meditate beforehand how to answer, for I will give you a mouth and wisdom, which none of your adversaries will be able to withstand or contradict. You will be delivered up even by parents and brothers and relatives and friends."[5]

There was stunned silence on the other end of the phone. I was now well aware that I had been shamelessly doing nothing more than speculating; we both had.

"Now I understand why I was to give to you that scripture," Erik said. "This passage isn't *about* you, Micah, but it is *for* you in this time. God has given an answer through His living Word, a pattern He has and will continue to use throughout your life. God has laid before you a blueprint of what is to take place, and now you must have faith that He will give you strength to do what He is asking. This is God's message to you of how to prepare. You need to read it again before you go."

I could feel my heart beating heavily. "Erik," I asked, "do you think this is what's going to happen to me? Could the Church really be planning to confront me for what I have discovered?"

"I wish I didn't, Micah. But this will be your time to bear witness of what God has done in your life. There is no more hiding it. This, therefore, is your test of faith. Only you can decide if it is time to take up your cross and follow Jesus Christ as the disciple that God is calling you to be. Even though you are weak, His grace will be sufficient for you. Trust the Lord. He loves you. There is nothing to fear."

Nothing to fear? Maybe he was right. Once again, I felt encouragement from my friend.

"I better get ready to leave, then," I said, not wanting to get off the phone. "I love you, Erik. Pray for me. I'm so scared. I feel weak and helpless."

"I will, Kid. The Lord is your Rock. Call me as soon as you can."

As I hung up the phone, I slumped to my knees onto the blue shag carpet and began to sob. My head was pounding and my throat was so dry that my pitiful wails came out sounding like the distant honks of a lonely Canadian goose. My ship was sinking, and I knew that the earthly consequences of my newfound faith in Jesus Christ were far greater than I could fathom. I felt afraid, broken, and alone.

Once I had poured out my tears until none remained, I slowly stood up and finished getting dressed. My hands were shaking as I tied the Church's decorative noose around my neck and completed the garb by dropping my nametag onto my suit jacket pocket—perhaps for the last time. Even though I had put on a tie and gone out nearly every day for the last two years and fought the world for the sake of my testimony, I knew this would become the greatest test of faith in Christ that I had ever been given, or perhaps would ever be given. Was I ready?

Lose Your Life

"What's going on?" I heard behind me.

Oh yeah…Lucas! I was so caught up in the moment I had not only forgotten my companion was there, but I had also overlooked how he must have felt while hearing a confusing and frightful one-sided conversation on the phone. I turned and looked into his terrified eyes.

"We have to go to Leesburg so I can meet with President," I said curtly.

"But why do you have to meet with President?"

Perceiving his anxiety, I smiled at him and put my hand on his shoulder. I spoke with as calm and soothing of a voice as I could muster, as if suddenly realizing I had just been cornered by a startled bear.

"I don't know, Luki-Bear, but you don't need to worry. Everything will be fine. I promise. This has *nothing* to do with you."

Lucas gave me his characteristic half-smile, his head tilted. I pinched him under the arm and he dropped his nervous front, chuckling and looking once again like a big, harmless teddy bear.

"Why don't you wait for me in the living room? We need to leave soon." Lucas was not yet satisfied that everything was okay, but he submitted, nodded, and slogged out of the room.

After I finished preparing myself, I went into the study, plopped down at my desk, and stole precious moments to compose myself and clear my head. The gravity of my situation weighed heavily on my thoughts. I supplicated with God to help me understand all that was expected of me now that I had been born again.

"Lord, if ever there is a time I have needed You, it is now. I am so afraid I can't do this. Give me strength. Please give me hope through Your Word."

I stared at my Bible in front of me on my desk. The leaves were torn and tattered—I had spent perhaps a thousand hours or more poring over its pages daily for nineteen consecutive months. And through it all, God's love had been poured into my heart through the Holy Spirit.

With my hands quaking, I opened my Bible to the place where it had all begun, and although my concentration was shot, I was soon drawn to these words in Matthew 16:

> Jesus told his disciples, "If anyone would come after me, let him deny himself and take up his cross and follow me. For whoever would save his life will lose it, but whoever loses his life for my sake will find it. For what will it profit a man if he gains the whole world and forfeits his soul?"[6]

My heart and mind were racing as I processed Jesus' words. I knew that I had been washed by the water of the Word of God, saved by grace through faith, redeemed by the blood of Jesus Christ, and forgiven of my many sins. God's immeasurable love had filled the gaping chasm in my heart. But now, Christ was beckoning me into discipleship, petitioning me to take up my cross and follow Him—even to the loss of my life.

The mere thought of the high cost I had to pay frightened me and made me feel guilty. After all, every facet of my life was so deeply entrenched in my religious identity: my family, friends, school, career path, relationships, reputation, hopes, dreams, earthly aspirations, culture, respect, and more.

I couldn't even fathom a life outside of that which I knew. Was I willing to walk away from everything the world had to offer?

Amidst my endless questions, I was certain of one inexorable truth: If I forthrightly told the mission president about my transformative rebirth—along with my new foundation of faith—I would undoubtedly lose the only life I had ever known and loved.

"God, what do I do? Show me!" I beseeched as I flipped just two pages forward and my eyes caught this inspiring passage: "Everyone who has left houses or brothers or sisters or father or mother or children or lands, for my name's sake, will receive a hundredfold and will inherit eternal life."[7]

Immediately, the Word of God imprinted itself on my heart, and I wept silently to the point I could hear the teardrops hitting the pages of my Bible. I couldn't maintain the quiet for long, because my chest heaved forcefully as I tried to repress my emotions. The more I thought about what I had just read, the more I lost control and sobbed. This was not a cry of despair, but rather, a cry of joy. God had answered my plea by giving me exactly what I needed to hear at the moment I needed to hear it.

Through His Word, God had reminded me of this simple yet profound truth: Jesus was worth the loss of all things because His love was all-sufficient to satisfy my every need and grant me eternal life. Therefore, it didn't matter what I gave up, what I walked away from, or what my personal cost of discipleship would be. What I had found in Christ was infinitely greater than anything the world—or my religion—could ever offer me. Jesus was enough!

After I had unleashed my torrent of tears, I stood up filled with hope and looked out the window at the beautiful citrus tree in the backyard that was bearing fruit. It was now my time to bear fruit for God, and through His strength, I knew what I had to do: surrender my hopes and dreams, and submit my will to His. My life would no longer be focused on my pursuit of the world, but on Christ living in me and working through me as His vessel.

My journals sat next to me on my desk and I began fidgeting with my very first diary, nervously flipping through its pages. I stopped, at random, to one of my earliest entries and read. For two years now, every day, I had written about everything God had been doing in my life:

> March 21, 2004: I am so excited to be a missionary of the
> Lord! (1) I know that I am in the true Church of God… (2) I
> know Gordon B. Hinckley is a prophet of God. (3) I know
> that Joseph Smith suffered greatly to restore the true Church
> on the earth in these latter days… (4) I know that the Book of
> Mormon is the Word of God. I know that it is another testa-
> ment of Jesus Christ. Temples are the house of God and fam-
> ilies can be together forever…[8]

This was the sincere testimony of a young and enthusiastic missionary
that was so far removed from the man that stood in his place; I no longer
recognized him. At the time I had believed those declarations with all my
heart, but over the past two years, my testimony had morphed from four
insecure pillars into one solid Rock.

Shaking my head in embarrassment, I picked up my most recent journal and turned to one of the last pages so I could see just how far I had
come on this journey:

> January 12, 2006: The more I find myself falling into the grace
> of Christ, the more the things of this world fade from my heart.
> I cannot turn my back from Christ and go against what I know
> I must do in my life. My heart is fixed on the Savior…It is my
> life that I place on the altar as an offering of love to Him who
> placed everything on the altar when He gave His life for me. I
> will give my life for Him. I am a disciple of Jesus Christ.[9]

The clock struck 11:00 as Lucas and I meandered to the car. It was a
beautiful day outside, with a hint of a breeze that alternated between very
hot and surprisingly cold as it drifted ever so gently over me. In poetic ways,
the wind washed and refreshed me. Standing in the warmth of the sun, I
closed my eyes and lifted my face toward heaven. I took in a lungful of
air and then slowly breathed out, struggling to calm my overactive nerves.

During the entire hour-long drive to the chapel, Lucas and I were
silent. Inside my head, however, a deafening battle raged on mile after
mile, each one marking a life-altering event over the past two years that
had led me to this point.

My heart broke as I stole a glance over at my companion. He looked petrified. In his innocence and naivety, he probably thought this had to do with him—that I had ratted him out to our superiors and was now deviously spiriting him off to the gallows. It didn't seem to matter how many times I told him otherwise. Sadly, he had experienced a long history of such betrayals during his time as a missionary.

We arrived at our destination and pulled into the empty church parking lot. Large willow trees gave shade to the sprawling property. As I sat in the car for a moment to gather the strength to face what lay ahead, I could see Lucas observing my every action with suspicion and misgivings.

"What's going on?" he probed as we climbed out of the car.

"I don't know, Elder. But you'll be safe. You don't have anything to worry about, okay?"

"Okay," he said, forcing a smile.

I turned around and looked up at the empty steeple on the large religious edifice. As I did so, I reached up to my chest and grasped, through my shirt, the cross necklace that I wore as a not-so-hidden symbol among my peers of my faith and devotion to Jesus Christ.

"Here we go," I said under my breath.

We walked up to the door and entered the building. Elder Lucas plopped down on the couch near the entrance and sighed, crossing his hands over his chest until they slipped down to his waist. Taking my seat beside him, I leaned over and rested my elbows on my knees, which immediately began bouncing out of control—a telltale sign of my nerves being beyond restraint.

Sitting there while awaiting my fate, the emotional drain on me was almost more than I could bear. I closed my eyes and tried to relax as I gripped the cross even more tightly in my hand. I could feel it digging painfully into my palm, but rather than paying it no mind, I gripped it even tighter. I understood that Jesus Christ had carried that heavy cross for me, and as His disciple, it was my turn to take up my cross, however small and simple, and follow Him—not by my strength, but by His.

Just as I opened my eyes, I heard a door open and close at the opposite end of the long hallway and I could feel a lump form in my throat. Even though I wasn't looking, I knew Sorensen was here.

CHAPTER 3

GOD'S ARMY

Provo, Utah | *February 11, 2004*

My time had finally come. I had waited my whole life for this moment, and now a tsunami of anticipation rushed over my emotions. I tried to look confident, but my facade stood as a dam destined to burst. Starting today, my life would never be the same.

There was a spattering of snow on the ground on this chilly February day in Provo, Utah, as we followed the tradition of my immediate family of sending their young men off on missions to exotic foreign lands. After a few minutes, that goal was in sight.

"There it is, Son!" my dad exclaimed as we approached our destination. His shaking voice rode the tide of his own swelling emotion as he tried vainly to suppress it by clearing his throat.

There was no doubt my dad was as excited as I was. Not only was I the uncanny spitting image of my father when he was my age, but in a strange sort of alternate reality more than twenty-five years in the making, I was living the last relics of his dream.[10] Any of the desires of his heart that had gone unfulfilled were now left up to me, the third and final one of his sons to be cast out to sea on a two-year voyage in which each member of my family would share sacrificially.

For Dad, seeing all his sons voluntarily indentured and pressed into service for twenty-four months was not getting any easier, and the full weight of it was pouring itself out in silent anguish. I, too, was so overloaded with emotion that I had to look away from him, knowing that I didn't need his unspoken sorrow to push me over the edge.

As I sought for an escape from my spiraling sentiments, something out of the corner of my eye captured my attention. It was the sign I had been waiting for. I pointed at it with exaggerated exuberance, as if I had just sighted Sasquatch.

"We're here!" I called out. I read aloud the words etched in beautiful granite: "The Missionary Training Center."

Ten-foot walls surrounded the massive complex, and once we were inside the protective fortifications, I took note of the numerous brown buildings that comprised the campus. To the outside world, this must have looked like an internment camp, but to me and countless others, it was the place where we would prepare for the greatest two years of our fortunate lives. The mere sight of it cracked my ever-weakening dam and a few tears escaped my eyes.

The MTC, as they called it for short, was a mecca for Church missionaries. Here, I would commit myself to being sequestered from the world and instructed, along with thousands of other faithful young men and women, to preach the restored gospel of Jesus Christ. It was in this place, over the course of the next nine weeks, that I would be rigorously trained to teach and defend my faith as a full-time representative of the only true Church of Christ on the earth.

For a young man nineteen years of age, this was no insignificant experience—this marked the official commencement of my transfiguration to spiritual adulthood. During these next two years, I would be endowed with a special power and authority unique to the upper echelon of our religion, holding the honored title of "elder" along with the fifteen highest leaders in the Church. For me, this was an event unparalleled in the civilized world.

As I marveled at the breathtaking sights before me, I reached into my jacket pocket and unfolded the copy of the missionary letter I had received directly from the Prophet[11] just three months earlier, indicating my worthiness for this undertaking. I reviewed its inspiring words:

You have been recommended as one worthy to represent the Lord as a minister of the restored gospel. You will be an official representative of the Church. As such, you will be expected to maintain the highest standards of conduct and appearance by keeping the commandments, living mission rules, and following the counsel of your mission president.

You will be expected to devote all of your time and attention to serving the Lord, leaving behind all other personal affairs. As you do these things, the Lord will bless you and you will become an effective advocate and messenger of the truth. We place in you our confidence and pray that the Lord will help you meet your responsibilities in fulfilling this sacred assignment.[12]

"Leaving behind all other personal affairs" meant forsaking my family, friends, girlfriend, school, work, and home for twenty-four months. In addition, I would be required to sever all regular contact with the outside world (with the exception of writing handwritten letters to friends once a week) and live a disciplined lifestyle dedicated to my missionary duties. Communication with my immediate family would be limited to weekly emails (through the Church's email system) with the luxury of only two phone calls *per year*—one on Mother's Day and one on Christmas.

Our commitment would incorporate a complete severance from worldly entertainment: no TV, computers, magazines, newspapers, movies, or dating. I would be required to retire to bed at 10:30 p.m. and wake up at 6:30 a.m. every day (with no exceptions) for 730 consecutive days. I would labor intensely for nearly twelve hours each day, earnestly seeking potential converts by knocking on strangers' doors and proselyting on the streets. I would be in a strange land where I had never been, with exotic people I didn't know, speaking a language I hadn't fully absorbed. This would be the paramount undertaking of my life.

I was not unfamiliar with the magnitude of the cultural and religious implications of this venture. I knew full well this would not be an easy experience. But if I remained faithful for the duration of the two-year commitment—completing my mission with honor—I would bolster my widely recognized reputation for zealously serving in the Lord's Church and continue to establish my right standing with God.

Up to this point of my life, by all outer appearances, I was a perfect and obedient member of the Church. I had proven myself ready to face the world as one of the best and most powerful warriors in God's army, being convinced through early personal revelations that I would become the Jason Bourne of missionaries. In fact, our family as a whole was the prototypical picture of our religion: Dad was a well-respected high priest, Mom was a professor at the prominent Brigham Young University (BYU), and the four of us children had faithfully followed their well-established archetype.

My personal religious resume was not unimpressive either: I had held every leadership position possible through my teenage years; read the Book of Mormon multiple times and received numerous spiritual witnesses about its truthfulness (based on the strongest of emotions); and had been a full-time temple worker for the six weeks leading up to this critical juncture of my service. I put everything I had and was into preparing for my mission and developed—through prayer and study—what I knew was an unshakable testimony of each of the five pillars of the Church.

To my congregation back in Alpine, Utah, I was seen as the quintessential role model for righteousness—the standard by which they set their religious bar. It was regularly conveyed to my parents by their contemporaries—and then to me—that I was everything they wanted their kids to become, and the young man that all the mothers wished their daughters to marry. For Mom and Dad, my dedicated service over the next two years would only keep the spiritual and temporal blessings coming.

An Uncertain Call

At the time, my older brother, Matt, was finishing up the last days of his mission in Denmark and had taken on a reverence from me that was like the frosting on the proverbial cake. I hadn't seen him for almost two years, and I missed him so much that my heart ached. I longed for him to share this time with me like I had with him, and it never occurred to me—in all my fantasies of this moment—that he would not be present for one of the greatest events of my life. Another two years would pass before we would be reunited, and I loathed the thought of such a long separation. I swallowed hard, pressed on, and tried to put the pain out of my mind.

My eldest brother, Josh, had recently returned from his mission to Russia, but our difference in age had dictated that we were not nearly as attached throughout our childhood, although we had developed a strong friendship over the past few months. The inspirational and wondrous chronicles that he and Matt had written had motivated me to want to be the greatest missionary the Church had ever seen.

As my older brothers had paved the way for me across the globe, I knew that God had a special mission for me as well—a place predestined for me specifically to share His truth to a people in need of the restored gospel. I was called by God—through the Prophet of the Church—to serve full-time in Mexico City, Mexico. (As prospective missionaries, we had no say in the destination of our two-year enterprise. Our orders were executively handed to us from the top down. It was even rumored in the Church that the Prophet and the Apostles chose where each individual missionary would serve through direct revelation from God.)

Although I possessed an undying faith in the leadership of the Church and naturally extended that trust to their calling me to serve in Mexico, deep within I harbored a secret I never divulged to anyone, including my parents. From the instant my eyes scanned the words in my mission letter, something didn't sit quite right in my heart: "You are assigned to labor in the Mexico City West Mission. It is anticipated that you will serve for a period of 24 months."

No matter how much I yearned for spiritual confirmation from God that Mexico was to be my divinely inspired place of destiny for two years, I couldn't overcome a feeling of uncertainty that I would never step foot in that foreign land. In all my ceaseless zeal, I suspected that God had a different plan and purpose for me; one that was yet to be revealed. However, fearing the embarrassment that would result should I reveal my thoughts, I concealed them from my friends and family.

For months, I vacillated between feeling confident about my call to feeling conflicted, but I finally convinced myself that my feelings were off—I was taught to trust the revelation of my leaders with unwavering loyalty. No matter what my gut was telling me, God *had* called me to

Mexico through the priesthood hierarchy, and the journey would begin today.

The Torture Chamber

As we approached the unloading zone, I could see young men and women like myself unloading bags and suitcases, whom I watched until they evaporated into the reflection behind the sliding glass doors. Sitting there in the car, I was like a kid in a candy store with my face pressed up against the glass, my breath causing the window to fog. Just moments from joining the ranks of the most incredible force on Earth, the final memories of my life up to this point were now fading away almost as quickly as the last visible residue of my breath on the window.

We parked near the entrance of the campus. As my father unloaded the car, my heart started pounding uncontrollably. Within the hour, I would be removed from my family for the next two years. The inevitability of our separation was terrifying me, causing me to reach out and grasp tightly ahold of the retreating moment like a baby realizing that he was going to be ripped from the arms of his mother and forced to spend the rest of his life at the day care center. Even so, my zeal for service went on to squelch my fear.

I glanced over at my fifteen-year-old sister, Katie. Up to this point, she had stuck to me in the back seat like glue. However, to my surprise, she ejected herself out of the opposite door like a jackrabbit on a catapult and flew around the car, all the while never taking her eyes off of me.

I opened the car door and stepped out into the frigid air, which caught in my throat. "Here we go!" I said excitedly as my sister jumped into my arms, me catching her fast-moving frame expertly. I set her down gently, then gave her a tight squeeze. She smiled as she attempted (with her much shorter legs) to match my long stride.

The four of us ambled up to the entrance, with me dressed in my dark suit and tie, hair short-cropped and parted to the side. I attempted to carry myself with as much divine stature as I could muster as I toted my sister along with me while she clung on like one of the Russian Gypsy children my brother had mentioned in his letters home.

Passing through the sliding glass doors, we entered a welcome area and were promptly greeted by several older women.

"Why, hello, Elder! What's your name?"

"Micah Wilder," I told them with ever-swelling pride.

One of the women smiled at me, then turned around and combed through a box. After a few moments, she spun back around with the tangible symbol of divine power and authority: my nametag. "Elder Wilder" was engraved in white letters on a shiny black background, with the Church's name in Spanish underneath: "La Iglesia de Jesucristo de los Santos de los Ultimos Dias." After putting a bright orange dot on the nametag, the woman enthusiastically slipped it over my jacket pocket while radiating an infectious smile. As she did, I felt as if I were floating. Now I was truly a missionary!

I looked at my family with a glowing smile and hugged them. "We're so proud of you!" my mother choked out as she wiped away the tears from her eyes. "You're going to be an incredible missionary."

With my supernatural ID proudly displayed on my chest, my family and I snapped a few photos to forever immortalize the moment before making our way down the hall to the orientation room. Along the wall to the right was a large map of the world, surrounded by young men and women who were standing near it, searching earnestly and then pointing hastily at various discovered locations. I spied Mexico out of the corner of my eye as we passed, but didn't stop.

We followed a massive flow of people like a migrating herd of wildebeests, which led us through large double doors and into a spacious meeting room that my parents—after their previous experiences dropping off my brothers—had affectionately referred to as "the torture chamber." The cathedral-sized room had high ceilings and was dotted with religious paintings on the walls. At the front was a stage and a pulpit. Missionaries were filing in with their families and taking seats. It was an awe-inspiring sight.

We sat down and the commotion of the missionaries and their loved ones was nearly deafening. After a few minutes passed, an older gentleman stood up at the pulpit and the room immediately became so quiet that all you could hear was the rustling of the suits and the sniffles of the mothers who were struggling unsuccessfully to contain themselves.

"Elders and Sisters, my name is President Johnson, and I am the president of the Missionary Training Center. I am humbled and honored to have this opportunity to join with you in this great work for the Lord. The coming months and years of your life are going to change you in ways that you cannot imagine. Our Heavenly Father has amazing things in store for each one of you, as long as you remain faithful to Him."

My knee bounced violently up and down. I was so consumed by my thoughts of what the next two years would bring that I was having a difficult time staying focused on President Johnson's discourse. I kept glancing over my right shoulder at the door on the other side of the room. I knew that once I crossed that threshold, there was no going back.

After an inspiring video about missionary work, the orientation concluded, and it was time to embark on my rite of passage. My family would go out one portal, and I another, and we would be ripped apart and kept in that state of detachment for the next twenty-four months.

As I slowly stood up to deliver my final farewells, I was overcome with emotion. I closed my eyes, clenching them tight while tears gushed down my face. I turned to my sister and embraced her first.

"I love you, Katie," I wailed as she nestled her head into my chest. She hugged me back, sobbing so hard she couldn't speak.

Katie and I had become best friends while growing up, an affection that was forever cemented due to unspeakable tragedy in her life—her best friend, at age ten, had crawled into her mother's arms and died unexpectedly. Seeing my sister suffer such a harrowing loss had been one of the most painful experiences of my young life. Through that heart-shattering trauma, Katie had grown to depend on me and love me in an exceptional way, seeing me as her protector and comforter. I loved her in a way words could do no justice. I was going to miss her.

I turned to my mother next, who was struggling to hold back tears as she confronted the reality that her third and final son was leaving for two years.

"You'll do great," she said as she hugged me. "I love you more than you know, Son. You are a special person. God is going to do marvelous things in your life."

My mother had been my rock without fail. Even in my uncharacteristic lapses of rebellion she had loved me unconditionally—always beckoning me home with a grace like that which God had shown to the prodigal. Not until the last year or so had I truly begun to comprehend the depth of my mom's love and grace toward me as I was growing up.

On the emotional spectrum, my dad was at the opposite end of my mom. In fact, I had seen him cry only once—when his mother had passed away. Typically, he handled emotional separations with a spice of humor. But today, the pain of impending division had muted that.

Dad wrapped his arms around me firmly and cried in gentle heaves that grew ever so slightly as he pressed his head to mine. "I'm so proud of you, Micah," he blurted out. "I love you so much. Serve with all of your heart."

"I will, Dad," I burst out through my sobs.

Although my mother had reached into her handbag for a tissue to comfort herself, by this time the situation had pickpocketed any hope for me to find a way to consolidate my own emotions. I was left with having to endure a very inconvenient runny nose that I wiped on my sleeve.

"Well, this is it," I said with a puffed-up chest, half inflated with confidence and half filled with fear. "I love you all so much. I promise I'll serve with all of my heart."

I embraced each of them a final time, then turned to walk toward the door that marked the beginning of my journey. As I approached it, I stopped abruptly with my back still toward my family. I tried to control my tears before facing them one last time, but my suppressed sobs were causing my body to spasm. I was choking out involuntary grunts that got worse the more that I sought to subdue myself.

Summoning all the strength I could, I spun around one last time to catch a glimpse of my family before they walked out the door and out of my life. I spotted them through the sea of people and was surprised they hadn't moved an inch, apparently wanting to savor the last vestiges of me before I disappeared.

I put both my hands in the air and tried to speak, but I could only mouth a silent "Hooray!" My father exuberantly returned the gesture with tears gleaming on his face. He then froze motionless with a slightly deflated posture while trying to hold on to the moment. I took the last snapshot of them in my mind, then turned and walked through the magical portal, ready to begin the most extraordinary journey of a lifetime.

CHAPTER 4

THE BAND-AID MISSION

Provo, Utah | March 1, 2004

Ball, ball!" I shouted from the top of the key while clapping my hands rapidly.

I savored these moments to solidify myself in the MTC sports Hall of Fame…well, maybe it was a far cry from my glory days of high school basketball, but it was a nice break from the long and monotonous days in the classroom learning Church doctrines in Spanish.

Elder Robinson, seeing that I was wide open, faked a pass down to the block and launched a missile right to my chest. I elevated and released the ball at the peak of my jump and…swish.

"Nice shot, Wilder!" Robinson said while high-fiving me as the game ended.

"Thanks. Nice pass!" I replied while resting my hands on my hips to catch my breath.

As I stood there, a sharp and almost unbearable pain shot through my back and lodged itself deeply into my chest. I collapsed to the ground, and as I came down hard on one knee, I thought death was certain.

"Wilder, are you okay?" I could hear the echoing voice from behind me as someone tried to help me up, but I was as dazed as I was confused.

Things seemed to be going in slow motion. I gasped for air, tried to talk, then settled on desperately trying to breathe.

"My…chest…" I said as I clutched my left side. With the help of a fellow missionary, I hobbled over to the athletic trainer.

"I…think…something…is wrong…with me," I managed to utter without the aid of even an ounce of air, while pointing to my chest and then my back. I struggled to pull in air with all my might, but it was as if there was nowhere for it to go.

"Hmmm…" the trainer said. "It sounds like you might have a broken rib." The look on his face betrayed him, however. We both knew I was a dead man. There was no way I had broken a rib; I hadn't had any physical contact with anyone. Whatever had happened came out of thin air, as if God Himself had poked me in the back with His almighty finger.

"We need to send you to get some X-rays," he said. "I will arrange a transport."

I arrived at the clinical examining room and with the pain nearly unbearable, I entered a mild state of shock. The medical personnel rushed me as if I were in a life-or-death situation and immediately took X-rays of the left side of my chest and back, manhandling me like a sack of potatoes.

As I lay on a padded slab, certain I was destined for the morgue, the doctor came in and examined my X-rays. "Ah, yes," he said while gazing at his clipboard. He turned toward me (while conveniently avoiding eye contact) and proceeded to serve up my death sentence rather coldly: "It's a primary spontaneous pneumothorax."

Dear Lord no! I thought to myself. *I'm going to die!* I had had no idea what his prognosis meant, but it sure sounded hopeless.

As the doctor was nonchalantly exiting the room, he glanced over at me and, in a rather routine style, declared, "Oh. Your lung collapsed."

"Oh?" I said sheepishly. His heart may have been in the right place, but his bedside manner needed a little polishing.

In God's Hands

I spent the next few days in the hospital for treatment and observation, and my parents were graciously given permission to visit me. Though only three weeks had passed since we had separated, I was euphoric to see them, and their presence promptly brought much-needed comfort and familiarity.

"Dad, do you think they are going to let me serve my mission?" I nervously asked. Before he could answer, my mom dove in front of him as if she were blocking a bullet and took me by the hand.

"I can answer that for you, Micah." She sat down on the side of the bed and took to telling me a story as if she had been waiting to do this all her life.

"Let me tell you about my little miracle. I was home one day and about sixteen weeks pregnant with you when I stopped feeling you moving inside me. I became alarmed when this went on for some time, so your father decided to take me to the clinic. Once there, the doctor examined me and then left the room without saying a word. Upon returning a few minutes later, he informed me that he could no longer hear a heartbeat. I was mortified.

"I started praying to God with all of my heart. I prayed and prayed. The nurse later told me that when the doctor stepped out of the room, he leaned against the wall and prayed before coming back in to give me the news. After he admitted what he had found, it was right then and there that I knew what I had to do. I had to make a sacrifice. In that moment, I gave you up for adoption to God, Micah. I promised Him that if He would not take you from me that I would commit your life to Him, and from that moment on I would raise not my child, but His." Tears were coursing down her face.

"So you see, Micah, I kept my promise, and I know God will keep His. He still has so much to do in your life, and I have no doubt that going on a mission will play a significant part in shaping you for your future."

My mother's emotional account of what had happened during her pregnancy convicted me. I closed my eyes and mustered up the strength to confess to her the secret that I had been hiding—and perhaps the real reason why this had happened.

"Mom," I said softly, "I never really got any confirmation about going to Mexico." Then, forgetting to take in any air, I forced out, "I faked it." I took a deep breath as I acknowledged my shame.

My mother, looking at me with compassion, asked, "Well, where did you think you would be serving, Micah?"

"I don't know, Mom," I said, trying to hide the tears welling up in my eyes.

"Well, I always wished you would go to Florida so you could convert your grandfather. But know this: You are in God's hands, Son. Everything will work out as it should."

After the doctors felt they had stabilized my condition, I was returned to my missionary quarters with a batch of painkillers and instructions to rest, although the directives were a waste of time. I didn't have to be told—the strong drugs they had prescribed had freed me from all my earthly burdens.

And so, for the next few days, I was detained in a room with a companion (which was rather unfortunate for him, considering that, at the time, I was busy flying all over God's creation).

"Are you excited to go to Orlando?" I asked Elder Rigby.

"Yeah," he said with a smile as he tossed a ball into the air while sitting at his desk. "I think it'll be awesome. I've always wanted to go to Disney World!"

"I went there for my eighth-grade class trip!" I said proudly. "It's pretty awesome. Do they let you visit as a missionary?"

"I don't know. But I've heard some weird stories about the Orlando mission. I guess it has a reputation for notoriously disobedient missionaries. I've also heard that Orlando is nicknamed 'the Band-Aid mission' because so many missionaries with physical and mental health problems are sent there. Apparently, it's some sort of convalescent rehab center," he explained.

Evidently, as Rigby had heard through the pipeline, missionaries with latent health problems (or even emotional misfits) were generally sent directly or reassigned to Orlando to serve out the remainder of their service for the Church in a sunny and temperate climate that was perhaps more conducive to recovery.

"Interesting," I replied. "Good luck with that!"

As the medication wore off and I gleefully floated back down to Earth sometime near the end of the week, I was summoned to the MTC doctor's office while still sporting a hangover—a little grumpy and having little idea as to who I was, who he was, or what he wanted.

"Good to see you again, Elder Wilder. How are you feeling?"

"I'm feeling a little better, Doctor, thank you. Though at times I'm still finding it painful to breath." *You got any more of those pills?* I wanted to ask. But I was far too shy to say that.

"Well, Elder, we are keeping a close eye on things to make sure that you are healing properly." He then seemed somewhat hesitant, as if concealing something from me. I braced for devastating news as he rustled through some papers before he spoke up. This could *not* be good.

"Elder Wilder, I have been talking on the phone with your Church leaders. They and I feel it would be best to…limit your travel," he said as he scribbled in what looked like reformed Egyptian on a piece of paper. As I tried to translate his encryptions, his next words caught me totally off guard: "We don't think it would be best for you to leave the country in your current condition."

In that moment, it was as if God had poked me in the back all over again. I panicked. What did he mean I couldn't leave the country? For how long? I was supposed to go to Mexico. God had *called* me to go there, and the call came directly through the Prophet; I had worked so hard and come this far. How could that change? Was this the end of my mission?

"So…you mean I will stay here for a while until I am well enough to go to Mexico?" I asked rather pleadingly.

I could tell the doctor felt badly because he dropped his gaze, shook his head, and took off his glasses. He hesitated while rubbing his eyes, then looked directly at me. The words he spoke came out in perfect, measured beats.

"Elder, you are no longer going to Mexico…at all. I have discussed this at length with your leaders, and we feel it is best for your health and safety. Your mission will be reassigned somewhere here in the States, where it will be easier to monitor your ailment."

I heard what he said, but his words weren't registering. As the significance of his pronouncement began to take hold, I put my hands on my head, breathing slowly and deeply.

So many tears had been spilt trying to convince myself I was going to serve the Mexican people and bring them the restored gospel. I had prayed incessantly, begging to receive confirmation from God concerning my mission call. It took some time, but eventually I submitted to the priesthood, trusting my leaders and humbling myself by accepting my disappointment and doubts. I recognized that the problem was with me and not my authorities. And now, just when I thought things were back in control…wham, I was knocked off balance again. I was so confused. Was this confirmation that I might have been right all along? Probably not. Most likely, I was paying the price for my lack of faith. Where now…Idaho?

"I know this is difficult," the doctor said with kindness. "But Elder, you just need to trust your Heavenly Father. Everything will work out. I don't know when you will find out where you will be reassigned, but continue on working as you have, and leave it all in God's hands."

The Happiest Place on Earth

The intercom crackled to life in the classroom and I turned my ear toward it as I pretended to be paying close attention to the lesson plan. For some reason, I knew the message would be for me.

"Elder Wilder, you are needed in President Johnson's office."

I immediately became nervous as my mouth dried and my palms started sweating. An anxious smile crept along the left side of my mouth. As the whole class roared with excited commotion, the adrenaline started flowing and my smile grew into a big, prideful grin.

I looked over at my companion, daring him, and then stood up and bolted from the room, leaving the boy commissioned not to leave my sight trailing behind me like the greyhound after the bunny. For nine days now, I had been waiting to discover where God had chosen for me to spend my two-year mission.

I arrived at President Johnson's office, and he wasted no time.

"Hello, Elder. Please take a seat," he said.

I dropped into the chair eagerly.

"We have heard back from the Brethren,[13] and they have reassigned your mission call. You will be serving in the Florida Orlando Mission."

As soon as I heard those words, I leapt with elation. In my overjoyed state, I almost shook President's hand off.

"Thank you. Thank you!" I said as I flung the door open, coming face to face with Rigby.

"I'm going to Orlando too!" I yelled while giving him a vibrant high-five. "No way! Awesome!"

The Band-Aid mission was going to be my home for the next twenty-two months. And unlike my previous mission call, I was certain this was where God wanted me.

I wasn't going to Mexico; I was going to the happiest place on Earth!

CHAPTER 5

SON OF
SUFFERING

I could hear the quick tempo of footsteps clattering down the stake center hallway. Knowing they were coming for me, I was snatched back to the moment. That magical portal I had passed through almost two years ago had miraculously teleported me across the great divide—a spiritual-event horizon of sorts—only to deliver me unexpectedly to this very day and this very place. Everything in between was now nothing more than a blur.

God, in His wisdom and foresight, had sent my life on a breathtaking course correction by puncturing my lung with His tender finger. Although excruciating at the time, He had meticulously guided me to the place where I would be healed of my spiritual infirmity and be forever reflated through an encounter with the Breath of Life.

I don't think anybody—myself included—entered the mission field expecting to face what I had undergone throughout the course of a two-year-long journey through the wilderness, during which God rebuilt and defined His relationship with me. From illnesses to pastors; teachers to friends; through hurricanes, tragedy, death, demotion, and a whole host of betrayals; I had traversed this vast and terrifying wilderness all while sporting a veil over my eyes, during which my only means of navigation came through the Word of God. Through it all, however, my path had been gracefully filled with indelible markers that were crafted and placed by God to reach past my blindness and mercifully lead me directly to His ultimate expression of love.

With my heart nearly pounding through my chest, I glanced up from my seat and saw President fast approaching through the hallway. My oncoming executioner was a distinguished-looking man in his seventies. He wore a dark blue suit, his brown and slightly graying hair was parted down the side, and his shoes shone so brightly that the light reflecting off them was nearly blinding. He always looked so dignified and professional no matter what the time of day or the occasion. As he strolled casually yet determinedly toward me, his wiry glasses and methodical movement gave him the look of a seasoned medical doctor (which he was), and the brief-case at his side only added to the spectacle.

President was an interesting and at times intimidating man, despite (or maybe because of) his small and thin stature, soft-spoken voice, and tranquil demeanor. In fleeting moments over the last two years, I had seen him as he presented himself to be—a father figure, of sorts, to myself and the 120 missionaries over which he was given spiritual stewardship.

I genuinely loved and respected President, and I'm certain that for the greater part of my mission, he felt the same way about me. But regardless of the cordiality in our relationship, there had seemed to be a mutual aloofness between the two of us that had grown exponentially over time. President, by his own admission, was a man of science and logic, and I think I left him no doubt that I was a man of spirituality and faith. Thus, from the onset we had a defined difference in the way that we approached missionary work, which eventually triggered several divisional strains over the course of our professional relationship.

Seeing him now, despite the complexity of our history, my heart longed for him to understand what God had done in my life while under his guardianship. More than that, I desired to take him by the hand and lead him to the same waters that I drank of so freely, which had quenched my thirst and now flowed out of my heart. I had found God's truth, one page at a time, in precept after precept, and now I had the opportunity to witness of that truth to the very Church to which I had devoted my life.

Although I was fully aware that several of my discoveries from the Bible contradicted the fundamental doctrines of this religion, I could only hope that my testimony of God's Word to this man could spark a reformation in the Church.

As for me, I, too, was found to be dressed for the occasion as the typical warrior in God's army, wearing my full missionary armor: a white shirt and tie, black pants, black shoes and socks, and metaphorically bulletproof undergarments. My hair was short-cropped and properly parted, yet so naturally wavy as to give me the ultimate in proprietary distinction. And of course, the cherry on top was the one item that quickly singled us all out from an embarrassingly mistaken identity with those silly Jehovah's Witnesses: our trademark nametag. For special functions like this, a black dress jacket would accompany our garb.

I stared at my shoes while vigorously bouncing my knee until I heard his footfalls come to an abrupt end, and my heart sputtered as I silently said the world's shortest prayer (which some might have mistaken for me taking the Lord's name in vain). I had no doubt that my fate was finally upon me and I could no longer delay the inevitable.

I closed my eyes for a second, took a deep breath, arose from my place seated next to Lucas and greeted President as cheerfully as I could. Even though my lean 6' 3" frame towered over him, I could not have felt more small, insignificant, and alone. Finding myself in the flesh at that moment, I quickly forgot the One who had promised to fight my battles.

"Hello, President," I said as I shook his hand, mustering as much outward confidence as I could. I glanced down at his jacket and noticed that even his nametag seemed to shine particularly bright this day. "President Sorensen; Mission President," it read, with the commanding Church logo on the bottom: "The Church of Jesus Christ of Latter-day Saints."

"Hello, Elder Wilder. How are you today?" he asked as he held on to my hand for an extended time, looking directly into my eyes while slowly pulling me closer to him. He seemed to do this with every missionary that he greeted, most likely to demonstrate his spiritual ability to discern through his divine calling. No matter what the purpose, the axiomatic legend persisted: President could truly peer into our souls.

"I'm doing well, President," I answered.

As my personal emotion pendulum swung, President turned and looked down into the childlike face of my companion. Since the fateful call earlier that morning, Elder Lucas had convinced himself that this tragic scene was somehow all about him. He had remained seated and avoided all eye contact from either President or me, looking much like a frightened puppy.

"Elder Lucas, if you could just wait out here, I would like to talk to Elder Wilder alone," Sorensen gently instructed him.

My Deliverer

As President began walking down the hall, I tried to resolve the situation and comfort Lucas, but when he saw me looking at him, he snapped his head defiantly away from me and closed his eyes as if he could turn invisible. How ironic that he was clueless to mourn for me as I was about to begin my own walk to the gallows.

Before I could think of what to do to alleviate Lucas' fear, President's footsteps once again suddenly halted as he reached the end of the priesthood chain that still bound me to obedience. I peered over my shoulder and he was gazing back at me with a slightly impatient stare. Then he gave a verbal tug on the leash.

"Follow me, Elder Wilder," he said as he turned, motioning for me to hurry along.

For a moment I halted in fear, and having the slightest of second thoughts, the weight of the situation became almost too heavy to bear. Every fiber of my being wanted to turn tail and run. Instead, I found myself sluggishly dragging my spiritual cross down that passageway, grumbling as I selfishly savored the last remnants of my old life. I questioned whether I could really give it all up. I was assessing the cost of building my tower,[14] and feared I couldn't pay the full price.

Shamefully, for a moment I entertained taking the easy way out. All I had to do was placate President by telling him what I knew he wanted to hear: confirm my testimony in the pillars of the Church and repent of my love-centered rebellion. Then I could be freed from the cross that was about to collapse me with its weight. If I did not, my life would change dramatically. Everything I had ever known would be sacrificed on the altar, and I would be forced out into the great unknown.

God, I need You so much right now. Please, do not forsake me. Show Yourself and strengthen Your weak servant! I cried out in my soul.

As I attempted to repress the fear that was consuming me, I recalled the spectacular and transformative events in the middle of a sleepless night, just days ago, that had completely altered my understanding of the nature of God. It was there, in that epiphanous moment, that God had so mercifully revealed to me the supreme love I had been searching for my entire life as He bestowed upon me His steadfast and everlasting forgiveness. This memory reinforced my faltering soul, for I knew, without a shadow of a doubt, that God had not and would not forsake me in my hour of need. I found myself ashamed that I had ever doubted His love and protection for me. I didn't have reason to fear; the God of Israel was my deliverer! He would sustain me in my weakness, and by His strength I could do what He had called me to do.

Psalm 18:1-3 came to mind, which I had memorized in past weeks:

> I love you, O LORD, my strength.
> The LORD is my rock and my fortress and my deliverer,
>> my God, my rock, in whom I take refuge,
>> my shield, and the horn of my salvation, my stronghold.
> I call upon the LORD, who is worthy to be praised,
>> and I am saved from my enemies.

A Man of Sorrows

Resolute in God's grace, I followed President down a long stretch of hallway. Along the way, there were numerous representations of Christ hanging on the wall. The light-skinned, blond haired, blue-eyed Caucasian man depicted was beautiful, well dressed, and by all outward appearances, flawless. He was the religious manifestation of Jesus that I had come to know through my teenage years as a Latter-day Saint: This was the Jesus whom I had served with all my heart while a devoted member of the Church.

In these impeccable portrayals of His earthly ministry, Jesus had a physical perfection about Him that was captivating and, on mere sight, easy to love. However, it was clear to me now that this Jesus, as portrayed, was not the Son of God I had come to know after poring over the pages of the New Testament nearly a dozen times over the past nineteen months—not only in His physical appearance, but in His very likeness and nature. The individual who appeared on these walls was not the Son of Suffering and the Man of Sorrows who had opened Himself up willingly to vulnerability, the Messiah that was unveiled so tenderly in Scripture. This was indeed a different Christ from the Lord I now loved and avowed.

As we progressed and I gathered my thoughts, I passed the restroom I wished I had seen earlier, and this caused my mind to wander again until it was encircling its own marker, a milepost from my past no doubt related to an inconvenient call of nature that brought me head-on with a Jesus I did not want to recognize and a man whose words I did not want to hear—an experience that began my personal march toward a Man who "had no form or majesty that we should look at him, and no beauty that we should desire him" (Isaiah 53:2).

CHAPTER 6

MUD IN
MY EYES

Apopka, Florida | *June 4, 2004*

E lder Wilder, I need to find a restroom, ASAP!" came García's pleading voice as he barreled down the small hill in my wake.

The relentless Florida sun was beating down upon us and it must have
been ninety-five degrees outside. I was sweating bullets. Before turning to
my companion and responding, I stopped and took a sip of water that by
now could have been labeled a hot drink. I smiled while wondering jest-
fully if I was violating the Word of Wisdom.[15]

As missionaries, we were always paired in teams of two, with an experienced missionary matched up with a less experienced one. This was done
for accountability purposes and so we could use each other as human
shields to protect ourselves when we were over our heads in dealing with
combative Christians. This was a tried-and-true system that worked well.

How could he need the restroom again? I thought. *This guy needs to toughen
up.* I was still getting accustomed to being in the brutal heat and humidity
all while wearing black pants, a collared shirt, and a tie while trekking on
foot going door to door. Even after spending nearly two months in Florida since leaving the MTC, the climate was still insufferable.

I glanced back at my comrade and caught him staring at my bottle of water with a pained look on his face. I wasn't sure if he was (1) annoyed that I was drinking; (2) contemplating hitting me over the head with the bottle; or (3) considering stealing it from me to use it for something to pee into.

"Alright, Elder García," I huffed, "let's head for that shopping center."

Taking the handlebar in one hand and the water bottle in the other, I pointed the way with my lips (as the Latinos had taught me) and coasted on the slight downhill toward the center until it flattened out. Losing momentum, I stood up and peddled furiously. The run-down center seemed to be our only option for finding a suitable solution to my companion's impending problem, which by now had become a ticking time bomb.

As we approached the dilapidated building, it was just as I had expected—the old shopping complex appeared deserted. "I think we are out of luck, Elder!" I yelled.

I was resigned to moving on while he—indubitably committed to finding a remedy for his threatening condition—quickly abandoned his bike by letting it crash to the ground. My suddenly eagle-eyed and highly motivated companion then spotted one section in the center that he hoped would have some life in it and progressed to limping out ahead of me and holding his lower abdomen like a woman in full labor.

"This way!" he grunted without even looking in my direction. He hobbled in short strides straight for a double-doored entrance, above which were the words "Faith and Power."

I corralled both of our bikes against a post and headed for the doorway, trying to catch up to my companion. I overtook him just in time to tug at the ill-fitting door, which opened to a small welcome area.

As my eyes adjusted to the dim light, I discerned unusual objects and paintings on the walls. The subject of the bizarre portraits was an unassuming man who was healing the sick, walking on water, and raising the dead. These were obviously depictions of Jesus, but not ones that I was accustomed to seeing. This Jesus was homely and unattractive. As we pressed on, I was mesmerized by the portrayal of a dark-skinned man who looked like he had been beaten, bruised, and battered, and there was not the least bit of beauty in him at all. I was mortified. My Christ, as depicted in the rendering that was approved by the Prophet of God, was light-skinned, well adorned, handsome, and beautiful. I immediately felt uncomfortable, as though we had walked into a cultish church of some sort.

During my short six weeks in Florida, I had yet to confront a pastor or attend another church, although targeting and hunting Christians seemed to be a beloved pastime among some of the more seasoned and gutsy missionaries. However, neither Elder García nor I were quite yet equipped for such a bold undertaking. We had entered by accident, and my discomfort grew with every ticking second. I had no idea how a pastor would react to our uninvited visit, and I was poorly hiding the fact that I was far out of my element. I just wanted to find the restroom quickly and get out.

We continued to explore the seemingly vacant area until we spotted the office. Hoping to find someone so we could ask for permission to use the facilities, I poked my head around the corner like a seasoned sniper. "Hello?" I said, feigning to get someone's attention. "Is anyone here?" There wasn't a soul in sight, and if anyone was, given my feeble attempt, they wouldn't have heard me anyway.

García was now in desperate turmoil and I knew we had to do something fast. As if by providence, I spun around and spotted the sign for the restrooms toward the back of the building. Pointing again with my lips, we headed determinedly toward our goal, hoping not to be noticed as we invaded the inner sanctum of the enemy.

We next entered a spacious room with elevated ceilings. To my left was a large stage with drums, electric guitars, microphones, and speakers. Centered above the stage and mounted on the wall, like some kind of trophy, was a ginormous cross that loomed eerily overhead. Rows of chairs, facing the rostrum, filled the room. It was all so strange and new to me. Our church services were limited to piano and organ. Using rock-music instruments for worship seemed…inappropriate.

My distressed companion spotted his coveted destination and quickly left my side, making a beeline into the restroom while leaving me vulnerable. As I anxiously stood on guard outside the door and kept a keen eye out for intruders, my neck hairs were on full alert. (This is precisely the point in every horror movie where the audience begins yelling, *No—don't go in there, stupid!*)

Saul of Tarsus

Suddenly, a door on the other side of the room flung open. A large, middle-aged black man who looked as though he knew full well that I had been there all along headed straight toward me. My fight-or-flight intuition was saying, *Run for your life!* I wanted to do nothing more than sprint into the restroom, throw Elder García over my shoulder, and make a clean break for it. The problem was that my feet were frozen in place.

While I turned to locate my companion, the man was already upon me and had placed his hand firmly on my shoulder, negating any attempt to escape. I noted through wide eyes as I spun around that he had on a blue-gray suit jacket and pants, a gold watch, and a gold cross necklace held up by a chain that could have easily suspended my companion from around his neck. Oddly, to make things even more uneasy, this football-linebacker-of-a-man was baring his teeth broadly.

"Pastor Matthew Shaw," he said in a deep and pleasantly raspy voice.

"Nice to meet you," I replied, trying not to sound too intimidated, which became even more difficult after he swallowed my hand in his hungry grasp.

"We...we were just stopping in to use the bathroom," I stammered. "I hope you don't mind. We tried to find someone to ask."

He looked at me and smiled from ear to ear, still enveloping my hand in his firm grip. "You're welcome here any time," he said. "You don't have to ask."

While we traded ever-tightening yet nonaggressive squeezes, he looked deeply into my eyes. "Young man, do you know the story about Saul of Tarsus?" he asked.

I thought to myself, *Oh yeah, I hear that story every day when I am lost and alone and I am approached and held captive by a very solid and intimidating black man. It is quite the conversation starter!* Before I could open my mouth to respond, he continued.

"Saul was a young religious man, not unlike yourself. Passionate about God, he went about trying to destroy the church of Christ, believing that what he was doing was the work of God. He went door to door, persecuting those who were saints and disciples of Jesus and bound them in prison. He was even involved in the stoning of a great disciple, Stephen. He was an enemy of the church of God."

I couldn't understand why he was telling me this, but I kept glancing over my shoulder toward the bathroom, hoping that would let him know I was in a hurry. Striving to free myself, I looked down at our still-clasped hands and tugged a little. On cue, he released his uncomfortable hold on me.

"But one day, Saul, on his way to Damascus, was visited by the resurrected Lord Himself," he said with animated hand motions. "The Lord said to him, 'Saul, Saul, why are you persecuting me?' And Saul was afraid, and said 'Who are you?' And the Lord replied, 'I am Jesus whom you are persecuting. Go into the city and you will be told what to do.' There and then Saul received a great revelation, and he ended his persecution of the church. He became Paul, the apostle of the Lamb, a great defender of the faith and minister of the gospel of Jesus Christ!"

Pastor Shaw smiled at me as my mind trailed off for a moment and confusion was plastered all over my face. I had no clue how to respond.

"So, what are you doing dressed up so nice?" the charismatic minister asked, as if the last couple of minutes had never happened.

"Well, we're missionaries from the Church of Jesus Christ of Latter-day Saints. Some people know us as Mormons."

"Is that right?" he responded with a childish grin while looking down at my nametag.

Just then, in a flash, my much-refreshed companion glided up next to me, and I was grateful to have some backup. Pastor Shaw looked at Elder García and introduced himself.

"So, you're both named Elder?" he laughed. "That's quite a coincidence!"

"Well, actually, elder is a title; it's not our name," García chimed in.

"Oh, I see," he said, putting his hand on his chin. "You're elders of the church. You look a little...*young* to be elders."

Seeing our lack of reaction to his humor, I think he could tell we were far out of our comfort zone, so he quickly changed subjects and assumed a more serious tone.

"Tell me, gentlemen, what is it that the Mormons believe? What are you teaching people as 'elders of the church'?"

My companion and I both looked at each other. He gave me a slight nod, and on that silent cue, I began teaching.

"We teach people about the restoration of the gospel and the true

Church of Christ to the earth in these latter days. Jesus Christ gave His apostles a special authority, the priesthood of God. When the apostles were killed, this priesthood authority was lost and the world fell into darkness. There was a great apostasy from the truth, and the Church of Jesus Christ was lost from the earth for a time. But because God loves us and doesn't want us to be without His truth, He called a prophet in these latter days to restore His Church again to the earth and make salvation possible to mankind once again."

My discourse was the summarized company line as a missionary. It's what had been drilled into my head my whole life and reiterated at the MTC. It's what I believed with all my heart.

The Law and the Prophets

Pastor Shaw rubbed his goatee and looked at us, as if deep in thought. He nodded and gave a borderline smirk that turned into a smile as he saw me take note of it.

"Interesting. And tell me, why do we need a 'prophet' today?" he inquired.

"Well," I said, "just like God called prophets in the Old Testament so that the people would know His Word and will for them, God has called prophets today to teach us His Word for our time—to give us commandments and reveal new Scripture. God is the same yesterday, today, and forever, and that is the system He established through Adam, and the system by which He reveals His truth today."

Pastor Shaw looked at us and squinted. He then tilted his head to one side and broke into a large, patented toothy grin. With his deep, raspy voice, he launched into a long tirade that was proclaimed with so much rhythm that it seemed to command authority.

"In the Bible, it says that when Christ died on the cross, the veil of the temple was torn in two. Do you know what that means?" I had no immediate answer, and neither did my companion. Even if we did have a retort, Pastor Shaw gave us no time to respond.

"It means that the need for a man to intercede between us and God is over. We now have direct access to the Father through His Son, Jesus," he said, again with vibrant hand motions.

"You see, when Jesus died, there was a change in the law. Every part of the law, including the prophets, was to prepare us for the coming of Jesus, who would offer Himself up as a sacrifice for our sins. Once He did that, the old law was fulfilled, and the prophets along with it. Do you understand?" He looked us both straight in the eyes. I think he detected we were perplexed.

"Follow me, gentlemen. In Hebrews, it says that even though God spoke to us in the past through the prophets, He has now spoken His Word, once and for all, through His Son. So we have the eternal truth of the gospel forever through this book," he exclaimed while holding up the Bible, shaking it as though he was showering us in holy pixie dust or something.

"We no longer need prophets to speak to us for God. That is why God has given us the Holy Spirit in the church today. The true 'prophets' today are those who have the gift of prophecy and the testimony of Jesus."

When Pastor Shaw finished, neither Elder García nor I knew what to say. He had bloviated a lot of information in a short amount of time, and I was having a hard time making sense of it all.

I thought Pastor Shaw was finished patronizing us and I was ready to make a hasty withdrawal, but before I knew it, he had set off to baring his teeth again, once again asking questions without giving us any time for rebuttal (like a kid offering candy then snatching it away just as his victim reaches for it). I was getting irritated. After all, what if I did have an answer? I couldn't have gotten a word in edgewise. I soon zoned out and tried to ignore whatever nonsense he was spewing. This guy was a nut job of the highest caliber.

Noticing that I was not paying attention to his sermon, Pastor Shaw leaned uncomfortably into my personal space and placed his massive hand on my right shoulder while looking deep into my eyes.

"Elder Wilder, if you hear nothing else, hear this: *All* the law and the prophets hang on the new and great commandment, which is to love God with all our hearts and to love our neighbor as our self. That's what matters. Love fulfills the law." He then placed his other hand on my left shoulder and pulled me to within inches of his face. "Do you know *love*, Elder Wilder?"

Deaf Will Hear

I didn't know what to do. This madman was testing the boundary of my patience. In the moment, I couldn't contend with what he was saying. I couldn't even grasp what he had been pontificating. In such a predicament, I had been instructed (in the MTC) to share my testimony of the Church, so I followed my directive obediently.

"Pastor Shaw, even though I can't explain everything through the Bible, I know through the Holy Ghost that the church we represent is the only true Church of Christ. The Book of Mormon is the Word of God and another testament of Christ. Joseph Smith was a true prophet and restored the true gospel and Church to the earth. We do need prophets, priesthood, and temples today. God's Church is that of order. No matter what the Bible may say, that is what I *know* to be true."

Pastor Shaw became more serious at that point. He looked at me and lowered his voice as if he was going to tell me a secret: "Do you know what the biggest difference is between what you believe and what I believe?"

I had to lean in a little to hear him. "What?"

"You believe in a different Jesus than I do." He then turned up the volume and turned on his charismatic tone. "I believe in the Jesus Christ of the Bible who died for my sins and gives me salvation as a free gift—by His grace through my faith, not my works. I don't know who your Jesus is," he said as he poked me in the chest so hard that it smarted.

In an instant, Pastor Shaw had cracked my sugar coating and reached the sourball hidden inside. I was furious. Even though I never moved a muscle, I lurched at him in my mind to the limits of the invisible chain that held me back and barked at him viscously with teeth bared and religious slobber flying. I was prepared to cut him off with authority, throw my arm into the square, and do this man a favor by commanding the demons to come out of him. (There was no doubt in my mind he was possessed.)

As I tried to contain my fury, I looked over at Elder García, who was paralyzed and silent as could be. But I would not remain quiet. This man told me I didn't believe in the same Jesus as he did? I would not stand for this! I was handpicked by an apostle of God to be a missionary and representative of Christ Himself. This was a claim he could not equal.

My chest was now painfully heaving, yet I couldn't seem to gather sufficient breath, so I barged forward without it and stood tall in my shoes with my chest puffed out in a schoolyard bully bluff.

"You have no right to tell me I believe in a different Jesus!" I screamed. "I *do* believe in the same Jesus as you. My Jesus *is* the Jesus of the Bible. I love Him with all my heart. You have distorted His true gospel, and that is why you are blind to the truth. I am a disciple of the Lord!" I bellowed with heat rising in my ears.

For the first time, the tables had turned, and Pastor Shaw was left without words as he looked at me with his mouth slightly ajar. Uncertain as to what to do next, he then peered deeply into my eyes just as the edges of my peripheral vision darkened. I was left with tunnel vision, and I could see nothing but him.

"I could do something with you," he said to me in a gentle voice as he nodded. "God *will* do something with you."

As I stood there looking at him through the shaft, the world closed in around me and I could see that he was now talking to me and only me. His eyes darted back and forth, peering, searching, looking at me until he seemed to lock on to my very soul.

"You're different than all the other missionaries I have met over the years," he said affectionately. "Though you are now as Saul, you will one day be as Paul—a minister to the world of the true Word of God and the gospel of our Lord Jesus Christ!"

For a giant of a man, Pastor Shaw—for the first time—looked surprisingly fragile, exceedingly tender, and eloquently compassionate. This should have been an equally warm moment for us both, but I didn't know how to interpret what he had just said. Wasn't I already a minister of the true gospel? Isn't that what I was doing as a missionary? I was conflicted by his seemingly paradoxical statement. Was he complimenting me while implying that I was actually *persecuting* the Christians like Saul? This made no sense to me. I presumed Pastor Shaw had just insulted me while disguising it as praise and that he was telling me—in no uncertain terms—that I was leading people away from the Bible and the Jesus of the Bible, binding them to a gospel and Jesus who were not of God. Now I knew for sure that even though he may appear to be sincere, he was an irrational nutcase.

Right then, Pastor Shaw placed his massive arms around García and me. "Young men, let me pray for you," he volunteered. We didn't have any choice, but the good news for me and the consolation prize for this meeting was that my beating at the hands of this charismatic minister was about to come to an end, and I was grateful for that.

"Almighty God, we thank You this day for bringing these two young men here, and for the desires in their hearts to teach what they believe is Your Word. God, I pray to You for this young man, Elder Wilder, that You will guide him to Your truth. Give him a great revelation as You did Your servant Paul." He tightened his grip as if to squeeze the devil out of me.

"Father, I pray to You in faith to bind the spirit of blindness that is upon this young man. Remove it, mighty God! I pray that Your Word will be fulfilled—that the deaf will hear and the blind will see, so that one day he may know of Your marvelous love through Your Son. In Jesus' name, amen."

Pastor Shaw smiled, opened his arms wide, and engulfed me in a deep embrace. His act of charity was quite unexpected and seemingly contradictory to the hurtful words he had hurled at me.

"God be with you," he said to me as he abruptly turned and walked away.

As I tried to dust myself off from the whirlwind that had just battered me, he turned back and raised one hand into the air. "Don't be a stranger now," he said. Then he disappeared through the same gateway from whence he had come.

García and I quickly made our way out of the building and into the sweltering heat. As we mounted our bikes, I glanced over at him with a slightly aggravated look on my face. "That was weird," I said while taking a sip of water and then shaking my finger at him. "Next time, just hold it."

CHAPTER 7

FOR BY THIS

President Sorensen went straight for a door that opened into a large, mostly empty classroom. I couldn't help but identify it for what it was—a carefully set courtroom for my upcoming interrogation and subsequent execution.

At the back of the room sat a table with two chairs facing each other on opposing sides. As I walked toward the judge's bench cautiously surveying the landscape, I noticed a poster on the wall with the heading, "The House of the Lord," and underneath it, a picture of the ornate Salt Lake Temple. Next to it was a second poster, a rendering of a teenage boy kneeling in the woods with a bright light shining overhead with the caption "BELIEVE."

As I continued to assess my surroundings, I detected two more religious depictions on the opposite wall. One was a collection of portraits of the fifteen highest leaders of the Church with the quote, "What I the Lord have spoken, I have spoken…Whether by mine own voice or by the voice of my servants, it is the same."[16] Adjacent to that was a poster listing the books in the Book of Mormon. While still gazing, I tittered nervously to myself at the thought that my first impressions of the room had been accurate. This was indeed the effective scaffold for a calculated hanging.

"This should do," President said as he sat down amidst his props, crossing his legs and placing his hands on his knee. I took my place across from him, neither of us flinching as we sat in silence staring each other down, like we were waiting for the other to give away his twitch that he was about to draw his weapon.

He finally broke the deafening silence, and I was grateful.

"How about we begin with a prayer to invite the Lord's Spirit here? I'll say it," he volunteered, even though it was customary for him to do this as the priesthood authority. I followed his lead and we both knelt on the ground with our elbows resting on the chairs, in true missionary style.

"Our dear and gracious Heavenly Father," he began quietly and reverently, "we humbly come before Thee and give Thee thanks for all Thou hast done…"

A Good Samaritan

I couldn't help but drift for a few seconds as President's prayer in perfect King James English echoed in my ears. In his briefest moments of hesitation, I was sucked back through the wardrobe portal into my own personal Narnia, revisiting vital points of time during the past two years when God had transformed me through the work of His Spirit. Each lesson I learned was brought back to remembrance in a clear picture and narrative. I now had no doubt that God had been relentless in His pursuit of me from the onset of my mission—my entire life, in fact—His steady hand watching over me, deliberately placing me in circumstances that He would use to gently guide me to His truth and open my eyes. God's love found me where I was, but the effects of His love didn't leave me there.

As I drifted further away from the present reality, my thoughts were littered by the aftermath of the Jesus bomb that had been dropped on me by a loving minister who bear-hugged me and prayed for the spirit of blindness to be removed from my eyes. It was now apparent that Pastor Shaw—a gentle but intimidating man—played no insignificant role in God's plan for my life. God used him as a catalyst to set my conversion into motion by taking the first swing at the pendulum to start a perfectly timed clock. As painful as it was then to hear the hard truths he spoke to me in my state of blindness, I now recognized that he had wanted to help me more than I could have understood at the time. He saw me in bondage and desired to set me free. And he knew that only the Son of God could release me from the shackles that held me bound.

Pastor Shaw did what few people on my mission had chosen to do: He loved me as a Christian is called to love. He was my Good Samaritan.[17] When I was a stranger in a foreign land—even his very enemy—he exhibited compassion by feeding me with the bread of life when I was starving. He gave me living water to drink when I was thirsty. And just as Jesus had done to the blind man in John 9 as He spat on the ground, Pastor Shaw put mud in my eyes, preparing me for the cleansing that would come through the water of the Word of God.

Although Pastor Shaw vocally disagreed with our message, he obediently fulfilled the scriptural mandate to correct his opponents with gentleness.[18] The confirmation of his discipleship was revealed through the grace, love, and truth that he bestowed on us—elements that were all but missing during my many encounters with so-called "Christians" as we walked from door-to-door.

Even though I had met countless people who professed to be disciples of Jesus during my nearly two-year tenure as a missionary, the majority of them were barely distinguished as such by their actions toward us. An all-too-common response when we approached Christians at their homes was, "We already know the Lord Jesus, and you guys are in a cult and are going to hell! Now get off our doorstep and don't come back. We have no interest in the message you are sharing!" Their tirade would end with the door slamming inches from our faces. I would often walk away shaking my head in disgust and thinking to myself, *If that's what a Christian is, I don't want anything to do with them.* Their behavior only further solidified my testimony in the Church and drove me deeper into my religious convictions.

Ultimately, God's immense love is what had changed me, but it wasn't just God's love revealed through His Word alone; it was His love manifested through His disciples—His body of believers. Pastor Shaw was the first of three uniquely chosen loving vessels whom God used to radically change the course of my life when I was a lost and dying man. Unfortunately, the benevolence demonstrated by these few godly individuals was not commonplace in my experiences as a missionary. In the thousands upon thousands of people I had engaged with, I could count—perhaps only on one hand—the number of Christians who not only displayed to me a genuine Christlike love, but also proclaimed the gospel as revealed in God's Word.

Looking back at this disheartening fact that so few Christ-followers made a concerted effort to declare truth to me when I was unsaved, I was determined not to harbor ill feeling toward them. Instead, I was resolved to use their lack of sympathy for me as my motivation to not repeat their unfortunate oversights. I was committed to loving the broken and beaten travelers God would place in my path because—as I had come to learn—love is the core of the gospel of Christ and the foundational attribute for His followers.

After Jesus sat at a table with His disciples in the upper room and instituted the Last Supper[19] the night before He was to offer His life as a sin ransom for the world—His ultimate display of love for mankind—He went out and proclaimed,

> A new commandment I give to you, that you love one another:
> just as I have loved you, you also are to love one another. By
> this all people will know that you are my disciples, if you have
> love for one another (John 13:34-35).

Christ set the paradigm for His church: Love others in the same way He loved them. This genuine, selfless love was to become the characteristic mark of Christians and their Founder. Love would identify those who were disciples of the Nazarene, and love would separate His body from the world. Therefore, everything a Christ-follower does must be done through the lens of love. Without love, we are *nothing*.

Paul confirmed that high standard when he declared,

> If I speak in the tongues of men and of angels, but have not
> love, I am a noisy gong or a clanging cymbal. And if I have
> prophetic powers, and understand all mysteries and all knowl-
> edge, and if I have all faith, so as to remove mountains, but
> have not love, I am nothing. If I give away all I have, and if
> I deliver up my body to be burned, but have not love, I gain
> nothing (1 Corinthians 13:1-3).

As part of the body of Christ now, I, too, was commissioned as a follower of Jesus to love my neighbor as myself, beginning with the man kneeling across from me. How? By mercifully giving him God's Word as it had been mercifully given to me. After all, as it states in Romans 10:17, "Faith comes from hearing, and hearing through the word of Christ." How is President—or anyone, for that matter—going to hear unless someone shares with them? How can others know Christ if He isn't preached? If I see someone in spiritual bondage but don't share truth with them, do I really have love in my heart? Contrary to what the world seems to preach, true love is not affirming others in their sinful and lost state, it is proclaiming the Christ who can liberate them from captivity. Therefore, my greatest calling as a Christian is to be a conduit of God's love to unbelievers by proclaiming to them the grace and truth found only in Jesus of Nazareth.

As I pondered my peculiar encounter with Pastor Shaw, I had long been confounded by his unusual pronouncement as he disappeared through that door and out of my life: "Don't be a stranger now,"[20] he said. It took a long time for me to discover just how much of a valuable message was tied up in a seemingly offhand parting of words. I now knew that he wasn't so much inviting me to visit his church as he was urging me to become like the Good Samaritan—to no longer be a stranger who is in need, but rather be transformed by the gospel of Christ into a neighbor, like the Samaritan was to the stranger, like Pastor Shaw was to me, loving others as Christ has loved us all. He was inviting me to be a follower of Jesus and partake of the Lord's Supper. Finally, I found myself at the table.

Four Pillars

As I returned through the wardrobe and back to the room, I was nearly hypnotized by President's droning voice.

"We thank Thee for giving us the fullness of Thy gospel to lead us in these latter days. (1) We thank Thee so much for Thy servant Joseph Smith, and all he has done to bring us Thy truth. (2) We thank Thee for the Book of Mormon, and the guidance it gives us to know Thy will and follow Thy path. (3) Father, we give Thee thanks for our beloved prophet President Gordon B. Hinckley and for the instrument he is to teach us Thy Word in these latter days.

"Oh Father, we ask Thee to bless us with Thy Spirit, and lead us to the truth of these things, and to know that Thy gospel has been restored to the world, (4) and that this Church is Thy kingdom here upon the earth. Please lead us and guide us in all that we do, and help us not to be deceived by the ways of the world. Bless us now that Thou wilt show us Thy truth. These things we pray, in the name of Thy Son Jesus Christ, amen."

"Amen."

Whether it was premeditated or not, President had prayerfully stressed the exact points of doctrine that were no longer incorporated into my testimony—a testimony which, publicly born only two days ago in this very building in front of fifty missionaries and President himself, had most definitely contributed to my current predicament. My religious superior had named four of the five pillars of the faith, and not surprisingly, had left out his testimony of Jesus Christ.

I slowly opened my eyes as President finished his lengthy prayer and the brightness of the room was overpowering. After a lifetime in spiritual blindness unable to see, the light of the gospel of the glory of Christ had pierced through my darkness. I could see, and I could understand, and after having washed my eyes with the water of the Word of God, I was a new creation in Christ. The dichotomy between who I was and who I had become was astonishing, filling my heart with praise and thanksgiving to God for His mercy toward a pitiful man like me.

I climbed back into my seat directly across from President Sorensen. As I observed him and he scrutinized me, I realized that everything in my life had reversed. Only three weeks after Pastor Shaw had taken his place in my spiritual training, I found myself staring at a man who graced me from the opposite side of his desk, and although he believed radically differently than me, he would lovingly pick up the torch it seemed Pastor Shaw had passed on to him.

The religious tables had turned—just as they had with Saul 2,000 years ago—as I was now preparing to defend the very same truth I had once fought so vehemently against.

CHAPTER 8

ZEAL FOR GOD

Winter Garden, Florida | *June 27, 2004*

W ell, here we are," I said, sporting a mischievous grin.

I glanced out the car window at the high steeple on the Dillard Street building just as my companion and I succumbed to a sudden urge to pull into the parking lot of Calvary Baptist Church on a rainy Sunday evening. I wasn't sure what stirred me to take note of the church, but the desire to put a Baptist minister in his place and bring him to the truth was born out of the ill-fated confrontation I had recently faced with Pastor Shaw, in which I endured a biblical pistol-whipping. This was my opportunity for redemption.

With less than three months' experience in the field, I was still quite green but already emerging as one of the mission's young leaders. The willingness to charge headfirst into a Herculean battle against a Goliath that represented the forces of veiled evil would prove that I was worth my salt.

I was not alone in my venture; there were many missionaries who fantasized about converting a Baptist preacher to the Restored Church (yet few would ever admit it or be driven to do this). Rumors would circulate about miraculous instances of missionaries converting and baptizing leaders of other denominations, and they, in turn, would convert their whole congregation. Although I doubted the veracity of these accounts, I was convinced I could make this happen. After all, I wasn't an average run-of-the-mill missionary. If anyone could accomplish such an implausible scheme and convert a Baptist minister, it was going to be me.

My propensity for outward confidence was spoon-fed to me in the Missionary Training Center for weeks as it was communicated to us that, as missionaries, we had been given exclusive authority from God to act in His name. Naturally, our confidence was unparalleled. All I had to do was arrange a time to meet with this pastor and the power of our message, delivered with breathtaking authority, would sweep him off his feet. He would have no choice but to beg for baptism! Once we had converted him, he would then assist us in converting the remainder of his congregation. It was a foolproof plan that, once executed, would launch me into legendary status and enshrine me in the missionary Hall of Fame.

As we were slowly devoured by the side entries of the Christian citadel, we were greeted by a couple of sentinels guarding the inner sanctuary doors. If they were the least bit surprised at seeing us, they hid it well. "Good evening, young men!" they said as they blitzed us with warm, infectious smiles. I couldn't help but also bare my own pearly whites and reciprocate the gesture.

As we made our way down the center aisle, we were overcome by dozens of people from all directions. To make matters worse, some gracious Christian women shockingly stole hugs, while their husbands slapped us on the back with one hand and plunged the other at us like a serrated dagger. I handled the situation as skillfully as I could, turning this way and that while shaking the men's pawing hands with enthusiasm and waving off the innocent embraces of the womenfolk by using their own men adeptly as human shields. After all, contact with women (other than a handshake) was strictly forbidden in our missionary culture, and I felt like I had been placed in an active minefield.

Eventually, we found an out-of-the-way place to plant ourselves. As we sat down with my knee nervously bouncing and my eyes scoping out every conceivable avenue of escape should one be needed, I observed the impressive sanctuary: high ceilings, stained glass, and in the front was a large cross. Yes, there it was again, the same graven image we had seen in Pastor Shaw's church. I was so confused about why "Christians" placed so much emphasis on the cross. It always made me feel uneasy and had the effect of mildly repulsing me. After all, as I had been taught, Christ's primary suffering for our sins took place in the Garden of Gethsemane the night before, and not on Calvary. Why celebrate and glorify an instrument of death?

As I turned my attention away from the offending cross, the service began, and the congregation arose to sing the opening hymn, *The Old Rugged Cross*. I chuckled to myself.

> On a hill far away stood an old rugged cross
> The emblem of suffering and shame
> And I love that old cross where the dearest and best
> For a world of lost sinners was slain
>
> So I'll cherish the old rugged cross
> Till my trophies at last I lay down
> And I will cling to the old rugged cross
> And exchange it some day for a crown

A Pure and Simple Testimony

As the song ended and the congregants took their seats, a well-dressed Lebanese gentleman approached the pulpit. "Brothers and sisters, my name is Charbel, and it is an honor to be here today. I am privileged to be able to report to you that the gospel of Christ is being advanced in all parts of the world, no matter the cost."

He proceeded to share story after story about his missionary journeys to Baghdad, Iraq, where he had been a pioneer in establishing Christian churches since the fall of Saddam Hussein's regime. He recounted many heartbreaking instances of the persecution the Middle Eastern Christians endured because they would not recant their faith in Jesus of Nazareth, to the point of suffering beatings, rape, torture, and even death. Their dedication to Jesus Christ shook me to the core. I was inspired by their faith.

Charbel then showed a stirring video of poor Christians in broken communities worshipping in homes and basements, humbly gathering wherever they could with other believers to praise God and read the Bible together, even with the threat of execution over their heads.

As the video came to an end, I could hear a chorus of sniffles throughout the room. After a brief pause—perhaps to suppress his own emotions—Charbel approached the pulpit and passionately shared his testimony of Jesus Christ.

"Friends, the gospel of Jesus does not call us to tangible wealth and treasures. Following the Lord does not mean that our lives get easier in the worldly sense. Our brothers and sisters in other parts of the world are evidence of that reality. To follow Christ is to take up our cross. To follow Christ is to be hated by the world, persecuted, and often suffer for His name. False teachers propagate a counterfeit gospel that believing in Jesus means our houses get bigger, our cars faster, and our bank accounts larger. No! The gospel calls us to eternal, spiritual riches in Jesus Christ—and an inheritance as adopted sons and daughters of the King.

"I would like to believe that if I was ever put in a situation like my brothers and sisters are—to have to suffer all things, even my own life, for Christ—that through the grace of the Lord, I would persevere, because He is my treasure and He is worth my life. And if I can be faithful to Jesus, and if ever I am given a crown of glory by the Lord, I will take it off and cast it at His precious feet, and worship Him with all my heart. He alone is worthy because He shed His blood for me."

By the time Charbel finished his testimony, a flood of tears had been unleashed from my eyes. I turned away from García, uncertain what he might think about me shedding tears in a Baptist church. More so, I was unsure what the *Baptists* might think.

"Praise the Lord God for His goodness and grace!" the pastor said as he stood up to the pulpit, his voice cracking slightly. "God is good, isn't He?" His statement was followed by an explosion of "Yeahs!" and "Amens!" from all around me. This was so unexpected and abrupt. Never in my life had I heard a peep from our congregation. There were people in our ward[21] who would choke to death without uttering so much as a squeak lest they interrupt a service.

"Christ's gospel is being preached across the world, and it is only by His strength that it is being done. We need to recognize the freedom we have in this country, praising God that we don't face the same persecution for our faith as do many of our brothers and sisters from all corners of the globe. But let us hold fast to the same hope that they have, that Jesus is worth the loss of all things, because in Him we have our everything."

For a split second, the pastor glanced to the back of the chapel and looked into the eyes of me and my companion. "We will now have our missionary youth share testimonies about their recent mission trip," he said. I was momentarily suspended in place, questioning our presence in the church and giving healthy consideration to making a run for the door—until he released me from his gaze and I realized that he was not referring to us. I breathed a sigh of relief.

One by one, the youth of the church stepped up to the pulpit, sharing testimonies of their different missionary experiences and witnessing of their faith in Jesus Christ. It was characteristic of what I saw in our church during fast Sunday, when once a month the members of the congregation would share their testimonies of the five pillars of the Church. There was a glaring, distinct difference between the two ceremonies, however: There was no Joseph Smith, no Book of Mormon, no prophets, and no recitation of "I know the Church is true"—all of which are the central components of our religious foundation. The total focus of each testimony by these youth was rather astonishing: a simple and pure affirmation of the Lord Jesus Christ.

I was emotionally overwhelmed by what I heard, and feeling shame for something that I couldn't put my finger on, I buried my head from public view. I was amazed—but conflicted—at how deeply impacted I was by the service. After all, these were the people I was seeking so desperately to convert to my religion; yet they had an obvious and zealous passion for Jesus Christ and an unwavering testimony in Him. I was unsure how to reconcile this dissonance.

Finally, after experiencing a nonstop rush of emotions for an hour, we sang the closing hymn, *Nothing but the Blood.*

> Nothing can for sin atone:
> nothing but the blood of Jesus.
> Naught of good that I have done:
> nothing but the blood of Jesus.
>
> O precious is the flow
> that makes me white as snow;
> no other fount I know;
> nothing but the blood of Jesus.

Divine Appointment

As the song came to a close and I thought hard about my next move, I tried to eradicate my feelings of guilt and focus on my daring undertaking: converting these sincere—but lost—people to the true Church, starting with the leaders.

My stomach began to swell with butterflies as my companion and I made our way up to the front of the sanctuary to introduce ourselves to the pastor. Along the way, I swayed and bobbed, using the men once again as shields so that I could reach around them and offer my hand to the women (instead of my bosom). As we made our way through the sea of people, I was fighting an uneasy feeling that reminded me of my earlier experience with Pastor Shaw. I was trying hard to maintain confidence. I didn't want a repeat disaster.

Just then, an arresting gentleman approached us and greeted us with a bone-crushing handshake.

"Pastor Martin," he said assuredly with a wide smile. "I'm the youth pastor here at the church. It's nice to have you with us!"

"We really enjoyed the service," I said.

"Thank you," he responded. "God is doing amazing things all over the world, preaching His gospel to those who are lost. All we are doing is spreading the Word to those who do not know it. God gets all the glory!"

As I was contemplating my next strategic action, another man approached and my heart skipped a beat—it was the head pastor. He was a striking individual, probably in his mid-thirties, and was well-dressed in a black suit, white shirt, and tie.

"Pastor Benson," he said as he shook my hand firmly.

There was undeniably something intimidating about this pastor—he had a demeanor about him that made me less certain about my ability to turn him to my side.

"I'm Elder Wilder, and this is my companion, Elder García. We're missionaries from the Church of Jesus Christ of Latter-day Saints."

Pastor Benson smiled with a subtle, almost imperceptible twinkle in his eyes. His behavior and his countenance puzzled me. Even so, I continued in my pursuit.

"We would like to share a message with you about the gospel of Jesus Christ," I petitioned.

"Well, we would *love* to sit down with you young men and talk to you about the gospel," he answered enthusiastically. I couldn't believe it. He was already coming around before we even made our presentation!

"Why don't you gentlemen come by my office Tuesday morning at eleven o'clock. Does that work with your schedule?"

I was so excited. Quite frankly, I was dumbfounded by how kind, gracious, and respectful Pastor Benson had been to us. I was unaccustomed to this manner of treatment. In my short time in the mission field, I had bottles thrown at me, guns pulled on me, dogs let loose on me, and every profanity known to mankind hurled at me. I'd even had a driver try to run me over. Benson's kindheartedness was clear evidence that God had prepared his heart to receive the message of the restored gospel.

"Sounds great, Pastor Benson. We'll see you then!"

———

For the next two nights, I sat at my desk with all my Scriptures and books sprawled out in front of me. I welcomed the time to brush up on the "discussions." Principally, these were the tailored teachings of the Church that we had spent hundreds of hours absorbing at the MTC. To me personally, the discussions were the restored gospel of Jesus Christ. I had never once in my life doubted or questioned these sacred truths as they had been imparted to me from my parents and Church leaders. This is what I had been taught from my youth, and I believed them with more zeal and fervor than anyone I had ever met.

As I sat at my desk and pored over the teachings of the Church, I sensed an inexplicable feeling I couldn't eradicate. Something was different about this Pastor Benson fellow, yet familiar all the same. I couldn't tell whether I loved him or hated him, but something drew me to him, like a moth to the flame.

I laid in bed restlessly that night trying to quench an unnerving feeling that had built up inside of me. Attempting to eliminate my anxiety, I rehearsed over and over what I was going to say and how I was going to say it. I carefully reviewed every point of doctrine and every scripture that supported each point, tying each precept into a tight little package. I must have fallen asleep doing so, because the next thing I remembered was the throbbing sound of my alarm at 6:00 a.m.

CHAPTER 9

FIGHT THE
GOOD FIGHT

June 29, 2004

Waking up at the break of dawn before the required time, I enthusiastically went through my morning routine, knowing today was my chance to demonstrate that I was no longer a lightweight in the faith. Doing pushups to oxygenate my brain, I felt like Rocky training for his epic match with the Russian Ivan Drago, and I had no doubt that I would be the victor, because—like Rocky—I, too, was the protagonist of this story. Unlike my experience with Pastor Shaw, I had entered this bout willingly, and this time I would be prepared to fight the good fight and make my mark as one of the all-time missionary greats.

With the opening bell quickly approaching, Elder García and I were ready to face the odds and our opponent head-on. We said a prayer as we left the apartment and headed out on the short five-minute drive to the church. My heart pounded and my palms sweat as I nervously sat in the passenger seat of the car, savoring the last few precious minutes to prepare my mind and heart for the upcoming contest.

As the hot sun beat down on me through the windshield, I became detached from reality and found myself daydreaming of the most spectacular performance of a lifetime. Hitting, jabbing, bobbing, ducking. I was throwing beautiful right hooks and landing left jabs with jaw-dropping precision. As Pastor Benson was retreating off-balance after a flurry of blinding speed hits, I cocked back with full force and delivered the proverbial knockout punch: I bore the most beautiful, sincere, and powerful testimony of the restored gospel that had ever come from my lips (and perhaps the world itself had ever seen), and Benson broke down in tears while collapsing on his knees, repenting, and begging to be baptized into the true Church of Christ. I raised my hands in the air as the crowd chanted my name in a chorus so glorious it was as if the angels of heaven themselves were cheering.

A broad and confident smile crossed my face and comforted me for a split second, but then I was quickly brought back to reality as we hit the speed bump entering the church parking lot. It was eleven o'clock, the sun was shining brightly, and the heat and humidity of the day were quickly rising. Even though my stomach was in knots, I convinced myself I was ready for the fight.

As Elder García and I sat in the car seeking the strength to confront our foe, we said a prayer. "Heavenly Father, we ask that Thy Spirit be with us, and that Thy message may touch the heart of this man who is in darkness. Open his eyes to see Thy truth. In Jesus' name we pray, amen."

I stepped out of the car and slung my backpack over my left shoulder. In it I carried the missionary essentials for battle: my "quad" (a thick single-bound book containing the four "Standard Works"[22] of Church Scripture canon), Church-sanctioned books, and tracts to hand out to unsuspecting pedestrians on the street.

I slowly walked toward the west entrance of the building as García trailed behind, and with determination in my eyes, headed to the door that was marked "Office." As we entered, a middle-aged woman sitting at the front desk greeted us with a friendly smile. She was smartly dressed and stood up sharply as she introduced herself. She eagerly led us to Pastor Benson's office and gently tapped on the door.

"Pastor Benson, you have some visitors!"

"Come on in!" I heard in a rather enthusiastic voice from the other side. *This is it,* I thought as the door swung open and we entered our corner of the ring. It was taking all the strength I had to suppress my nerves.

Pastor Benson was sitting at his desk in his corner, leaning back in his chair. He smiled as we entered and stood up to greet us.

"Hello, gentlemen," he said in his seductive pastoral drawl, a voice I had heard over and over in my head over the past two days like a broken record.

"Hello, Pastor Benson," I stated cordially while sizing him up. His light brown hair was combed to the side and he was wearing brown slacks with a blue shirt and tie. Benson's clean-cut appearance and spiffy attire (typical of my Church's leadership) did not put me at ease; rather, the poor impersonation of my headship quickly set me on guard. After all, Lucifer himself was said to have been the most attractive of all of God's angels.

As we greeted each other with universally ritualistic pleasantries, I inspected Pastor Benson's office with my wandering eyes, trying to gather clues about my opponent, attempting to figure out any way to gain an advantage over him. His meticulously maintained space gave me no helpful hints, although the plethora of religious books filling his bookshelves seemed to indicate he was well-educated.

"Please, take a seat," he said, pointing to the chairs facing him. "Make yourselves at home." I knew *that* wasn't going to happen, so I took great pains to position the chair as carefully as I could away from his desk, to give myself a clear shot at the exit in case Benson became argumentative. In such a scenario, we were instructed to give a heartfelt testimony and beat a hasty retreat.

As I continued to gaze at the surroundings, I noticed pictures of a woman and young kids that I assumed were his family; this humanized him for the first time and gave me a way to connect with him on a personal level, as we had been trained to do.

"You have a beautiful family," I said passively.

"Thank you. I love them very much." He paused for a second, and an awkward silence filled the room. I looked over to my companion, who was quiet as usual, and he once again gave me no aid. As I sought for something to break the emptiness, Pastor Benson spoke up.

"Gentlemen," he said, "let's pray, shall we?" He took command of the prayer in a traditional Baptist fashion. "Oh Lord God, we just thank You so much Lord for the gift of Your Son, Lord, and the grace and mercy that You give us every day, Lord God…"

Ready to Rumble

After he finished the prayer, Benson initiated some informal chitchat, perhaps in an attempt to subdue our nerves he could no doubt sense from a mile away—he had made more than one glance down at my bouncing knee, which by now looked like it was driving an oil well under his desk.

"So, where are you gentlemen from?" he asked, beginning a string of inquiries about our homes, families, and lives prior to becoming missionaries. He seemed genuinely interested and rather intrigued by the sacrifices we had made for our full-time service to the Church. Perhaps he did this to be polite, but it had the effect of putting us on equal ground, which was a stance that few Christians had taken based on my experiences with them.

After a few minutes of small talk, it was time for the main event. We touched gloves and the bell rang.

"Would you young men like to tell me a little bit about your church?" he asked. His interest seemed so genuine that I was immediately filled with hope. *This is the opportunity of a lifetime,* I thought. *All I have to do is bear testimony of the true Church, and the Spirit will change his life.*

I fervently prayed in my heart as I retrieved my Scriptures from my backpack. I was both eager and nervous for the unique opportunity that God had placed in front of me. I had prepared an arsenal of Mormon Scriptures to prove to Pastor Benson—beyond a shadow of a doubt—that the Church was true. And most importantly, I had perfected my secret weapon: a sincere testimony of the restored gospel.

"Pastor Benson, God is our loving Heavenly Father and we are all His literal spirit children. We lived with Him before this life. He sent us to Earth to learn and grow. He loves us, and He wants us to return to live with Him again. Because of that love, He has always called prophets like Noah, Moses, and Abraham to teach us the gospel so we know the way to return to His presence." This was the same company line we had delivered to Pastor Shaw.

"Jesus Himself came to the earth to atone for our sins. He also came to establish His one true Church. Through that Church, we can have the correct authority to perform the ordinances necessary to be able to live with God again. Jesus Christ also chose His twelve apostles and gave them a special authority, the priesthood, to preach the gospel to the world and to perform saving ordinances such as baptism and the giving of the gift of the Holy Ghost.

"But when Jesus and His apostles were killed, that priesthood authority was lost, and the Church became corrupt. Men no longer had guidance from God and the simple truths of Christ's gospel were lost or distorted. There was no authority to guide Christ's Church or receive revelation."

I paused for a second, curious to see how Pastor Benson was holding up. I had given him some small jabs, but he just kept his gloves up. He looked stone cold and didn't bat an eye. Unsure of how to interpret his lack of response, I nodded at my companion, and he entered the ring.

"The earth was in darkness for centuries," Elder García shared in his serene voice. "The truth was lost. No one had knowledge of the gospel for nearly two thousand years. There was a great need for a restoration of the truth. Pastor Benson, in the year 1820 there was a young boy named Joseph Smith who was searching for answers. He wanted to know which church was the true Church of Jesus Christ. He went from church to church, yet he saw that they all interpreted the Bible differently. He was so confused. We see that same confusion in the world today.

"In the Bible, he read in James, 'If any of you lack wisdom, let him ask of God, that giveth to all men liberally.'[23] Joseph Smith knew that the only way he could know the truth was to ask God directly. One day, he went to a grove of trees and prayed, in humble sincerity, and God and His Son Jesus Christ appeared to him in person. He asked them which church he should join, and they said to join none of them, because their creeds and doctrines were an abomination in His sight. The young boy was then told that he would restore Christ's Church to the earth, and that he would be called as a prophet, just like Moses and Abraham.

"In Amos 3:7, we read, 'Surely the Lord GOD will do nothing, but he revealeth his secret unto his servants the prophets.'[24] God is unchanging. He is the same yesterday, today, and forever, and if He called prophets in the Old Testament, why would He not call them now to lead and guide

His children? The heavens were opened, and God's truth could once again be on the earth."

I smiled at García in approval of his performance and then turned my eye to Benson, hoping to see that our punches had landed on target. After all, we had been crystal clear in our presentation. If his heart was pure, he would feel the Spirit through our message and know that it was true. I had to trust the process.

However, I was disheartened to observe that Benson's reaction hadn't changed one iota, and his emotionless face was difficult to read. He just sat there, rigid, and stared at us with unwavering eyes. He didn't punch back. He was unnervingly still, and his behavior made me uncomfortable. We had no choice but to continue, so I retook the reins.

"Pastor, I know that Joseph Smith did indeed see God the Father and His Son Jesus Christ. I know that the true Church of Christ was restored through this humble and simple young man. Because of the restoration of the priesthood keys and authority, salvation is now possible to all who come to the true Church and follow the laws and ordinances established by Jesus Himself!" I exuberantly proclaimed, half expecting Benson to jump up and down at the good news we were delivering to him. This was the greatest message in the world!

Pastor Benson leaned back in his chair. His hands were together up against his mouth as he sat and listened intently to every word. *I think we're getting to him,* I thought, so I continued with my ardent proclamation.

"Pastor Benson, it's amazing!" I stated with zeal. "Christ's Church is on the earth again, and the priesthood authority to perform ordinances necessary for eternal life—such as baptism, conveying the gift of the Holy Ghost, the sacrament, and sacred temple covenants—has been restored. We now have the only true authority to do God's work on Earth!"

By the time I finished my oration I was nearly yelling. There was no doubt, even to the depths of my soul, that everything to which I had just born witness of was true. I knew it. That certainty only grew stronger within me each time I shared my testimony. The restoration through Joseph Smith had opened the door for eternal life once again, making salvation possible through the fullness of the new and everlasting gospel as revealed through a fourteen-year-old boy.

I was convinced that Pastor Benson's stillness was evidence that he was deeply contemplating the truths we had been imparting to him, so I prepared to give him the silver bullet—the foundation of our message and the keystone of our religion.

"Pastor, we know a prophet by their fruit. We have the fruit of the Prophet Joseph Smith," I declared while proudly holding up a Book of Mormon. "The Book of Mormon is a record of God's dealings with the people of the ancient Americas, and it contains the fullness of the gospel of Jesus Christ. The Bible has become corrupt over time and some of the plain and precious truths have been lost. But God has given us His truth in the Book of Mormon, and a man will get nearer to God through the Book of Mormon than any other book. It goes hand in hand with the Bible and is a second witness of Christ."

Pastor Benson slowly shook his head as I finished my sentence, and for the first time I had seen but the slightest reaction from him. I pounced on the opportunity.

"Have you heard of the Book of Mormon?" I asked in excitement.

"I have," he replied. "In fact, I have read most of it."

I knew it. I knew it! God had prepared his heart to receive the message of the restoration and in His divine wisdom had sent me to this man's office for a purpose. I continued with zeal.

"Well, Pastor Benson, there is an incredible prophecy about the Book of Mormon in Ezekiel chapter 37," I stated while flipping open my Bible. "This book, the Book of Mormon, is the stick of Joseph, which is prophesied of by the prophet Ezekiel. The stick of Judah is the Bible. I now hold the stick of Judah and the stick of Joseph in my hand, as the Bible says." I confidently held up my missionary quad high into the air, making my not-so-subtle point. Pastor Benson looked at the thick book and then back to me with a befuddled grimace.

"Pastor Benson, you, too, can know if the Book of Mormon is true, and thereby know that Joseph Smith was a true prophet and that this is indeed the true Church of Jesus Christ on the earth today. There is a promise at the end of the Book of Mormon by which we can receive an answer directly from God. All you have to do is ask God—with a sincere heart—if this book is not true,[25] and He promises to answer you through the power of the Holy Ghost!"

Benson slowly squinted and scribbled a note on a piece of paper in front of him. I tried unsuccessfully to decipher what he had written, then primed myself for the final punch, which I was certain would end the match: my testimony.

"Pastor Benson," I pleaded, "I know with all my heart and soul that what we are telling you is true. Through prayer, God has told me in my heart that these things are true. He has witnessed to me through the power of the Holy Ghost." I looked him square in the eyes without flinching.

"I know that the Book of Mormon is true. I know that this Church—the Church of Jesus Christ of Latter-day Saints—is the only true Church. I know that Joseph Smith is a prophet of God, and I know that we have a prophet today to speak for God," I testified with an animated and forceful conviction. "I am begging you, Pastor Benson: Open your heart, read the Book of Mormon, and prayerfully ask if it is true. Then you will know, as I do, that this is the only way to get back to the Father and live with Him forever."

Bam. I had delivered the perfect knockout punch with flawless execution. The bell chimed, the round was over, and I was certain I was victorious.

As I sat stationary in my seat with my heart pumping heavily, I looked up at Pastor Benson, hoping that I would visibly see a miraculous and instantaneous change in his life, that my punch had met its mark. I half expected to see tears rolling down his face...but no. He was sitting back in his chair, demonstrating impeccable posture while appearing very contemplative. There was nothing defensive about him that alarmed me. He gave nothing away. I didn't know what to think. Maybe he was so impacted by the power of our message that he was simply left speechless?

My knee was bouncing out of control. This was the moment of truth, when I would find out if I had been drilling a dry well after all.

CHAPTER 10

ENEMY OF THE CROSS

P astor Benson leaned forward in his chair as if to speak, and my eager-ness quickly rose. My examining eyes focused on his body language, searching for any clues as to his state of mind, and my ears strained for his words. I found myself dangling at the edge of my chair, perched in a painful and dreadful anticipation.

Then in a very delicate and deliberate manner, Benson spoke up. The bell chimed, and round two began.

"You are both certainly devoted to what you believe, and I respect that," he said. "There is no doubt in my mind you are sincere in the things that you teach. You are both zealous for your religion, and I commend you for giving up two years of your young lives to go door to door and share what you believe. Honestly, I wish more Christians had the same type of zeal for their faith that you Mormons do for yours."

I leaned into the very edge of my seat, so nervous that I had difficulty breathing. Could this be it? Was he going to confess his sins right here and now and ask to be baptized? Was I about to become a hero of the faith?

"But I must tell you that I *strongly* disagree with your message. It is not the gospel of Jesus Christ as revealed in the Word of God. Gentlemen, what you have shared with me is not good news."

Benson had lulled me into a false sense of security before he came out swinging in full force, and his first words out of the gate gave way like a ton of bricks on my heart. I had let my guard down as the Christian air bag exploded in my face, and I realized right then that I had enthusiastically plowed into an immovable object. I did *not* see that coming.

Everything I had just taught and testified of was all in vain with this stubborn, deceived man. I had poured out all I had—every ounce of my heart—in testifying to him the tenets of my faith. Now I would be rewarded by having to endure his doctrinal jabs and swings, all while mirroring the same respect that he had offered me. With my heart now crushed and delivered into his unyielding grip, I readied myself to take his fire.

"Elder Wilder, I want you to know that I care about you. I can see something different in you. You are a genuine young man with an admirable zeal for God. Both of you are," he said diplomatically while nodding at García. "But there is a big difference between you and me, and what we believe."

My mouth starting twitching slightly as I delivered a smirk, straightening my posture in defiance of Benson's advantage over me, determined not to let on that I was wounded in any way. He continued.

"I put my faith in the Word of God—the Bible—and in the Jesus of Nazareth as revealed in the Bible, not in man," he declared while holding the Bible in his right hand. "I believe the gospel as delivered once for all to the saints: 'that Christ died for our sins in accordance with the Scriptures, that he was buried, that he was raised on the third day in accordance with the Scriptures.'[26] From what you have shared with me, I fear that we are not proclaiming the same gospel, and we do not know and serve the same Jesus."

I defiantly shook my head in disgust and could hardly contain my now-visible resentment. *Of course* we served the same Jesus! What a ridiculously cruel accusation to make—the second time now in a matter of weeks this slander had been spewed out against me. I was growing tired of hearing this fallacious falsehood. *Has the whole world gone mad?* I thought. My Jesus *was* the Jesus who died for my sins and rose from the dead. I *did* believe in the same Jesus as this pastor. How could he say I did not?

I desperately wanted to retaliate right then and there, but Pastor Benson had yet to fully puncture my courteous shell and so I sat paralyzed, holding my hands in front of my face, cupping my chin in a defensive position. He continued before I had time to organize my argument and take a swing back.

"I must respectfully refute many of the things that you just shared with me. And know that my foundation of doctrine lies in the inerrant God-breathed Word, the Bible, which is my sole source for truth. What you have told me, as sincere as it may be—and as much as you may believe it in your heart—contradicts the saving gospel as revealed in Scripture, and for that reason I must call into question the validity of what you young men are teaching."

I wasn't sure what to say or do. My ever-sinking heart was quickly being flooded with a mixture of anger and pride; I was now drowning under wave after wave of crushing disappointment. How was I going to get out of this? I had nothing to say, and in fact my mind had gone blank, so I silently called out to God for help and then locked the door on my now-shattered heart. I resigned myself to listen politely and endure Benson's turn as respectfully as he had offered his attention to me.

The Christian Iceberg

"You taught me that all people are literal spirit children of God, yet the Bible teaches that we *become* children of God through our faith in Jesus Christ. In fact, mankind is all conceived in sin and because of our sin, separated from God—and in this state, we stand in condemnation before a holy and just God. We, by nature, are enemies of God and are not reconciled to Him except through the blood of Christ," he said as he opened his Bible. "But God's love is lavished upon us by adopting us as His own children and making us righteous through our faith in the finished work of Jesus. John teaches us, 'To all who did receive him, who believed in his name, he gave the right to become children of God.'[27]

"You emphasized that God called prophets to teach His Word and mediate from God to man, and in the past, He did. But wasn't the purpose of prophets in the Old Testament to prophesy of the coming of the Messiah? To point toward the hope in the One who would come to take away the sin of the world and fulfill the law? As Hebrews 1:1-2 says, 'Long ago, at many times and in many ways, God spoke to our fathers by the prophets, but in these last days he has spoken to us by his Son, whom he appointed the heir of all things.' Jesus is now our only mediator with the Father, and only through Him do we have access to the throne of God's grace. As Paul wrote to Timothy, 'There is one God, and there is one mediator between God and men, the man Christ Jesus.'"[28]

Benson paused as I was fighting an emerging offense triggered by his direct and cutting words. I had been passionately pleading to him the good news of Christ's Restored Church just minutes ago, and he was now sitting there (although politely) bashing my faith and me along with it. I had to ask myself: *Who could call themselves a Christian and do such a thing?* Jesus would *never* condone condemning someone else's religion. I was convinced this was all a part of the lies and propaganda put out by the enemies of the Church. I made every attempt to close off my heart as Benson continued coming at me.

"You zealously claim that your church is the 'one true church,' and the very institution Jesus Himself organized while on the earth. But Scripture teaches us that the church is not a physical organization or institution, but the body of Christ comprised of all believers who have a saving faith in Jesus and have been born-again—those whose names are written in the Lamb's book of life. This worldwide body of believers encompasses followers of Jesus from all corners of the globe, representing countless denominations, congregations, and fellowships—yet one Lord, one faith, and one baptism, all adhering to the Word of God as their standard for truth. And each one working together to glorify God through the building of His body. As Romans says, 'For as in one body we have many members, and the members do not all have the same function, so we, though many, are one body in Christ, and individually members one of another.'[29]

"You also assert that there was a great and total apostasy, and that the gospel of Christ was lost from the earth for centuries. But when was God's Word ever lost, Elder Wilder? For nearly two thousand years, faithful disciples of Jesus Christ have preserved the Word of God—many to their own martyrdom. At unspeakable costs, devoted Christian missionaries have been proclaiming the good news of Jesus Christ to nations all over the earth. Jesus said, 'Heaven and earth will pass away, but my words will not pass away'[30] and 'Upon this rock I will build my church, and the gates of hell shall not prevail against it.'[31] Does God lie? God's Word *has* been preserved, and the Holy Spirit has been working in the church since the day of Pentecost."

I was starting to feel as though God had abandoned me. I kept glancing over at my companion to see how he was reacting to this whole charade. As was his nature, he appeared nervous, scared, and remained quiet. I felt sick to my stomach. My boat was sinking after foolishly declaring that it was unsinkable, and I had set out on a blind run in defiant confidence only to strike a Christian iceberg. I desperately sought for my companion to throw me a life preserver. However, he was the proverbial deer caught in the headlights and, not knowing what to expect next, he had surrendered to fear and had frozen while bracing for impact. He wouldn't be capable of rescuing me; he couldn't even save himself.

Pastor, unwilling to relent, continued mercilessly in wave after wave to pound at the rift in my bow with a torrent of water.

"You boldly testify of the restoration of Joseph Smith, yet it seems as though he 'restored' everything that Jesus Christ fulfilled. Every element of the old law was expressly to foreshadow the coming of the promised Messiah, the Mashiach of God. Adherence to the old law could never save us, but rather existed to show man that we could not be reconciled to God by our own righteousness. It exposed the nature of our sin and showed us the hopelessness of our state and our desperate need for a Savior, who is Jesus Christ.

"Therefore, when Jesus ushered in the new covenant of grace, He fulfilled all the priesthood, prophets, temples, and ordinances of the old covenant when He paid for our sins on the cross. And as He did, the temple veil was torn in two, signifying the end of the separation between men and God and giving us free access to the Father through the righteousness of the Son. He then gave us all the royal priesthood as believers, He became our high priest and prophet forever when He offered Himself as the final and ultimate sacrifice, and His body is now the temple of God. Christ, on the cross, fulfilled the old law. 'For Christ is the end of the law for righteousness to everyone who believes.'[32]

"So then, as Christians, we are not justified by works of the law or any of its ceremonial rituals. The law died with Jesus Christ, our debt was nailed to the cross, and now we live by a better promise: the new covenant of grace. As the Bible teaches in Galatians: 'We know that a person is not justified by works of the law but through faith in Jesus Christ.'[33]

"Gentlemen," he beckoned as I was frantically trying to endure my spiritual waterboarding, "eternal life cannot be earned by the merit of our own righteousness. You can never do enough to make yourself worthy. You'll never be good enough. There is no amount of works, ordinances, laws, and commandments that you can do, perform, and follow that will ever make you right with God outside of faith in Jesus alone. The Bible says in Romans 3:23-24, 'All have sinned and fall short of the glory of God, and are justified by His grace as a gift, through the redemption that is in Christ Jesus.'"

Benson's ruthless "anti-Mormon" tirade seemingly had been building to a crescendo, and I squinted as I instinctually saw him take aim at me as if preparing to coldly deliver an arrow straight into my heart.

"Salvation is in and through the cross of Jesus Christ—by His once-for-all offering on our behalf, and in no other way. Anyone who teaches otherwise is an *enemy* of the cross."

His words pierced me with a pain that ran through my chest. My lung felt like it had collapsed all over again and the mighty finger of God had poked me straight through my heart and right to my soul. In an instant I was filled with an overwhelming dread and anxiety. What if what Benson was saying were true? What if I *was* an enemy of the cross of Jesus Christ? And what did that even mean? Aside from being confused and scared, I had no passion left to draw on. I was emotionally and physically exhausted, and it all manifested itself into the only defense mechanism I had left—anger.

Agape Love

I wanted to condemn this man for his blasphemies against the Church of Jesus Christ, rebuke him with the power of the holy priesthood that I held, and dust my feet by his door. But before I could muster up enough strength to confront him with a counterpunch, he resumed his diatribe.

"On the cross, Jesus Christ came to set mankind free through the offering of His own body as a ransom for our sins. He died in our place as our substitute, satisfying the demands of God's law that stood against us by shedding His own blood to cleanse us from sin—doing for us what we could never do for ourselves. In Ephesians 1:7, Paul states, 'In him we have redemption through his blood, the forgiveness of our trespasses, according to the riches of his grace.' Through His death, we find life."

Pastor Benson paused for a moment, looking down at his desk while taking in a deep breath. He seemed thoughtful and, for the first time, at a loss for words as he fought back his emotions. His slowly lifted his head again and his eyes met mine with laser focus. His next words came forth from his mouth with a slight tremble.

"God's love is so…vast, so immeasurable, and so deep. It surpasses all knowledge. My desire is that you truly know God and *His* love, a love that is like no other." He closed his Bible and folded his hands in front of him.

"Elders, did you know that there are actually four distinct types of love talked about in Scripture? *Eros* is the romantic love most of us come to know; *storge* is an affectionate love we share with our families; and *philia* is a brotherly love we share with our friends. But the greatest of all, the apex of love—which describes God's love toward mankind in Christ—is *agape*. This is a perfect, selfless, sacrificial, unconditional love that encompasses all other love. I pray that one day you will come to know *that* love, which was demonstrated in Jesus Christ when He died for the sins of the world.

"It truly breaks my heart that you teach and believe that Jesus saves you 'after all you can do,'[34] and that there are certain works and ordinances that you must perform to become worthy of eternal life in the presence of God and be 'exalted,' as you say. But God's Word is so clear: There is nothing we can do to earn the free gift of eternal life. As Scripture says, 'By grace you have been saved through faith. And this is not your own doing; it is the gift of God, not a result of works, so that no one may boast.'[35] Our solitary hope is in Jesus Christ and His one act of righteousness for mankind. God's love for you is so much greater than you can truly fathom."

I was starting to see a pattern with these so-called "Christians" that I was meeting. From both Pastors Shaw and Benson I heard the same regurgitated proclamation, and they were obviously in cahoots with one another, teaching this ridiculous doctrine of "saved by grace" foolishness. Apparently they had never read James 2: "Faith apart from works is dead."[36]

Pastor Benson wouldn't concede and came at us again with lightning speed.

"Once we are regenerated through the Holy Spirit by faith in Jesus Christ, we are born-again as new creations, and we as Christians then produce the fruit of true faith, which includes the proclamation of the good news, the gospel of Jesus Christ. When one truly believes and has a saving faith, they will do good works as a Christian—not to be saved or to prove worthiness, but out of love because they have been saved. A Christian is compelled by the love of God, and we love Him because He first loved us. And so, we are driven by that love to respond in faithfulness to God, because—continuing in Ephesians 2:10—we have been 'created in Christ Jesus for good works, which God prepared beforehand, that we should walk in them.'

"Young men, God is truly gracious. It is a lesson you need to come to understand, and it pains me that you don't know the depth of His grace and mercy and love. The gospel you teach is not the true gospel because it is not rooted in His living and abiding Word. I can only pray that one day you will know the glorious gospel of the grace of God that is the power of God unto salvation to everyone who believes. Then, and only then, will you be liberated and set free from the bondage of men that now holds you captive. Heed the words of Jesus: 'If you abide in my word, you are truly my disciples, and you will know the truth, and the truth will set you free.'"[37]

My head was spinning at the plethora of scriptures Benson was reciting, the words of each verse assaulting me like 1,000 tiny cuts. Much to my dismay, the doctrines he spoke were involuntarily soaking into my soul like the first water to a dry sponge.

Benson had been speaking with such assurance and authority that I was left awestruck. I couldn't detect an ounce of uncertainty or hesitation in him; either I was sitting in front of Satan himself, or Benson was what he claimed to be: a disciple of Christ who was revealing to me a different gospel, the likes of which I had never heard before.

I quickly became aware that I was all alone on a great stormy sea in a sinking boat. I should have been bailing desperately against the crashing waves that were now breaking heavily over my bow, but I was immobile. I cried out silently once again for God to rescue me from my adversary. I was ready to jump out of my seat, raise my arm to the square, and sharply rebuke my antagonist. But before I could attempt such a brave action, Pastor Benson calmly and timely put another arrow in my heart that caught me off guard and sent me reeling.

"The biggest difference between you and me is that you believe in a different Christ. Your Jesus is not my Jesus," he declared. "My Jesus died on a cross so that all who believe may be saved through His blood. Did yours?"

CHAPTER 11

AS A CHILD

The entire time Benson was sermonizing, my blood was boiling hotter and hotter. Genuine fear had made me angry, but I didn't know how to defend myself. After all, everything he witnessed to me emanated straight from the Bible, from under his very own finger, which was tracing the words right from the mouths of Christ and His apostles. I had seen it with my own eyes. How could I dispute what he was saying?

I tried to shake off my doubts by reminding myself that he didn't have modern-day prophets to interpret the Scriptures for him, and he didn't have the fullness of the gospel contained in the Church's Standard Works; therefore, he couldn't have the truth as I had it. But rather than surrender a New Testament baptismal death, I altered my mindset and took on the offensive. I had to speak. I would endure no more of these unwarranted assaults.

"Pastor Benson, I know what God has revealed to me through the Holy Ghost. No matter what you or anyone says, this is the only true gospel. We are representatives of the only true Church. Joseph Smith restored these plain and precious truths to the world so that we can have salvation. The priesthood, temples, ordinances, prophets, and apostles are all necessary today."

"I do not deny that you are a passionate young man," Benson said sympathetically. "But you are blind to the simple, saving gospel. In trying to establish your own good standing with God based on the laws and ordinances of your religious system, you are ignorant of God's righteousness, which comes only through faith in Christ."

I had been beaten nearly unconscious, but the man would not give up. Would he keep belting me if I fell to the floor? There were now so many holes punched in my defense that my vessel could not have held one drop of water let alone a deluge of living water. It all came down to the fact that one of us was right and the other was dead wrong and there was no in-between. A clear and distinct line had been drawn in the sand; the problem was that we were both claiming the prize.

"I respect you for your dedication to what you believe to be the truth," Benson said gently. "If you could turn that passion and devotion toward the true Word of God, God could use you to proclaim good news to the world. But right now, you are caught in false teachings that come from man, not God. You have not tested the words of your leaders against the Bible."

He had cornered me, and I had no way out but to come out swinging.

"Pastor Benson, you have blasphemed!" I yelled with an authoritative voice. "You have spoken against the Prophet and Church of God. One day you will stand in judgment and be held to account for what you have said," I uttered almost out of breath as I put every ounce of energy into a final aspiration that God would rescue me from this dogged antagonist.

I took a moment to regain my composure. "I would like to read a scripture to you," I stated, my hands quivering as I opened the Book of Mormon. "If you believe in Christ ye will believe in these words, for they are the words of Christ...for Christ will show unto you, with power and great glory, that they are his words; and you and I shall stand face to face before his bar; and ye shall know that I have been commanded of him to write these things...for those words shall condemn you at the last day."[38]

I paused for effect and kept my head down for a moment. I had done it. I had pulled out my dual swords, expertly wielding and spinning them while heading right for Benson—a force that I knew would lay waste to him and cut him to pieces. He had brought this upon himself, and now, armed with the truth, if he chose to ignore it, he would stand in condemnation before God.

I looked up at Benson in confidence to discover a rather subdued look on his face. It was clear that he was unarmed. He had no more arrows in his quiver, no testimony upon which to defend himself.

"So…what you are telling me is that if I or anyone does not believe in the Book of Mormon as the words of Christ Himself, and accept the Mormon gospel as you have presented it, then he will be condemned?"

I couldn't back down now.

"Yes," I relented. "To deny the words of the Book of Mormon is to deny the words of Christ. There is no other way."

I was surprised at the bold manner in which I had so mercilessly come right at him, but Pastor Benson had left me no choice. That is what I had been trained to do. I was a soldier out to fight for the kingdom of God, to defend the honor of Joseph Smith, the Book of Mormon, and the restored gospel. I would not be trampled on as I had been by Pastor Shaw. I would uphold the truth with all my heart.

"Elder Wilder," Benson responded, "Jesus Christ was lifted up on a cross and was crucified for the sins of the world so that you, and I, and anyone who believes in Him could be granted the free gift of salvation. John 3:16 says, 'God so loved the world, that he gave his only Son, that whoever believes in him should not perish but have eternal life.'

"I feel true sorrow for your soul that you have not accepted that gift. You are a bright young man with such potential, but you don't yet know God's love. There is certainly eternal life outside of the Book of Mormon and your church, just not outside of Jesus Christ. He is not a religion. He is not an organization. He is the Way. He Himself is Salvation, and if you believe in Him as such, you will be saved by His grace."

With love and gentleness, Benson, in effect, pulled out his gun—hidden in its holster the entire time—and promptly dispatched me.

Read the Bible

Pastor Benson's words were passionate as well as elegant and inspiring…and deep down in my heart, I was drawn to the message he was sharing. His words had ever so subtly brought back memories of my relationship with God in my youth. But I had had enough. This man had absurdly called into question my status as a true disciple of Jesus and had so blatantly rejected the gospel that I knew to be true. I refused to endure any more of his gratuitous attacks, so I defiantly stood up without the final bell ringing, climbed under the ropes, and began to storm out of his office. I was done.

Not content with my premature withdrawal from our bout, Pastor Benson stopped me before I reached the door and gently set his hand on my shoulder. I turned to him while trying to hide the tears that were welling up in my eyes.

"Elder Wilder, I challenge you to study the Word of God; read it, feast upon it, and prove that what I have told you is wrong. I promise that if you read the New Testament as a child—with an open heart seeking for truth—God will open your eyes to His boundless love, and you will see for the very first time the beauty and simplicity of the good news of Jesus Christ."

He looked at me with kindness in his eyes. In that moment, despite all the anger welt up within me, I could sense a true, Christlike love from him. It softened my heart.

"Read the Bible like a child, young man," he pleaded, "and God will bring you out of the darkness and into His marvelous light."

My internal peace was short-lived. I was so angry with him for what I felt had been an embarrassing injustice against me, so I turned the challenge back on him.

"And I challenge you to read the Book of Mormon, and God will open your eyes, Pastor Benson! And you will realize you are wrong, and that it is *you* who is in the darkness!" I yelled weakly.

I had pounded against Benson for all that I was worth, and I was spent. I had read scriptures, born my testimony, and shared the very depths of my heart with this man, but whatever possessed him was immoveable. He had rejected everything I slung at him, seemingly without the slightest bit of doubt or forethought. What was most frustrating was that no matter what I said, he instantly dispelled it with ease, all by using the Bible.

I stormed out of Pastor Benson's office and stood under the scorching Florida sun offended, frustrated, and confused. I was convinced that he was wrong, but I didn't know how to prove it. *If that's the way we're saved,* I thought to myself, *then everybody would be saved, because who would be so foolish as to reject the free gift of eternal life?* Never in my life had I heard the gospel in the manner Benson had presented it to me. It seemed…too easy. Too simple. It *wasn't* the gospel I knew.

———

That evening, no matter how hard I tried, I couldn't escape the piercing challenge given to me, and its deafening tone rang in my ears over and over: "Read the New Testament like a child, and God will open your eyes." I had only two choices: I could shake off the entire experience and forget it had ever happened, or I could accept the challenge and prove him wrong. For a zealous man like me, there was only one option: I would study the Bible, substantiate my position, return to the ring, and demonstrate Benson's doctrine of grace as folly. I was greatly looking forward to the rematch.

And so—feeling bruised and battered—I sat down with the Bible in my hand, intent on reading the New Testament from beginning to end for the first time in my life. Not once had my religious leadership ever challenged me to read the New Testament all the way through, though the invitation to read the Book of Mormon—both personally and as a family—had been issued on numerous occasions.

But now I had a new task: prove the validity of the Church exclusively through the Bible, and in particular the New Testament. I was confident this could be easily accomplished and that God could indisputably defend His Church through the Bible. Once verified, I could then refute the many critics of Christ's Restored Church.

I knelt next to my desk, bowed my head, and sought God's guidance: "God, please lead me to Thy truth, and help strengthen my faith in the gospel through the Bible. Give me knowledge and wisdom."

I then opened my Bible to Matthew chapter 1 and began to read. "The book of the genealogy of Jesus Christ, the son of David, the son of Abraham…"[39]

PART 2

WINDS
of
CHANGE

CHAPTER 12

THE HOLY INQUISITION

"Elder Wilder…? Elder Wilder!" President growled out while continuing to dig through his briefcase like a determined badger. Repeating my name twice had distressingly grabbed my attention more than he could possibly have known.

"Sorry, President," I responded as my mind slipped fully into the present gear. Sitting across from this man, I was experiencing a twisted form of déjà vu, and I couldn't stop contemplating that fateful meeting with Pastor Benson or the gravity of all that had transpired since.

Considering what I now knew, part of me wished that my eyes had been opened that providential summer night—that once I opened the Bible and began reading, I received an epiphany and all of God's truth came crashing down on me, or a great pillar of light shone upon me and a commanding voice came out of heaven, saying, "Micah, Micah, why are you persecuting Me?" But that is not how God opted to train me. No, His work in my life had been much more delicate and gradual, no doubt due to my ignorance, stubbornness, and pride. Through it all, though, His longsuffering toward me had been unmistakable.

Erik once told me that God's hand was best observed at a distance, and now as I looked back on my life, I couldn't help but be amazed at how God had been at work the whole time. Almost humorously, the catalyst for the miraculous change that took place in me came through my own pride—through my attempt to prove Pastor Benson wrong by seeking to solidify my five-pillared religious foundation through reading the Bible. It was because of self-confidence that I had initially accepted his challenge, and yet God used me against myself by revealing the majesty of His Son to me while I was on my own road to Damascus. I had no idea Benson's simple yet profound challenge to read the New Testament like a child would eventually open the floodgates of the overwhelming grace of God, mercifully drowning the former man and raising a new one in his stead.

I also could never have known that as far as the Church was concerned, I had opened a Pandora's box. One event started to magnify upon the next. Through Pastor Shaw, God placed mud in my eyes; through Pastor Benson, I was commanded to take upon myself the cleansing water of the Word of God to wash away my blindness; and through the help of Erik's insight, I solidified it all into one purpose. Now there was no longer any doubt that all these things had worked together as parts of a deliberate plan God had for me from the beginning—a plan that led me to here and now, preparing me to witness of His Living Word.

The McGuffin

President, appearing uncomfortable, seemed hesitant to begin the interrogation as he continued to sift through a stack of papers in his briefcase. I took advantage of this pause to petition help from the Lord. *God, please give me a mouth and wisdom. Help me to witness of the change You have made in my life. Father, I'm scared. Give me strength as You did David...*

As I prayed, I suddenly realized the rustling of the papers had ceased. President was peering over his open briefcase directly at me.

"How have you been, Elder Wilder?" he asked with an unnatural softness as he pulled out a yellow notepad.

"Oh, just fine, President. Busy, you know," I replied with a half-smile. My eyes struggled to hold his gaze.

"That's good to hear, Elder."

At the moment President seemed overly kind and polite, as if to lighten the rather somber mood. My former nemesis, Pastor Benson, had also begun his interaction in such a manner, so I couldn't take this as a sign that Sorensen's scolding would be any less severe.

President casually slid his briefcase aside while leaving it open. He then turned his attention to his notebook, which he nervously placed directly in front of him. For a moment he sat scanning his notes from top to bottom. Then he looked straight into my eyes. I was now confident the holy inquisition was ready to commence.

"So, Elder Wilder, what are your plans after you finish your mission?" he asked cordially. His question caught me off guard because it signaled the breaking of the missionary enchantment under which I had been living. No matter how pleasant President appeared, this was—without question—evidence that this was the last day of my mission.

"Well, I plan to come back to Florida to live and work for a short time," I divulged, "and then I'm going to return to BYU this fall and finish my schooling."

President didn't appear overly shocked. The way that rumors spread in the mission, it was no secret that I had plans to return to Florida to work for a season before continuing my schooling in the fall. Moreover, my girlfriend, Alicia, had already temporarily moved to Florida to work since completing her semester at BYU. This decision—and the reasons behind it—had created dissension between us and both of our families.

"I have been told you have a special young lady in your life. Have you made any plans with her for the future?" I was startled by the way President had seemingly pried open a way into my private thoughts.

Regardless of his cheery exterior, I was now certain President was stalking me like a wolf on the scent, searching to uncover my tracks, the hidden evidence to convict me of my crimes and claim a legitimate kill. Undoubtedly, this line of questioning wasn't at all about my plans after my mission—it was a McGuffin of sorts, a way to expose the true purpose of the trial and lead to justification for my condemnation. Inquiring about my post-mission plans was nothing more than a means to an end, and that end was President's uncovering of the four pillars of my former testimony that were now nothing more than a rubbish heap that had been pulverized against the Rock by a tsunami of living waters.

Panicking, I yearned to lead him in another direction to get him off my trail, but I didn't know where I could go.

"Well, President, we plan to marry in April," I conceded.

"That's wonderful, Elder Wilder. Congratulations!" he feigned, holding me in his sights. I remained motionless and hoped he would pass over his mark.

"Will you be getting married here in Florida?"

"Yes…" I answered as he hunted for his target.

"So, you'll be getting married in the Orlando Temple then?" Now he had zeroed in on his prey. I was cornered and had no choice but to face my pursuer head-on—either by fighting my way out or surrendering. Pleading to God in my heart for strength, I chose the latter.

"Actually, we're getting married at the First Baptist Church of Winter Garden…not the temple,"[40] I disclosed as I diverted my eyes from his and looked down at the table. I could almost hear the ordure hit the fan.

I knew what was to come next—it was plastered all over his face—as his smile quickly faded and he no longer had any pretense of being cheery and kind. Rather, he smacked his dry, quivering lips in a look of utter disgust—the same look I had seen just two days earlier at the zone conference as I publicly bore witness of my solitary remaining pillar of faith, Jesus Christ, while disregarding the other four.

"What is your *reasoning* for this decision, Elder Wilder?!" he blurted out.

"It's what God told me to do!" I retorted. This was certainly not the best answer I could have given, and I regretted saying it the moment it spilled out of my mouth. But it was the first thing that came to my mind, which was now racing at hyper speed.

My curt and direct response to President was an honest (albeit short) answer to a complicated array of events throughout my lifetime, which had risen to a well-orchestrated crescendo over the course of my mission. The amalgamation of each one of these precious experiences had molded and shaped itself like a heart-piercing arrow, spearheaded by two loving pastors and quivered by a Spirit-filled guide, climaxing in a life-altering epiphany that left me facedown on my bedroom floor.

It was in that baptismal moment that God had struck me with a spiritual lightning bolt: I would no longer need to walk a tightrope between

Mormonism and Christianity. The Holy Ghost sniper had found His target, and the gulf that had been in my heart for much of my life had been rapidly filled to capacity with the *agape* love Benson had explained long ago. Jesus was that perfect and highest form of the ultimate love.

As Scripture says,

> What no eye has seen, nor ear heard,
> nor the heart of man imagined,
> what God has prepared for those who love him.[41]

Upon recently coming to comprehend this great love, the unattainable burden of trying to make myself right with God had been lifted from my back by the pierced hands of Christ and placed upon His shoulders. After many years of working *for* my salvation, I had finally worked *out* my salvation in fear and trembling, and had been perfected in true love through the righteousness of God by faith in Jesus Christ. And now, I could rejoice knowing that I no longer feared whether my salvation was secure. My good standing with God was ensured through the blood offering of Jesus Christ alone.

And because of my recent understanding of the sufficiency of that perfect and loving sacrifice on the cross—as manifested to me through a startling revelation in the book of Hebrews just one week ago—I knew that physical temples (and all their contents) were no longer essential for my righteousness. In fact, by God's grace, I myself had become a temple of the living God, a house of the Holy Spirit, and a living stone being built into the body of Christ.

God had painfully but necessarily revealed to me that to honor the physical temple by way of ceremonial ordinances, as I had done with such fervor for many years, was to ignorantly disregard what Christ had done for me on the cross, thereby making His sacrifice in vain. It was through that finished work on my behalf that He had torn the veil of the temple, giving me access to God through the once-for-all offering of His own body.

So yes, in short, it was what God had told me to do.

One

"Why would God tell you to do something like that?" President asked.

Taking a deep breath, I knew this was my opportunity to bear the good fruit of a Christian, to take up my cross, and to witness of the good news of the Son of God. I was suddenly at no loss for words because the Word of God had filled me to overflowing.

"Have you ever considered that the church encompasses more than just us? More than this organization? How can we claim that we alone comprise the entirety of the body of Christ?" I daringly questioned while looking into President's eyes.

"President, I have been reading the Bible for almost my entire mission now, and God has opened my eyes to so many life-changing truths. The love of Christ has pierced my heart and changed the very core of who I am. God has moved in my life in a way I never thought possible."

President looked at me while squinting in confusion. "I don't understand, Elder Wilder. You believe that other churches have the truth? Is that why you are getting married in a Baptist church? You think they can offer you something that you don't have?"

"President, I already have everything I need in Christ! I am getting married in a Christian church because I am uniting myself with others who believe that salvation comes through faith in Jesus Christ alone, not a church. I'm not saved because of a church; I'm part of the church because I am saved."

President wiped his eyes with the tips of his thumb and forefinger. The facade of kindness was gone by now, and his frustration was clearly visible.

"Elder Wilder, that is foolish," he quipped. "There is nothing they can offer that equals what you can have here in Christ's Church through the fullness of the restored gospel."

I wanted to lash back at him, but God promptly reminded me of my own hypocrisy. The reaction I had received from President was the same reaction I had delivered in self-righteous condemnation many times myself. I couldn't blame President. I loved him. I *was* him for most of my life. I knew in my heart that my approach to him, and to everyone, needed to be centered on love and compassion—not attacking the individual, but gracefully witnessing the Word of God.

"President, why is it wrong to unite myself with other Christians by marrying in their church? I see them as brothers and sisters in Christ. If we hold fast to Jesus Christ as the foundation of our salvation and His Word, the Bible, as our source for truth, then we have unity of faith. We need to stop labeling ourselves and putting our identity in our denomination, and instead, put it in Christ Jesus alone."

"Why would you do such a thing?" he snapped. "Don't you realize that is what we are doing, gathering everyone to Christ's *true* Church?"

I had spent countless hours as a missionary trying to convince Christians—who professed to already being saved and redeemed by the blood of Jesus—that what they had in Christ alone was not enough, and eternal life could come only through the construct of our religious authority. The thought of this made me sick to my stomach. I had been wrong, and God had torn me down and rebuilt me on the foundation of Jesus and His Word. Now I could see that eternal life was possible outside of the Church, though not outside of Christ and His grace.

"President, I spent so much of my mission seeing missionaries focus on bringing people to the Church, but rarely to Christ—myself included, for a time. And it broke my heart. So much emphasis was placed on the organization and not on the Savior. Now I know that the Savior is so much bigger than the organization. The body of Christ encompasses so much more than I ever knew. Alicia and I have become a part of that worldwide church through our faith in Christ."

"Elder Wilder, that is wrong," he said. "Why must you compromise your standards and lower them just to please someone else? Christ has established His Church for a reason, and we are to live by the standards He has set. The temple is the ultimate standard. This is the only true Church, Elder. This alone is God's kingdom on Earth. Here, you have the fullness of the gospel."

President didn't understand that I wasn't doing this to please anyone other than God. I had the world to gain by pressing forward in my faithful life as a Latter-day Saint and *everything* to lose by forsaking the religion of my youth. Instead, I was surrendering everything that once defined me and trading it all for a pearl of great price: Jesus.

"I am not compromising my standards, President; I am establishing a new standard for myself: the Bible, and I am joining with others who hold to the same standard of truth and who have a saving faith in Christ. I feel called to proclaim the gospel of Christ to all people. Why is that wrong?"

The more I had been washed by the Word of God and transformed by God's grace, the more I found myself compelled to share the good news I had come to know. This wasn't a work or a duty that I had to fulfill. Rather, it was an irresistible compulsion I could not overcome. I had to witness as much as I had to breathe. I wanted to go out and teach, and to testify of Jesus and baptize everyone I could—not in earthly water, but in the Word of God, just as I had been. That's what I wanted to do for the rest of my life.

President must have realized that he was quickly losing ground, so he remained quiet for a few moments, as if to gather his composure.

"Elder Wilder, is this something you feel like you have to do?" he asked.

"Yes, President, it truly is," I said gently. "God has opened my eyes to the salvation that is in Christ alone, and I feel the call to help gather everyone under a united faith in Jesus through His Word. I want the whole world to know of Jesus Christ, the Son of God, who died for our sins. My desire is that the body of Christ can become one—unified by His Word to prepare for His imminent return."

President flopped back in his seat in an overly dramatic way. "That seems like quite a calling," he said sarcastically. "Don't you think that is what the leaders of the Church are doing?"

I was uncertain of how to answer his question without incriminating myself.

"I agree that they are doing their best, according to what they know," I said tactfully. "But there are so many pieces outside of the Church that need to be put together. This Church *could* be one of those pieces if it submits to the Word of God and rejects that which doesn't align with the teachings of Jesus and the apostles."

I stopped for a moment, then added, "I'm only doing what God has asked me to do. I can't change what He has shown me through the Bible. I may not know everything, President, but I know God loves me and He has saved me. I don't know why, but He does. This is what He's asked of me, and my greatest desire is to be faithful to Him."

President was surprisingly calm. Although he had probably heard enough to have condemned me at that moment, he would most likely take the chance that he could turn me around to repentance, and in doing so, salvage his reputation. After all, no mission president would want the embarrassment of an apostate on their permanent record. I was like a nuclear bomb that was leaking but had yet to detonate. He had to find a way to either defuse me or get me a safe distance away. If not, he had a lot to lose.

"And how do you feel He speaks to you?" he asked. "How do you feel you've been called?"

Now that's a story, I thought to myself, but I conceded to giving him the *Reader's Digest* version.

"Well, it's been a process, President. God has been answering my prayers through the Bible, and He has been giving me truth through His Holy Spirit. But every truth that has been revealed to me I have tested against the Bible. For the first time in my life, I am making sure that what I am told aligns with God's Word. Through that confirmation, I have the confidence that God alone has led me on this path. I waited my whole life to understand my purpose in Christ, and now that it has been revealed to me, there is no going back."

I think President was rather puzzled and uncertain of what to do with me, and during the moments he seemed to fear something about me, he had to admit I had done nothing wrong. In fact, he knew as much as anybody that I had been a hard-working, faithful, and obedient missionary, and my reputation for such was well known throughout the mission.

"President, God has made an amazing change in my life. I am now grounded in true faith and love, as the Bible teaches. I love Jesus because I now know how much He loves me!" I exclaimed as an overpowering love surged through my heart, causing me to lift my arms into the air—all to President's alarm.

"Elder Wilder, I don't doubt your sincerity that you believe God has led you on this path. You have always been a spiritual person from the time that I met you, and I have respected you for that. But you must realize that there is order in God's Church. Jesus Himself established this very Church as the vehicle for salvation."

His statement, in a nutshell, spelled out the disparity between what I once believed and what I had come to know through the Word of God: The Church was not the avenue to eternal life—Jesus was, and because I knew Jesus and followed Him, I had the assurance of my salvation in

Him, independent of any religious institution or authority. I had finally attained the righteousness I was futilely pursuing through the endless maze of works and ordinances in the Church. I was now right with God— not because of my faithfulness to the Church's laws and ordinances, but because of the righteousness of Christ that had been imputed to me by faith.

"Think about what you are giving up, Elder Wilder, if you follow this path," President pleaded. "Think of all the work God has done so that you could have the truth of the restored gospel. Think about those two missionaries who knocked on your parents' door so many years ago and brought them the truth. How would they feel knowing that you have lost your testimony? How would your mother and father feel?"

CHAPTER 13

SHADOWS
OF DAVID

W e're missionaries from the Church of Jesus Christ of Latter-day
Saints."

The first time the elders came knocking on my parents' door in 1977,
they were graduate students at Ball State University in Muncie, Indiana.
My mother was away teaching a special education class and my father was
home alone completing his master's thesis. Dad had been hungering for
a relationship with God (and wanted a break from studying) and enthusiastically welcomed the two sharply dressed young men into the house.

"We have an incredible message," they told him, which ignited and
then took advantage of his inborn desire to serve God. "The true Church
of Jesus Christ has been established through a living prophet!" In mere
minutes, Dad was held spellbound by their tale of the restored gospel.

My father—always a generous and loving soul—was prone to be
succored into such idealism because even though he had a love for God
already, his foundation of Christianity was built on an underpinning of
the fear of eternal damnation bolstered by the soapbox preachers of his
former legalistic community. Finally, he had found a religion that seemed
to give him a blueprint to follow from which he could measure his success and standing with God.

Before Dad could know of the complexity or impossibility of the Church's standards for righteousness though, he was immediately love-sick and blinded by pure devotion. My mom, however, was on high alert and took considerably more time to warm up to the missionaries and the exclusivity of their claims to hold the keys to salvation—an assertion that stood in stark contrast from the teachings of her Presbyterian roots. But as the months went by, she and my father studied multiple times a week with the missionaries and asked a million questions while struggling to decide what they should do. During that time, a tender bond formed with the elders.

One night, after months of prayer and Scripture study, my once-ever-so-slightly conflicted dad had a dream in which he vigorously defended Mormonism to his close friends and family. He interpreted this dream as a sign from God to join the church that was so desperately courting him. Though my mother was still tussling with a few of the Church's nontraditional doctrines, she trusted my father's intuition and they were baptized into the Church in October of 1977. (They had decided at some earlier point that whatever they chose to do in the realm of faith, they would do together, and whatever they did together would be done with whole-hearted dedication.) Over time, as she was groomed and fully indoctrinated in the Church, she, too, had her own spiritual experiences, which eventually developed into a steadfast testimony of the Restored Church.

For nearly thirty years now, my parents had devotedly served their religion and were consummate members of their faith. So yes, President was justified in posing the question. What would they think of what had happened to their esteemed son? I knew the answer: It would absolutely crush them.

The Heartland

Growing up in the small farming community of Yorktown, Indiana, we lived in a scenic old split-level wood and stone house built back in the woods on nearly eight acres of land. Most of our property played out along the White River. My siblings and I spent our summer days swimming, rafting, fishing, and catching all manner of wildlife that crawled, slithered, and swam through the riverway wilderness. We built forts, made ponds, and deliberately got lost from each other in the cattails and bulrush that grew over our heads. From June through August every year, the woods were our kingdom as we reflexively practiced for adulthood while establishing our sibling pecking order, tending fervently to our own idealistic childhood realm. From the moment we hastily abandoned our beds in the morning until Mom literally rang a rusted old bell calling us home for dinner in the evening, the riverside hideaway was our refuge. Life was good.

For my first few years of formal schooling, I attended Heritage Hall, a small private Baptist school in Muncie, Indiana. Being the only Mormon there, I knew I was set apart from my peers regarding my religious beliefs, but I didn't completely understand why. Nevertheless, I came to love this environment. Every day I learned a Bible story and memorized a new scripture. It was there that God groomed me, trained me, and planted seeds within me at a tender young age—seeds that I had no conscious recollection of for many years.

As a four-year-old boy, my schoolmate-turned-best-friend Nathan and I would have curious discussions about the religious dichotomy that separated us. (Although we didn't understand it or take it seriously, we were fully aware of its existence.)

"How come you don't come to my church?" he would ask me in direct innocence during recess. "My mom says that Mormons aren't Christians." Apparently, I had been of enough interest to the general Baptist population to have been a part of this family's dinnertime conversation.

"Well, I am a Mormon because Mormons are the true Church," I stated curtly. I didn't know what it meant to be the true church; the retort I gave was a compulsory reaction that had been embedded deep in my subconscious.

"How do you know that?" Nathan asked while focusing intently on the ant colony we were both poking at on the ground.

I sat back and thought for a moment until the answer suddenly hit me. "Well, because Jesus was a Mormon!" I said this with such honest naivety that Nathan almost bought it, because for a moment, he stopped his assault on the ants. Then he shrugged and returned his attention to the devastation he was inflicting.

"But where does it say that?" he asked.

"It's in the Bible!" I resolved with confidence. Although I was never explicitly told that, in my young mind I could only reconcile the two truths that I had learned from opposite ends of the religious spectrum: The Bible contained the truth (as taught to me at my Baptist school), and the Mormon Church was true (as taught to me at church).

If nothing more, I had dispelled—for the time being—Nathan's line of questioning by accidently taking advantage of his youthful inexperience. The passive battle ended with a shrug as the bell shrieked to indicate recess was over. Fortunately, we quickly moved on to far more important subjects as we ran back to the schoolhouse, discussing what transformer we would play with and which new dinosaur had been discovered.

The Shepherd Boy

Perhaps the most significant event that took place in my young life at Heritage Hall centered on a biblical figure who would become the impetus for my intimacy with God—one who, from the onset, intrigued me beyond measure and was seared into my mind.

"David, as a young man, was a shepherd of the flock, spending his days alone in the fields tending to his father's sheep," Mrs. Briner taught our first-grade class. "He would protect them at all costs. He even killed a lion and a bear to save them from harm." This was such a fascinating story that it gripped me with a passion. I was not only hooked, but my mind entered a full-fledged daydream complete with live narration.

"It was there that God was watching him and training him, and where David became a man after God's own heart. God had an exceptional fondness for him." Mrs. Briner's profession of David's special relationship with God quickly removed me from my daydream and found me seething with jealousy. I wanted what he had: intimacy with God—so much that my heart ached. I settled the matter by putting on his shoes and pretending to be him.

David, like me, was the youngest of his brothers. He trusted in the Lord and God found great favor in him. David—seemingly unqualified—was eventually called to be king of Israel, but first he was to be trained by Saul, the wicked king whom he was to replace. As David grew, Saul became jealous and tried to kill him. In time, I stopped being envious of David because I grew to feel that I understood him. I then went on to love and respect him. I wanted so much to be just like him; more so, I wanted all my friends to know all about my new hero—after all, he slew the mighty Goliath!

"David made a lot of mistakes," my teacher continued. "He broke God's commandments. David was weak in the flesh, and he knew he was a sinner. So what did he do? He felt godly sorrow for his sin and disobedience, but he didn't let his weaknesses ever stop him from worshipping and serving God with all his heart. He trusted in God's forgiveness and put his faith in the Lord's mercy, even though he knew he didn't deserve it.

"David showed that he knew God and His love were far greater than his sin, and even in his sin, his heart was turned to God. In the Bible, Jesus says that those who are forgiven more love more. We don't sin on purpose, but the beautiful thing about God's grace is that when we believe in Jesus, even if we do sin, we are forgiven through His love. David is evidence of God's mercy and forgiveness toward undeserving people. Just like you and me."

What Mrs. Briner showed me through David not only helped me identify with God's love, it also gave me confidence in His mercy. I wanted the same forgiveness from God that He had offered His servant David, because I knew that—just like David—I needed it. Even though I had not yet reached my Church's "age of accountability"[42] of eight years old, I could clearly see my imperfections and need for God's grace in my life. The story of the shepherd boy gave me hope that there was a God, He did love me, and I could be forgiven.

From that auspicious day forward, I planted David in my soul and carried him to my place of seclusion down by the river. In the solitude of the thick Indiana forests that surrounded my home I became king of my own land, and it was there that I longed with all my heart to be loved by God, just like David. (I had so much identified with him that I even fashioned my own slingshot and gathered five smooth stones from the river, firing them at the large trees cleverly confronting me with a laugh, as though they were the Philistine giant himself.)

For me, the forested expanse was more than just a place to live out my wildest daydreams. It was my own kingdom to enter and be with God

Himself. It was in my woodland refuge where, as a child, I began to know God and discover His love through my direct communication with Him daily. In the summer months, I would find myself running down to the river so I could be alone and talk to my constant Companion, as I imagined David would do while tending the sheep in the fields. Although He did not answer with words, I never, for a moment, suffered anything without knowing that He was with me, guiding and watching over me. I called on Him at the slightest sign of trouble, anguish, fear, or despair. He was my Best Friend. Our relationship was pure, simple, and uncomplicated.

One fateful day at church during Sunday school, my two independent worlds entered the same orbit and collided with devastating effects. As I approached my eighth birthday, I made the mistake of openly comparing myself to David to one of my friends, which was overheard by my teacher and brought the Mormon lesson to a standstill. The teacher charged at me with her mouth wide open and slid to a stop, towering over me. As she stood silently glaring overhead in sheer disbelief, I cowered under her shadow and didn't even know what I had done.

"David was wicked and disobedient," she roared while wagging her finger. "You shouldn't want to be like him in any way. David is paying a heavy price for his disobedience to the commandments of God. Because of his great sins against God, he lost his very own salvation!" she blasted out with fiery breath.

I was hopelessly embarrassed, humiliated in front of my peers, and torn apart inside. My role model and hero had been ripped from me, and the whole situation left me heartbroken. I found myself bewildered by the juxtaposition of the two viewpoints on the same person. The Baptists at school had taught me—from the Bible[43]—that David was forgiven and his life was a lesson on God's mercy and His willingness to forgive the unworthy. But at church, I was taught that he wasn't forgiven, lost his exaltation (eternal life in the highest kingdom of heaven), and his life was a lesson on the consequences of disobedience.[44] Which was it? I couldn't reconcile the two, and I knew better than to make any rebuttals or even to ask any questions.

Yes, David had committed horrible atrocities and sinned greatly against God—I knew that, and I had to think about that (and I did for a very long time). I didn't want to receive the punishment I was told that David was receiving, and I was given the prescription for true forgiveness by my religion: confess my sins to my priesthood leaders, follow their instructions for repentance, and then—through proper contrition—I could find forgiveness from God. I was also warned that if I sinned again, all my previous sins would return to me,[45] be compounded upon me, and I would find myself worse off than before. What hope was there for me in that? What if I couldn't keep myself clean? The thought terrified me because in only a few days, on my eighth birthday, I would officially be held accountable for my wrongdoing.

My Sunday school teacher did offer a glimmer of hope that, unlike David, I would be offered a second chance for my redemption, which would come after I was baptized into the Church on my birthday and my covenants with God were solidified. Even in my humiliated stupor I paid close attention to the remedy that she was spelling out like my (eternal) life depended on it: be baptized and confirmed as a member of the Church; remain active in my Church duties and meetings; solidify my testimony; tithe; obey the Prophet; receive the priesthood; perform temple ordinances; follow the Word of Wisdom; live the law of chastity; go on a mission; get married in the temple; and "endure to the end" by staying faithful to the laws, ordinances, and commandments of the Church for the rest of my life.

I was internally conflicted for a time, but my fascination for the Israelite king remained—although I carried our relationship underground and tucked it firmly into my religious duality. I was careful not to mention him to a Church leader ever again.

Frog in the Water

In the years to come, I continued steadfast in my Davidic pursuit as I sat down by the river. Time and again my heart would fill with an engulfing love for God as I contemplated His love for me. I was gradually morphing into a child after God's own heart, just like David of old. Stepping down to the riverbank, I would look at my reflection in the water… though there were moments it didn't seem like my reflection at all. Sometimes, if I squinted just right, I would envision a curly-haired boy who

looked much like me—but it wasn't me. It was someone seemingly familiar, and I pined for the reflection to be Jonathan, the beloved best friend
of David. As the years went on, I became accustomed to imagining the
other boy in my reflection in the dark water. I kept my reflective companion deep in my heart, praying that one day I would come face to face with
my own Jonathan.

When I was ten or so my parents—abruptly and without warning—
pulled me out of the Baptist school and I began my long tenure in the public school system. The secular realm was unfamiliar territory for me. No
endless Bible lessons, no memorizing scriptures, no more personal relationship with God, no more David, and no more internal religious conflict. My daily life was immediately less God-centered and now had all the
typical worldly trappings for someone my age: Pogs, yo-yos, Legos, model
planes, sports, and even girls.

As I entered middle school, I became increasingly enamored by the
world around me, and although I would spend countless hours down by
the river, I was no longer alone with God. My new best friends—Schuyler
and Ryan—would accompany me on adventurous escapades of swinging
on an old rope into the river while pursuing all manner of childish mis-
chief. My purpose in traversing the banks of the White River was no longer to have intimacy with God and seek daily communication with Him,
but to enjoy the love and brotherhood of my comrades. My relationship
with my Creator was drifting from the forefront of my mind as my heart
began to pursue the accolades of the world—and my religion.

By the time I received the coveted Aaronic Priesthood[46] at the age of
twelve, I often would attempt to talk to God as I sat in the field by my
house, but something inside of me was drastically changing. The religion
of my birth was winning; it was capturing my attention and becoming
far more strident in my life. The Church's compulsory obedience contin-
gency that was now imposed on me little by little through the regimented
priesthood was slowly supplanting my relationship with God, much like
the proverbial frog being slowly boiled alive in water. In time, my own private kingdom was overgrown as well, with my path directly to God overcome by an impenetrable shroud of thorn bushes.

As I grew in age and gained the superior intelligence of a teenager, my mind and heart became more focused on the Church and unknowingly less on God because I was to love Him through the proxy of the leaders of the Church. The deeper I delved into the Church, the farther I drifted from the apparently incorrect childhood notion that I had an intimate relationship with God already. The process to communion with God was no longer direct and personal; rather, it occurred through the authority of the priesthood that now governed, by strict obedience, my standing with God.

Though I never saw it coming, by the time I was completing middle school, the once-beautiful and personal relationship I had with my Maker was becoming a mere echo. Though I felt His love on occasion, I didn't seek Him out like I had before. Knowledge of my sins was causing me to turn away from my first love and I started to see through a glass darkly, whereas at one time I saw face to face through the innocence of a child. The more I sinned, the more I was drawn into the Church by seeking forgiveness, and the farther I was being carried away from the outstretched arms of a God full of grace.

As my awareness of my sin debt increased, I grew less concerned about how God saw me and evermore worried about the perceptions of those around me. The filthy nature of my flesh was being revealed to me and I wanted to hide it at all costs. I focused on cleansing the outside of my cup for my parents and Church leaders, while my sin was festering within me. I was able to hide myself behind the exterior facade that I was righteous and obedient, yet inside my whitewashed tomb, I was full of bones.[47]

As time passed, though I strove to be a good person by any objective standard and had always been perceived as the quintessential church boy, I began to explore the polluted offerings of the world. Even with principled parents who had instilled in me a moral compass, I succumbed to the relentless pressures of my sinful desires. I fell victim to the expertly packaged and appetizing blind notions of the world that had snuck up upon me as easily as the sugarcoated cereal commercials that bombarded me as I watched the Saturday morning cartoons. There was a constant and raging battle between flesh and spirit—between what I wanted to do and that which I did. I was beginning to feel hopeless. My life was cascading toward an unavoidable shipwreck. David was but a mirage from my past.

CHAPTER 14

SECRET SACRED THINGS

My unlikely deliverance from worldly ruin came when I was fourteen years, three months, twenty-four days, and seven hours old, and my parents served up the most startling news of my young life: "Micah, we are moving."

Apparently my mother had just acquired a job at the prestigious Brigham Young University located in the heart of Mormonism. Not only were we being uprooted, but we were to be replanted in…Utah?! *Utah* of all places!

As the unexpected announcement sank in, all I could comprehend was that I would have to leave my home, my friends, my church, and everything I had ever known and loved to be cast out into a desert land. The panic caused by this thought raced through in my mind like a raging wildfire, and I pictured myself standing amidst the smoldering piles of my former life. To me, this was so unconscionable that I felt I had to do something.

I became so angry at my parents that in my mind's eye, I visualized myself as a B-17 in battle pitching bravely and wildly toward my mother, my props gaining speed and whining as they cut the wind while my bay doors opened wide and dropped every bomb at my disposal on my enemy.

To my own demise, my imagination quickly deviated from fantasy and into reality, and I said things to my own mother—including dropping the mother of all bombs, the infamous f-bomb—that would have made a drunken sailor blush.

The last I saw of Mom during the light of that day was her alarm, surprise, and gaping mouth as I realized I had foolishly not imagined the words in my mind but had actually said them aloud. I knew that as soon as she got over the initial astonishment and paralysis, I was going to be dead. I lurched, throwing my thin frame into a full tactical reverse and instinctively entered a full gallop in the opposite direction. My feet had taken on the task of saving me before my mind had fully comprehended the danger that a moment's indiscretion had placed upon me.

I ran out the door, dove over an embankment, and barreled through the briar patch. Without looking back, I sprinted to my river basin hideaway a quarter of a mile away, seemingly unscathed before the idiocy of my crime fully sunk in. Entering the river with water up to my knees so I could soothe the itchy wounds left from running through the thorn bushes, I crouched down and gazed at my unclear reflection in the stillest area of the murky water. Tears mixed with fear, sorrow, and anger poured from my eyes and into the babbling river. I was determined to hold on to the only life I knew.

My sixteen-year-old brother, Matt, soon found me, and in true and loving boyhood solidarity, he joined my immature all-out war against our parents. Even as we waged a futile campaign over the subsequent months (we had even planned to run away and live in a fort we had built in the woods, surviving off the land like grizzled old mountain men), there was nothing we could do to avoid the inescapable—we were moving to Utah, and no force on heaven or earth (including stubborn children) was going to change my parents' minds.

Zion: The Promised Land

In August of 1999, the Wilder family departed from the heartland and moved to the promised land: Alpine, Utah, a picturesque utopian town on the edge of the Wasatch mountains, with ninety-eight percent of the population comprised of Latter-day Saints.

The transition was challenging, and I grieved painfully each day for my friends and home 1,600 miles away. Every aspect of Utah was so foreign from the life I left behind—the people, culture, climate, geography, demographics. I struggled to assimilate to my new environment, and I found myself soaking my pillow with tears night after night, mourning for my Midwestern birthplace.

As the months passed and I was slowly baptized in the religious world of my new surroundings, I found myself gradually becoming infatuated by the distinctiveness of life in "Happy Valley."[48] I had never been privileged to be immersed in a culture with so many people who shared my belief system, and due to my overcompetitive nature, this quickly had the effect of motivating me to stand out as a faithful and obedient Church member among my peers. Determined to surpass my contemporaries as the most exemplary religious devotee in the region, I began to abscond from the worldly darkness that had held me captive in Indiana and started the long process of refocusing my life on God. In a few short months, moving to Zion had already begun to change my life.

As the days grew shorter and the nights stretched longer, the Utah winters provided breathtaking, crystal-clear views of the nighttime sky. For hours upon end, I would endure the bitter cold of the darkness with my telescope (a peace offering from my parents), peering into the majestic creation of God in reverent awe. Night after starry night, I found myself enamored by the endless celestial bodies that dotted the heavens, to the point that my days were spent in anticipation of the night to come. Deep down inside of me, God was rekindling a nearly forgotten flame of my past that had been all but extinguished by my flesh.

Through the small eyepiece, I could see so clearly the hand of God in His creation and I was reminded of the personal relationship I once had with Him on the banks of the White River. I desired to restore that intimacy and return to the heart of David and love God again. Peering into the endless firmament above invigorated me, and I was certain that God had a plan and purpose for my life, and more than anything, I wanted to know my place in the vast universe—and in the eyes of God.

As I became more deeply ingrained into my religious culture, my life became increasingly centered on faithfully serving God through the

Church—the two were intrinsically connected. My religious leaders in Utah seemed to take note of my unmitigated passion, and they consciously and deliberately groomed me to be a future leader in the faith. Much like the Catholic leadership's infatuation with Martin Luther, my leaders gave me so much special attention that I felt I was destined for greatness in the Church. Yet like Luther, I never would have imagined that my destiny would rip me away from the soil that held my ecclesiastical roots, and not plant me even deeper into it.

The Chasm

As I grew in the Church and received honor after honor, a gulf developed within me that only intensified over time. I had been Deacon's quorum president, Teacher's quorum president, first assistant to the Bishop in the Priest's quorum; I had served on the stake youth committee, on the seminary council at my high school; I received my duty to God award, and was as faithful to the commandments and standards of the Church as anyone could be. As to the law of my religious system, I was blameless.

Yet despite the measure of my piety and devotion to God through my religion, I never felt I had attained the love and intimacy with Him I had experienced as a child. I constantly felt disillusioned no matter how high up the ladder I climbed, as though I was going the right way on the wrong escalator, turning every good thing I had hoped for in my religious life into an unrelenting treadmill. No matter how hard I worked or what I accomplished, I was left wanting.

During my junior year of high school, I was confident my life was going to change and the massive hole inside of me would be filled once and for all. It was then that I would receive my patriarchal blessing—an outline of revelation directly from God to me through a patriarch.[49] Placing his hands on my head, he would verbally reveal my lineage as God's child and uncover to me my spiritual gifts and temporal blessings, disclosing my true calling and purpose in life—a road map to my destiny. The burning question of "Who am I?" would finally be answered.

I prepared for months for the momentous occasion. I prayed earnestly, read my Scriptures, and fasted religiously. I peppered my father with questions as I studied about the patriarch in the Scriptures and did everything that I was instructed to do with tremendous zeal. I was convinced this event would re-solidify the heart of David and reveal to me the surefire path back to my childhood relationship with God and His love.

Instead, I was met with a crushing disappointment that I could not hide from my father any more than the expectation of getting a bike for Christmas only to end up holding the helmet. Dad did everything he could do to console me, reassuring me not to be disheartened. He encouraged me to wait until I obtained the blessing in writing and, after careful observation and dissection, he was positive I would find the answers I was seeking.

A few days later, as I was seated on my bed reading the Book of Mormon, my mother burst through the doorway out of breath. In her hand she clutched an envelope that I knew right away contained my patriarchal blessing in written form. I ripped open the letter and read the revelation, turning it over and over, searching for any clues that I might have overlooked the first time around. The verdict: I was devastated. I walked over to my bed and flopped down on my face, crying into my pillow.

"This can't be it, Mom," I said.

In her tender love and compassion, my mom knelt next to my bed while gliding her hand over my back to comfort me in my disappointment. "Everything's going to be okay, Micah. I promise. God has a plan for you. I have no doubt. Don't lose faith."

In that moment, I had expected to receive a revelation from God—to truly know and understand my relationship with Him—and instead, I fell (literally) flat on my face. I became frustrated to the point that I grieved for hours in the solitude of my bedroom, crying out to God over and over, "Who am I, and what dost Thou want me to do in my life? Have I not done enough to show Thee that I am worthy and ready?"

Instead of picking myself up and pressing on, the fall had marked me; but rather than cover up the scars, I wore them as a badge of honor by using my disenchanting experience with my patriarchal blessing to motivate me more than ever to demonstrate my devotion to God. My heartache turned to zeal, and I worked tirelessly to establish my own righteousness through meticulous adherence to the law of my religious institution. My fervor was unparalleled and my testimony shone as a light for my peers.

Falling in Love

When I was seventeen and a senior in high school, I met a captivating and charming young woman named Alicia. From the first time my eyes beheld her beauty in Mr. Birrell's history class, I was smitten. She had the most stunning auburn hair and mesmerizing green eyes I had ever seen. She was soft-spoken, gentle, and kind. Once I had laid eyes on her, it was hard to think about anything or anyone else.

I eventually summoned the courage to ask her out on a date, and we spent an unforgettable evening together. I fell madly in love with this shy girl. It was love at first sight. At the end of our enchanted evening, we stood awkwardly on her parents' porch, and overwhelmed by emotion, I blurted out a daring and risky confession: "There is something special between us…something important is going to happen in our lives. God is going to do something amazing. Alicia, I think you are the one."

From that day forward, Alicia became an integral part of my life. Although we had certainly established a romantic relationship, first and foremost she became my best friend and spiritual partner. We would laugh together, cry together, and spend hours talking about God while looking into the night sky. I had never felt for any human being what I felt for Alicia. Her love was the most precious possession I had, and I was convinced I would marry her in the temple and we would live happily ever after throughout all of eternity. It seemed as though meeting this exquisite redhead had filled a portion of the gaping hole in my heart—but not all of it.

Stone Temples

My next and possibly greatest hope for finding complete fulfillment, I figured, would come from the temple—the opulent, sacred edifice known as the House of the Lord. Inside the walls of this hallowed building, I was taught, was not only the ordinances and blessings necessary for exaltation, but also the very presence of God on Earth. I yearned to be fully in His love and presence and reestablish, even perfect, the Davidic sanctuary I once knew as a child.

I had been enthralled with the temple throughout my teenage years, and my infatuation and love for God's holy house only grew stronger as I attended high school. During most of my senior year, Alicia and I would sacrifice sleep and comfort to attend the temple early mornings before school, performing consecrated works and ordinances to further establish our righteousness before God. Although I had experienced parts of the temple since I was twelve years old, certain rituals and knowledge were reserved for individuals of a special age and worthiness. That day, for me, was fast approaching.

As I neared my graduation and set my sights on my two-year mission, I began to seriously wonder about the secret—or rather, "sacred"—parts of the temple ceremonies of which I had not yet been privy. Not until immediately before my mission would I join an elite group of worthy Church members who would receive the pinnacle of God's blessings on the earth. It was there that I would make sacred and eternal covenants with God, all the mysteries of the universe would be revealed, and God would speak to me His plan and purpose for my life. To know God in such a personal way, I needed to prepare spiritually by making myself pure so I could enter His presence.

After I graduated, I started what was a long and at times arduous process of repentance in the Church, where I tearfully confessed my most intimate sins to my leaders so that they could guide me through the necessary steps of forgiveness. Only with them and through them, as my mediators, could God completely forgive me and I be made clean. Though the procedure of repentance was difficult and even humiliating, I was determined to purify my life.

Once I had satisfied the prerequisites established by my religious headship and had proven my penitence by keeping the commandments of the Church, I was bestowed my temple recommend—a small piece of paper, a sort of spiritual "passport" that indicated my worthiness to enter the Lord's House and ultimately heaven itself. I had earned my right to be counted among the few and the privileged.

As the day approached when I hoped to receive the greatest knowledge and revelation of truth in my lifetime, I cleansed myself by purging my life of all worldly influences. I stopped listening to the radio, discarded all my secular CDs, and engrossed myself in Church-sanctioned music. I expunged the world from every aspect of my life. I read the Book of Mormon and Doctrine and Covenants for hours upon end, prayed constantly, and fervently followed the Church's moral codes.

After months of rigorous purification, the blessed day to be endowed with knowledge and power arrived. I would finally uncover the answers to the questions burning in the deep recesses of my heart pertaining to my place in God's plan. On a frigid day in late November, my parents and I entered the Salt Lake Temple and I participated in the sacred ordinances therein.

Although I was reluctant to vocally admit it afterward (as I had done in the wake of my patriarchal blessing), I found myself plodding out of the temple somewhat confounded and even disheartened by the relatively anticlimactic event. It wasn't that the ceremony itself was not beautiful and even emotional—it was. I had savored each moment I was within the consecrated walls of the temple, and yet through it all, the void deep inside of me was still left unsatisfied. I wondered, *Is this it? Is there more?* I took in everything I was learning and searched for the hidden meaning, but couldn't disregard the hollowness reverberating in the deepest part of my soul. I wanted God and His love so badly but continued to feel as though He was barely out of reach. The chasm within me was not getting any smaller; rather, it was growing exponentially.

In the months leading up to my two-year mission and while attending BYU, I visited the temple unfailingly. My religious training and perfecting took far greater precedence in my life than any worldly accolades. Irresponsibly shirking much of my schoolwork and my student-related responsibilities, I would spend hours upon end in the temple—praying, reading the Scriptures, repeating the ordinances time and time again, searching for God's love and favor over my life. I saw my collegiate obligations as a senseless distraction from my relationship with God and my preparation for my mission. With reluctance I attended classes daily, pining for the freedom that would come at the semester's end so I could spend each waking moment in the temple.

After school concluded in December, I returned to the temple, but this time to submit a most unusual proposal: I wanted to work full-time in the sacred building, immersing myself in God's presence every possible moment I could. My religious leaders were shocked and even confused. Never had someone my age made such a demand. (Generally, temple workers were older retired men and women. It was simply unheard of for a young person—prior to their mission, no less—to serve in such a capacity.) Impressed by my zeal and dedication, I was deemed worthy of and set apart for the distinguished honor. Just weeks before my nineteenth birthday, I was told I had become the youngest full-time temple worker in the modern Church.

For the next six weeks leading up to my mission departure, I spent forty hours or more a week in the solace of the temple walls. I was so desperate for God's love, presence, and purpose in my life. While most of my eighteen-year-old peers were playing video games, hanging out with friends, and relaxing, I was not only earnestly seeking God, but chasing Him down with every fiber of my being. And yet, despite reaching the pinnacle of righteousness for someone my age, I still felt unfulfilled.

As my nineteenth birthday approached, I sensed that my last chance for redemption was wrapped up in going on a mission—perhaps then I would finally get the answers I was looking for. The passion to discover what God had in store for me became an obsession, and I was determined to make every effort to solidify my standing with Him as I prepared for my two-year journey. I strictly observed all the Church's commandments, obeying them as if my life, my future, and my love for Alicia depended on it.

After the long process of seemingly endless interviews, paperwork, and preparation, I was deemed worthy by my religious leaders to be a missionary. God had laid out my destiny for me, and as long as I remained worthy of the temple covenants that I had made, the trajectory I was on could not be altered.

I was convinced: my mission would change my life.

CHAPTER 15

WINTER GARDEN

Hunters Creek, Florida | April 20, 2004

Hola! Somos misionaros de la Iglesia de Jesucristo de los Santos de los Últimos Días, y témenos un mensaje acera del evangelio de Jesucristo…" SLAM! The door stopped just inches from my face as I turned and looked at Elder Shumway with a smirk.

"Just another day in paradise," he said while chuckling as we made our way to our next unsuspecting victim.

Knock, knock, knock.

"Can I help you?"

"Hi! We're representatives of the Church of Jesus Christ of Latter-day Saints and we have a message about how families can be together forever. You and your wife can be married for eternity!"

"No thanks, gentlemen. I think this life is long enough." SLAM!

The prolonged days of door-to-door tracting were brutal, but I had learned to cope with the harsh rejection the best I could after eight days in the mission field.

"So how are you enjoying your mission so far?" Shumway asked as we sauntered down the sidewalk to the next house.

"Honestly, it's been tough," I said. "I didn't know people could be so… mean! I wasn't prepared for this much rejection. But I do love it. I feel like Heavenly Father is teaching me incredible things every day. I can't wait to see what He has in store for me."

"That's awesome, Elder. There's a lot in store for you, that's for sure," Shumway said with a grin. "You'll see and hear some crazy things here in the mission field!"

"I bet," I replied. "What's the craziest thing you've seen or heard after six months?"

Shumway stopped and thought for a second.

"Well, I've heard about this guy, Erik, who is a recent convert to the Church. He owns this old hotel, and rumor has it he has 'spiritual' gifts," he offered up as we continued marching along the scorching sidewalk. "He has made some sort of a prophecy about a band that is going to put the Bible to music in helping prepare the world for the second coming of Christ, or something like that. Interesting stuff."

"That's impossible," I said incredulously. "No one can have those kinds of gifts of the Spirit but the First Presidency[50] and the Quorum of the Twelve Apostles.[51] He has no stewardship in the Church. Something like that could *never* be of God," I mocked.

For as long as I could remember, I had been taught that the only people on Earth with the gift of prophecy were the fifteen men who sat at the head of the Church. No ifs, ands, or buts. They alone were ordained as prophets, seers, and revelators. All revelation was possible only through the priesthood chain of authority; no one outside of that chain could give or pass any spiritual guidance or prophecy. God's line of communication to man could not and would not supersede the established authority. He wouldn't speak outside of the leaders of the Church. God was a God of order.

Despite my cynicism, Shumway's proclamation about this unusual man piqued my interest. I interrogated my lanky companion as we continued walking door to door, trying to understand how he felt someone like Erik could exist within the structure of the Church.

The widely circulated story among the local missionaries was that Erik had made a "prophecy" about a music ministry that God would call out of Central Florida, formed in part by former Church missionaries who would fulfill a very specific purpose, with the core undertaking of the band being to put the Bible into music.

Setting aside the questionable prophecy about this band, Erik himself was somewhat of an enigma to the missionaries (and by the minute was increasingly becoming so to me as well). Though he had just been baptized within the last couple years and was technically a member of the Church, he had recently become inactive, and the reasons for why were the source of unending speculation among my peers.

Rumor was spreading in the mission that he was—or was becoming—a mainstream "Christian" because he primarily emphasized the Bible, and not the other standard canon we adhered to in the Church. In addition, he had vocally tested the waters by expressing his uncertainty about Joseph Smith and the Book of Mormon, even when he was baptized. The position of the local leadership was that his concerns were nonaggressive and innocent, and they hoped his testimony would strengthen over time. Therefore, he was permitted to join the Church even without a strong testimony of each of the five pillars of the faith. One condition Erik placed on his baptism was that he not be baptized in the local chapel, as was tradition, but rather, at an outdoor natural spring. Adding insult to injury, he had refused to go to the temple despite enormous pressure by Church leadership. These facts, to me, raised a large red flag. This man was *not* to be trusted.

"Hey, you play the drums, right? Maybe you'll be in the band!" Shumway said with a smirk while playfully punching me in the arm.

"Yeah, right."

Though every part of me didn't want to believe and accept this Erik and his "spiritual gifts"—and in fact, my gut reaction was to try to expose him as a fraud—deep down, I couldn't shake my curiosity about him. But as the weeks flew by, I put my inquisitiveness to the back of my mind, knowing that God had a plan for me that had yet to be revealed.

Hour by hour, day by day, and week by week, I worked hard to be a dedicated and devout missionary, proclaiming the restored gospel to people whenever and wherever I could. On the streets, in the Walmart parking lots, door to door, on public sidewalks—I was establishing a fearless approach to missionary work that was even causing me to cross six lanes of deadly traffic to share our message to those in need.

Transfers
May 27, 2004

My first six weeks in the mission went by like the blink of an eye and anxiety was starting to build as I faced the frightful yet exciting gauntlet known as transfers: meaning that—up to the discretion of the mission president—a missionary would either stay in their current geographical area or get transferred to a new area and serve with a new companion. This process took place every six weeks.

One of the primary reasons for this exercise was to help limit the strong emotional connection that missionaries would develop for their investigators,[52] their mission companions, and Church members. Most importantly, it was to eliminate investigators from joining (or staying in the Church) due to their personal investment in the missionaries and not the organization itself. The objective was to convert people to the Church and its doctrines, not to the young men and women teaching about it.

Traditionally, as I had come to learn, we would be informed of our new assignment on a Saturday. And then, just three days later, on Tuesday, we would be jettisoned to our new home. In those short seventy-two hours, there would be just enough time to pack up our feelings along with our meager belongings and say our heart-wrenching goodbyes to the people we had come to know and love. Then we would arrange our own transportation and go wherever the Church chose to send us, having to re-form relationships with new people in a new environment. I was apprehensive about this upcoming ritual.

As I faced the potential changes coming at week's end, I also celebrated my first fruits as a missionary. Although still somewhat of a novice, I was finding relative success early on. Shumway and I had baptized our first convert, and President was in attendance for the joyous ceremony.

"How are you doing, Elder?" he asked while gripping my hand firmly and gazing deep into my eyes.

"I'm doing fantastic, President! I'm loving my mission so far," I replied.

"Well, are you ready to go serve in Winter Garden?" he asked matter-of-factly without the slightest hint of amusement.

Customarily, the directive of transferring to a new area was a formal process, executed from the top down in a regimented fashion. I wasn't supposed to have the privy information relayed to me for another two days. But President, with the authority he had, laid it right on me then and there.

"Uh…yes, President, that sounds great!" I said, unsure of what I had just heard or the significance of it all.

"You'll do great there, Elder," he said. "Good things are in store for you. I know it."

He promptly changed gears, turned away from me, and moved on. The whole situation left me baffled, yet at the same time, it permitted me a feeling of being relatively privileged. I had never heard of a mission president prematurely enlightening a missionary about where he would be serving.

I couldn't wait to tell Elder Shumway about what had just happened, so I trotted up pridefully behind him like a Clydesdale leading a parade and whispered excitedly into his ear.

"Something strange just happened," I said as I scanned the room to make sure what I was about to say would stay confidential. Seeing that the coast was clear, I leaned over and disclosed, "President just told me where I am being transferred."

Elder Shumway pulled away from me, brushing at his ear with exaggerated motions as if a bee had stung him. "What? You aren't supposed to know that!" He glanced around the room quickly as if offering up proof, in advance, of his willingness to keep this information under wraps before revealing his curiosity. "What did he say?"

"I'm going to Winter Garden."

Shumway's eyes lit up. "What? No way! You're kidding, right? Lucky!" he screamed.

"Lucky? What is the big deal? It's just another area. What do you mean?" I asked, confused about his response.

"Don't you know what's in that area?" he asked.

"No," I snapped with feigned annoyance.

He shook his head in disbelief. "You really don't have a clue, do you?"

Shumway now had the upper hand and he was not going to give it up easily. I strained to think until my head hurt, then I slowly shook my head with a not-so-committed *no* before I verbalized it.

"No…?" Shumway mocked, shaking his head with a dramatic flair along with me. I was tiring of his immature games. Noting my growing impatience, he leaned in and revealed, in a whisper, the second and most startling revelation of the day.

CHAPTER 16

THE EDGEWATER

June 1, 2004

W ilder, you are so lucky! In an hour, you'll be in Winter Garden. Say
hi to Erik for me!" Elder Shumway said while placing his arm over
my shoulder.

Standing next to the idling car, I couldn't believe I was already leaving
the place I had called home for my first six weeks in the mission field. Not
only was I departing, but I was heading to the most coveted of missionary
destinations, on a collision course that would bring me face to face with
the infamous Erik.

Shumway, with a sardonic smirk on his face, stuck out his hand as if to
give me an affectionate handshake. I looked at him, shook my head, and
wrapped my arms around him.

"I love you, Elder Shumway," I said as I hugged him. "I'll miss you.
Take care of yourself."

The man in the car grew tired of our sappy farewell pleasantries and
tapped on his watch. "Let's go!" he said curtly while honking the horn in
short bursts. I broke away from Shumway and jumped dutifully into the
back of the car as it started to pull away even before the door was fully closed.

Shumway, who had not finished his goodbyes, yelled after me. "Tell
me what happens!" he screeched. I turned to look out the back window
and couldn't resist giving him one last jab. I shook my head *no* with a

devious grin as Elder Shumway jogged alongside, nodding *yes*. The exchange continued until the car accelerated and left him behind. I chuckled as I heard the last of the muffled yelps of my now-former companion fade into the distance.

During the drive, all I could think about was my looming engagement with Erik. For weeks now, I had been painting a striking portrait of him in my mind: He was a well-dressed, good looking, and thin man. He was tall, dignified, and had appropriately parted his hair to one side, much like that of a Church leader. From the designer clothing and Rolex watch on his wrist (as he climbed out of his Viper to greet me like a returning war hero), there was no question that he was rich and powerful.

Ever since I had first heard about Erik, a civil war had been taking place in my heart. One part of me wanted to believe the rumors about him and the band, and the other part wanted to prove he was an impostor. The dichotomy wrestling within me frustrated me to no end. Despite my reservations and doubts, I subconsciously hoped that perhaps God could even use him—anyone, really—to help guide me into the intimacy with Him I had long desired. Nobody and nothing in my life was able to quench this ever-growing thirst—not my parents, friends, girlfriend, or religious leaders. My hope was that in Winter Garden, Florida, I would find what I was looking for.

You Have a Home

We arrived at our destination late afternoon, and the apartment complex was in a picturesque location right on the shores of the resplendent Lake Apopka. As we pulled into the parking lot, I looked out over the massive lakefront facility. What a beautiful sight!

The vehicle came to an abrupt stop and I got out. As I retrieved my belongings, I saw three young men in white shirts and ties advancing toward me. My pulse quickened. One of these men would be my companion for the next six weeks—maybe longer.

The rules for a missionary companionship were strict: We could never be separated from each other, which meant we were required to eat together, sleep in the same room, and always be within each other's sight. The only time of seclusion we were privileged to have was in the confines of the bathroom. The arrangement was comparable to a marriage, but unlike a spouse, we had no say in choosing our significant other.

I fabricated a confident smile as my new roommates approached me. One was a slightly portly Hispanic missionary with straight black hair slicked down against his head, and the other two were both tall and thin gringos. I glanced down at the nametag of the shorter individual: Elder García. He was to be my new companion.

"Hello, Elder," I said, trying to hide my nerves. "I'm Elder Wilder."

He smiled and seemed slightly bashful. "Nice to meet you," he said in a serene, somewhat nasally voice.

I introduced myself to the other elders, who in turn cheerfully presented themselves as Elder Rasmussen and Elder Larsen. They were both welcoming and their enthusiasm disarmed my anxiety.

After a few minutes of universal pleasantries, we headed up some concrete stairs that heaved and rattled at the slightest move that we made in step with each other. When we reached the top and entered the apartment, a tangy odor hit me in the nose. The smell that wafted up gently to greet me—which I recognized immediately—was the missionary kennel smell that I knew would be altered by each new tenant and could be counted upon to endure long after he had departed.

The front door opened into a living room with two old stained couches, likely acquired from a nearby curb. To the right was a dining area and a small kitchen with a calendar on the wall, next to which was a roster of names. (It was a tradition of sorts to leave behind one's name and even a little message—a lineage, so to speak, of all who came before. The list was short, so it did not take a Sherlock to know this apartment had only recently been turned into a missionary accommodation. Therefore, the pungency was all the more impressive.)

Straight ahead was a narrow hallway with four doors, two on either side. One led to a bathroom, two went to bedrooms, and one to an office. I was directed to place my belongings in the last room on the left. The small living quarters that I would call home for at least the next six weeks was largely unadorned. The chamber had two small beds, a dresser, and a messy closet—most likely used to quickly "clean" the apartment should there be a new missionary (such as me) entering the fold.

My place to rest my head was one of two twin-sized beds—by technical definition only—at opposite ends of the room that, from a quick assessment, most likely had recently boarded a small band of gibbons. As I was contemplating which side and then which end of the mattress had fewer sweat stains on it, I set my stuff down and began to unpack my meager earthly goods. As missionaries, we lived a simple and mostly possession-free lifestyle. The only truly indispensable items were our missionary attire, study materials, and pictures of loved ones from home.

At dinnertime that evening, I sat at a small, glass-top round table with my companion in complete silence while eating ramen noodles. It became apparent that I would have to take the initiative if I wanted to form a bond with the very shy Elder García. In a concerted effort to get to know him better, I asked all the typical new-missionary companion questions: "Where are you from?" "What do you like to do?" "How long have you been on your mission?" Elder García, as it turned out, was from Mexico City—the very location I was originally assigned to serve my mission. He and his family had immigrated to the United States when he was a child and had called Texas their home ever since. García had been on his mission now for twenty-one months and was a well-seasoned veteran.

The rest of the day was a blur—a new place, with new roommates and a new companion, compounded by my apprehension about meeting Erik. I was overwhelmed, and being that this was the first transfer of my mission, I was soaking it all in while fighting feelings of homesickness.

At nightfall, I headed to my new sleeping quarters, knelt beside the structure resembling a bed, and said my prayers. "Heavenly Father, please give me strength. Please help me to do everything that Thou hast prepared for me to do, and to learn everything Thou hast prepared for me to learn."

It had been an exhausting day. After I spent time like a dog circling over the mattress trying to figure out the best way to sleep, I succumbed to my destiny and laid down on the rather malodorous bed. I stared at the ceiling with a thousand thoughts coursing through my mind. It seemed like only moments after closing my eyes that the alarm buzzed, and I awoke to an uncomfortably wet chin that was resting in a sodden pool of fresh drool. I had officially claimed the bed for myself.

Breakfast in Brigadoon

It was 6:30 a.m. and time to start our monotonous rituals: say prayers, exercise, shower, eat breakfast, study, and then work. Our days were long and demanding, but I quickly became adapted to (and even enjoyed) the grueling schedule.

After I showered and donned my missionary apparel, I made my way to the kitchen to find some food to fuel me for the day. Just as I placed a bowl on the counter and began to pour a large helping of healthy Fruity Pebbles, Elder Larsen came out from around the corner and grabbed the milk.

"We're not eating here, Elder Wilder," he said with a devious grin.

"Oh?" I said as Larsen looked over at Rasmussen. "So, where are we going?"

Elder Larsen, who had a distinctive snicker and an ear-to-ear smile that was demonstrating its full range at the moment, simply responded, "You'll see."

The four of us headed out into the blinding and beautiful sunshine, loaded into the car, and sped away from the apartment in typical teenage fashion. We bounced uncaringly across the speed bumps without so much as slowing down.

After about a mile we turned onto Plant Street and entered the magical world of Brigadoon. I was instantly in awe of the brick-paved section that was lined with historic buildings, and for a moment I became lost in the surreal and timeless scene that rolled out ahead of us like a carefully built movie set. Along the side of the lane were well-manicured plants growing on either side of a bike trail. Shops and restaurants filled both sides of the street, and people milled around as if this were some sort of living museum exhibit. *This can't be for real,* I thought. It looked like a staged scene straight out of the movie *Pleasantville.*

When things seemed like they couldn't get any more unusual, we passed by an old clock tower with the words *Winter Garden* at the top. We then took a sharp left around the tower and pulled up to an old, three-story red brick building. On the front of the awning were the words Edgewater Hotel.

"It's Erik's hotel!" I blurted aloud. We parked in front and I leapt out of the car. I could hardly bear the anticipation as I followed the troop toward the entrance. This was the moment I had been waiting for.

The wooden front doors strained melodiously on their springs as we opened them, then slammed behind us as we walked into an open hallway with high ceilings. The dark, wooden wainscoting on the plaster walls surrounded us in an ambiance of years past. Turning left through a doorway, we entered a large dining area. An aromatic mixture of bacon, coffee, and toast filled my nostrils and I was transported back to when I was a child waking up at Grandma's house. (As Mormons, we could not drink coffee, but my non-Mormon grandfather unapologetically gulped it down like it was an intoxicating elixir along with his breakfast, and that made me wonder if coffee could possibly have tasted as good as it smelled. For the record, the one time I snuck a taste, I determined the answer was a solid no.)

We sat at a table and a waitress in her mid-fifties, with excessive makeup and browning teeth, approached rather quickly, as if she was familiar with our group. She walked with short little quick steps, and her pigtail bobbed behind her.

"What would you boys like to drink this morning?" she asked, then did a double take as she noticed me. "Well, who's the new boy?"

"Elder Wilder," I said as I extended my hand. "Nice to meet you."

As the waitress went around taking drink orders and fussing with crumbs on the table, I leaned into Elder Rasmussen. "How are we going to pay for all of this?"

"We just sign the ticket and Erik takes care of it, including the tip."

"Anything we want?" I said with wide eyes.

He nodded, then added, "As much as you want. Just be grateful to God. That's the only rule."

"Wow. No wonder missionaries want to come to Winter Garden," I said sarcastically. "Is Erik going to be here today?"

"Never know. Sometimes he is, and sometimes he isn't," Elder Rasmussen replied.

I glanced down at the menu and took note of the words across the top: "Edgewater Hotel, Est. January 26, 1927." *Hey, that's my birthday!* I thought to myself. *What a strange coincidence.*

After taking our orders, the waitress careened across the restaurant toward the back, and as my eyes followed her, my attention was taken to a man in the back of the room who was slowly making his way toward us. He was a tall, slightly overweight man wearing a Kermit the Frog T-shirt and jeans. He had a short-cropped yet shaggy beard, his hair was unkempt, and he walked with a slight limp. He looked plain and unassuming.

"Does Erik feed the homeless?" I asked while nudging Rasmussen and pointing toward the man with my head. The others at the table almost toppled over themselves and stood up in a half-circle in front of me to shut me up as the man came toward us.

"Hey Erik!" Elder Larsen said, hugging him. "There is someone we want you to meet. This is Elder Wilder."

My head started spinning. This wasn't Erik. This wasn't the guy. This *couldn't* be the guy. There's no way someone with so many supposed spiritual gifts, with such a reputation, could look like…well, *this*. I was confused. His appearance went against everything I had imagined him to be, and I was thoroughly devastated.

I stood up as Erik hobbled toward me. Uncertain of how to react and still wallowing in my disappointment, I opted not to hug him. Rather, I greeted him with a handshake. All the hope I had mustered for weeks about meeting the man who might be able to help me find my place in life was shattered in my heart like a glass mirror over a sharp rock. It was my patriarchal blessing all over again.

"Nice to meet you, Elder Wilder," he said as he shook my hand. His strikingly blue eyes and small, pinpoint-like pupils were so piercing I felt as though he could see right through me. He looked me in the eyes and squinted.

"Where have we met before?" he asked. Then, in an instant, something within him changed. His smile dropped and he abruptly averted his eyes and released my hand. He became pale, as if he had seen a ghost. He had obviously been startled, and I couldn't figure out why. Immediately, he turned away from me and began chatting with the other elders.

Erik's odd behavior left me bewildered. When he had first looked at me, I wanted to sink into the floor on my belly and scurry away. But after his inexplicable reaction to me, all I wanted was for him to flip me over and write ANDY on the bottom of my foot. *Where have we met before?*

What did that mean? I tried to get Erik's attention again, but he rather rudely ignored me and focused on the other missionaries.

"So, what are you guys up to today?" Erik asked.

"Probably going to go tracting this morning, and then we have a few appointments this afternoon," Elder Larsen responded.

"Well, I've got to get going. I just wanted to stop in and say hi."

I tried to make eye contact with Erik as he left the table, but he quickly headed to the rear of the restaurant and disappeared.

We finished breakfast and exited the nostalgic building. Even in my disappointment by Erik's physical appearance, something stirred within me that caused me to want to know more about how someone like him could exist under the authority of the Church. Though I didn't know him yet, I wanted to. For some reason, I now felt myself drawn to Erik.

As I stood in front of the hotel gazing out in amazement over the beautiful town, I heard the spring doors open and close behind me. I turned around, and Erik was standing there looking directly at me.

"It was nice to meet you, Elder Wilder," he said as he opened his arms wide and invited me into his embrace. Though still confused and even a bit restless, I cautiously hugged him. As I did, he imparted words that immediately penetrated my guarded heart.

"It's all about love, Kid. It's all about love."

CHAPTER 17

CHARLEY
(FREE MAN)

Winter Garden, Florida | August 12, 2004

I stood poised at the bottom of the stairs long enough to become aware that my backpack straps were cutting painfully into my hand. Irritated, I called up to the other elders.

"You ready?"

"Yep!" bayed Elder Olsen as he popped skillfully out of the door and rattled down the stairs. He was carefully balancing a bag of meticulously packed goods in each hand. Elders García and Rasmussen squeezed out of the doorway and trailed chaotically close behind.

"Hurry up," I urged as I stole a wary glance toward the sky, trying to mask my anxiety. "We really should get going!" At one o'clock in the afternoon, it was already getting dark. Strange, spiraling bands of clouds consumed the whole sky—they were quite beautiful, yet rather menacing. I had never seen anything like this before.

As the last of the wayward band of misfits reached the car, I hastily packed all our possessions into the trunk and crushed them down using the heft of my body like a garbage compactor. The task was accomplished more easily than I wanted to admit due to the thirty pounds I had gained on the complimentary all-you-can-eat breakfasts we had become addicted to at Erik's hotel.

Equipped with our doomsday necessities, the four of us loaded into the car and headed for the local chapel, where President, while giving no instruction or provision for food or otherwise, had ordered all the missionaries in the area to isolate themselves until the storm had passed.

As we drove to the church, rain began pouring down in short intervals so hard that it was difficult to see whether we were even on the road. I glanced over at Elder Olsen—Larsen's replacement—for some reassurance, who saw from the corner of his eye that I was looking at him and acknowledged me with a smile.

"This is exciting, isn't it?" I said with a poorly disguised quiver.

"The experience of a lifetime!"

After twenty minutes of driving on the oddly deserted roads, we arrived safely at the church building. Upon entering the doorway, we saw there were already numerous missionaries staking out territory like the Mormon pioneers who had crossed the plains in search of religious freedom, each one cleverly guarding their humble little patch of turf from the new arrivals by sprawling their stuff out.

Nearly everyone in the room was anxiously anticipating (some with glee) the arrival of the storm. A couple of the more electronically savvy missionaries were already busy monitoring the weather conditions with headphones and shouting out updates, having stationed themselves in the corners of the room on contraband receivers with all the seriousness of a military field radio operator on a battlefield.

"Hurricane Charley is expected to make landfall in Florida as a Category 4 hurricane, with winds of more than 150 miles per hour," one of the geeks informed us excitedly.

The violent hurricane was expected to strike sometime that evening. Being that for most of us this was our first experience with such a potential catastrophe, we all waited with conflicted enthusiasm and concern during the lulls in the play-by-play action.

Lemmings

As time passed by, the adrenaline had run its course and most of us had become jaded by the slow arrival of Armageddon. Missionaries were finding creative ways to occupy their time—taking pictures, playing games, reading books, writing letters home; but far too many were irreverently goofing off. The whole situation seemed to be cascading into disarray faster as the minutes ticked by. The full tempest had not even broken upon us, and already our orderly little Lord of the Flies society was breaking down.

Personally, I had been quietly reading the Bible in a small corner of the foyer while trying to drown out the noise of the rabble-rousers who were gaining membership by the minute.

> God, being rich in mercy, because of the great love with which he loved us, even when we were dead in our trespasses, made us alive together with Christ...For by grace you have been saved through faith. And this is not your own doing; it is the gift of God, not a result of works, so that no one may boast (Ephesians 2:4-5,8-9).

It took every bit of concentration I could muster to focus on the words in front of me, but as I did, I was intrigued by the simplicity of the passage, which triggered a memory in my mind: Pastor Benson had read these exact words of Scripture during our encounter.

When a sudden outburst of laughter broke my attentiveness, I became perturbed. It was impossible to stay focused. *That's it! This is not how it's going to be!* I reprimanded them in my mind. The actions of my fellow missionaries as representatives of divine brotherhood agitated me, so I approached Elder Olsen, who was both my friend and zone leader,[53] about the situation.

"Elder, what should we do? Do you want us to sit quietly and read the Scriptures?" I asked in a somewhat self-serving way. I was eager to get back to my reading of the Bible, which—after nearly six weeks—was consuming my daily thoughts and was calling out to me like water to a parched man in the desert.

"That sounds like a great idea. Why don't you have everyone do that, Elder," he commanded, thus commissioning me to relay the message to the unsuspecting missionaries. I dutifully obeyed my charge, and despite the third-grade moans and groans from everyone upon hearing my announcement, things did quiet down.

I returned to reading the Scriptures with eagerness and joy. I was learning marvelous things as I read God's Word with earnest for the first time in my life and had developed a passion to read and learn from it due to the challenge given by the nefarious Pastor Benson. I could sense—ever so slightly—that something was changing in my heart. I was beginning to understand love in a new way, and God was filling my heart with a desire to serve and love others. I was being drawn to something beautiful I didn't understand—but whatever it was, I wanted more. In the subtlest way, the chasm inside of me felt like it was starting to be filled.

As I continued reading, I was struck by these words:

> ...so that Christ may dwell in your hearts through faith—that you, being rooted and grounded in love, may have strength to comprehend with all the saints what is the breadth and length and height and depth, and to know the love of Christ that surpasses knowledge, that you may be filled with all the fullness of God (Ephesians 3:17-19).

As I struggled to fathom the depth of God's love for me, fate intervened. After about half an hour or so of good behavior, the submission bottle popped its cork and some of the missionaries began to get downright stir-crazy. Out of the corner of my eye I saw the first traitor get up enough nerve to drift outside with all the caution of a rodent about to cross a busy highway.

I sat in silence the entire time as one by one, most of the elders disobeyed their orders and bailed out of the building without even the slightest pretense of restraint. I watched dumbfounded as the last one of them scampered out into the coming storm as the tail end of a trail of lemmings.

I was so angered by their disobedience that I found I was reading the same Bible passage over and over, incapable of comprehending even the slightest bit of what it said. I struggled not to look up as I heard some of my peers return, chattering with excitement like the entire group of lemmings had now discovered a cache of nuts and were willing to tender some of them to me as a peace offering, as if that would somehow make up for all their foolishness.

"Wilder...Wilder...you've got to come see this!" one of them pleaded. I defiantly turned away, keeping my focus on the page before me to convince them I was spellbound. As they stared me down in silence, I finally glanced up and was shocked to see that the force of missionaries wanting me to go outside had become an army.

One of them, for whom I had an exceptional fondness, was Elder Warren. I found it hard to resist his childlike and angelic charms. In the short time we had known each other, he had become my all-time best and truest missionary friend. The moment that we met at a district meeting in Clermont, I felt like I had known him my whole life. I knew there was something about him that was different, and I was drawn to whatever it was. I was confident—and hopeful—that he would play a significant role in my life.

Elder Warren was tall, gangly, and of traditional Nordic heritage that early puberty had not blessed. He looked like he was twelve years old and was pale as a ghost. His powdery white complexion gave each of us unrelenting fodder for our own childish amusement that often ended with us taking friendly shots at him: *"Put your shirt back on, Elder; you might blind someone!"*

"Come on, Elder Wilder—you have to get a picture of this!" Warren urged while motioning me to follow, building it up with such enthusiasm like he was about to part the Red Sea.

"Elder Olsen told us to stay inside and read the Scriptures," I said. "I don't want to get in trouble. Just tell me what it is," I proposed, acting annoyed yet half interested. But he wouldn't give up.

"Oh, come on, Wilder. Olsen doesn't care. Just check it out!" Though this should have gone against every good feeling inside of me, I relented to the pressure of my persistent friend.

"All right, just for a minute," I said as I stood up. "Then we need to get back in here and settle down!" With a jubilant cheer like I had just bought a round of rum for the entire lot, the eager tally of bandits agreed to my terms, and we all headed outside. I was relieved that I could participate yet still act like I held the high ground.

The Fountain of Youth

Though it was only four or so in the afternoon, the sky was eerily bleak. Dreadfully dark clouds—with a strange green tint—greeted us menacingly. As I marched along now as a conformist being led by my little army, I was escorted to a small gray pipe—in the shape of a *u*—that stuck out maybe two feet from the ground. The other missionaries pointed at it, and I was confused.

"This is it? You dragged me out into the storm for...*this*?"

"You'll see," Elder Warren said, sporting a huge grin that piqued my curiosity.

He signaled expertly and one of the elders grabbed a hold of the pipe with both hands, then proceeded to lay flat on the ground while two other missionaries picked up his body, one holding each leg. He was suspended in the air clinging onto the pipe, giving the illusion he was hanging on for dear life with the ferocious wind threatening to blow him away. Another elder held a camera and took a side shot from his waist up, making it appear to friends and family back home that he was in peril.

Warren could barely contain his glee as he raised and lowered his eyebrows, studying my face like it was a treasure map, hoping to find where *x* marked the spot. The stunt was so stupid, immature...and dang...it was funny! They had totally caught me by surprise, and I reacted by letting out a loud and most inconvenient childlike chuckle.

"Hey, Elder Wilder, it's your turn!" Warren said eagerly, yanking my arm.

"All right, all right" I surrendered. "Let's get it over with."

I grabbed hold of the pipe, lay down, and began to adjust my body on the ground. As I did, Elder Warren and his companion grabbed my legs and promptly grunted as they struggled to lift me into the air. To my horror, I could feel Warren's knees trembling under the heft of my weight. With some very uncomfortable effort they got me into position, but as the cameraman took his time in framing the sweetest of shots imaginable, the two lead lemmings squealed and complained for him to hurry.

"Go, go, go!" Warren exclaimed as his face turned beet red. I tilted my head to strike a pose, and then I heard the "SNAP!" But it wasn't the shutter. In the moment before my life passed before my eyes, I saw the white light—but it wasn't the flash. From the way I felt and where I found myself next, it was most likely my head striking the ground. I found myself facedown, being held in a wheelbarrow position with water pouring over my body and my whole front side covered instantaneously with mud.

The most horrific and unimaginable thing had happened—the pipe had sheared off completely from its mooring.

CHAPTER 18

WILDER AND THE WHALE

My missionary accomplices were still holding onto my legs while my upper body and face lay on the ground. They maintained me in this undignified position for an eternity as they froze in fear, not yet comprehending what had just happened as the water quickly rose around my nostrils. No one but me seemed to mind that I was spitting, sputtering, and drowning.

I quickly scrambled out from beneath the missionaries' shoes while expectorating out the muddy liquid from my first waterboarding. Climbing to my feet, I shared in their disbelief at the six-foot-high cascade of water gushing from the ground. The stunning scale of the damage rapidly robbed me of my desire to strangle every last one of them because all of us were now thrust into the same state of chaotic panic.

"I knew this was a bad idea!" I howled. And, of course, I—the one person who hadn't wanted to do this—was the one who had annihilated the water pipe. All we could do now was look at each other in pained horror.

"What do we do?" I cried out.

The others were staring back at me like I was the downing of the Hindenburg. Nobody knew what to do, nor did anybody want to take responsibility or remain close enough to the blimp that broke the pipe to get caught for this disaster.

Guilt rushed over me. I had sinned greatly against God. This was swift justice and God was giving me immediate punishment, as I would have expected, for disobeying my Church leaders and not maintaining order. I was supposed to be inside reading the Bible, and instead, had succumbed to peer pressure. The one who had sentenced everyone to sit in his nest and read the Scriptures was now the one caught in a trap of his own design. I wasn't a lemming—I was a glorified rat! I just knew that God was disciplining me for my wrongdoing. *I'm going to get sent home,* I thought.

I glanced sheepishly toward the church building just in time to witness Elder Olsen poking his head out the door. So much for hoping no one had noticed. He looked at me for a moment, then shook his head. My heart sunk deeper than the Titanic as I turned quickly to expose my comrades and passively share the blame with them, but to no avail—they were all gone!

Because all the instigators had scrambled for the lifeboat, I was the only one left standing awkwardly by the church's new fountain. I felt as if I had a big flashing sign on my forehead that read "Guilty!"

This gusher was no small problem. I quickly realized that we...well, *I* had just cut off the water supply to the entire building. There were now twenty-plus missionaries staying overnight who had no running water. After tracking down and pressing each guilty party back outside by the nape of the neck, we spent the next two hours trying to fix the pipe—or at least shutting off the water so there wasn't a giant geyser in front of the building. Our efforts were of no use.

When all hope was lost, there came a moment when we realized we may have had an escape from our predicament: we could simply blame the destruction of the pipe on the storm, and no one outside of this band of accomplices would know the difference. Or...we could tell someone. For me, however, the first proposal was a pleasant fantasy but for a fleeting moment.

"We *have* to tell someone and get this fixed," I pleaded with the other missionaries, who seemed a lot less enthusiastic about Plan B.

"Elder, if we do, we will be in serious trouble. We should just let the storm pass and keep quiet. Nobody will know it was us."

I felt as if my missionary life was draining out of me along with every gallon of water that spewed out onto the ground. I *had* to take responsibility and get this fixed. I feverishly searched every corner of the building for answers, calling every maintenance number I could find, but to no benefit. Any hope of repairing the damage tonight was (literally) a pipe dream. We would have to live with the guilt of our crime for the coming hours while awaiting a sure execution from our Church leaders. This was second only to the fear of facing a group of hot and uncomfortable missionaries who had learned that it was our fault they had no running water. I felt like Jonah, who had brought the wrath of God to all who carried him aboard their vessel. My best hope now was a total annihilation of the entire region!

We went inside armed with the knowledge that if the storm obliterated the pipe anyway, then any premature destruction was rendered moot. I found myself now self-servingly rooting for the storm for all I was worth. In the meantime, I located a quiet room away from the accusatory eyes of the missionaries who were not involved yet were bound to suffer the consequences. I buried my head in my hands and began to cry.

Eventually I fell on my knees and pleaded for God's forgiveness. For what seemed like hours I begged God to exonerate me for my terrible sin. I knew I couldn't receive a full pardon until I confessed to my leaders. Only then could the burden of my guilt be lifted from my shoulders.

I had come out on my mission to save the world, and now I could do nothing more than allow my pudgy self to be cast off the ship by my cohorts and into the storm, only to be swallowed up by my own personal whale—a whale wearing a T-shirt that said, "Save Elder Wilder."

Confession

Sometime the following day, an "anonymous" call was made to the local Church leaders and the water pipe was repaired. But repairing my guilty heart was not going to be so easy. In the days that followed, I could not shake off the feeling of guilt nor could I feel true forgiveness from God. The breaking point for me came three days after the hurricane, while I was still held captive in the belly of the whale. It was during Sunday church service that the bishop[54] stood up at the pulpit for his weekly report.

"Brothers and Sisters, we are grateful to announce that there has been minimal damage to people's homes and property from Hurricane Charley.

We have a sign-up sheet for those of you who would like to help in restoration efforts. Also, we are pleased to announce that there was no considerable damage done to the church building...uh," he lowered his voice as if this was an afterthought, "except for a broken water pipe out front."

Crud! At that very moment, the whale chose to spit me out with an audible and embarrassing blat. I looked around me with all the guilt that I had committed a grave crime and buried my head in my hands. Elder García, sitting next to me, was the only one present who knew the true story.

"We still have not been able to figure out how this happened, but it might have been caused by debris from a tree." The bishop then raised his voice and moved on resolutely. "Either way, no one was hurt."

With heat rising in my body, I couldn't take it anymore. The guilt that lay on my shoulders was a burden I could no longer carry. I had to confess, even if it meant getting sent home. It took all I had within me not to get up and proclaim my guilt before the entire congregation.

I waited for the service to end. Then calling upon every bit of strength I had in me, I headed to the bishop's office. I took one last deep breath as a full-fledged missionary and knocked on the door.

"Come in!" said a cheerful voice from the other side of the door. I entered, and the bishop seemed surprised to see me.

"Elder Wilder, how are you?" he asked with a smile. "Good to see you. Please, take a seat."

I closed the door and walked over to a chair near his desk. "Bishop," I said, "I have done something terrible and I need to confess it to you. I have been holding it in for days."

His smile quickly faded and his eyes followed me as I dropped into the chair.

"Bishop...it wasn't the hurricane that broke the water pipe...it was meeeee!" I blurted out in utter shame as my eyes broke loose like sprinklers on a dry day.

There was dead silence. *He must be really angry,* I thought. I could almost make out my heartbeats as I awaited his angry outburst. But all I heard was the sound of a spring ever so slowly stretching to its limits, either from his chair or conceivably it was something far worse. Maybe it was a crossbow.

After what seemed an eternity, I stole a quick glance to see how Bishop was reacting. He had leaned back and clasped his hand over his mouth in astonishment. His face was red and he looked like he was about to blow a vein in his neck. After all, perhaps thousands of gallons of water had spewed out of the ground. I couldn't begin to imagine the cost.

But instead of yelling at me, a belching sound came out of his mouth that relieved him of whatever he was choking on. He broke out into a half-laugh, half-cough that left his composure as a bishop spraying all over his desk, baptizing me along with it. *Good grief, the insane man is laughing!*

"What a relief!" he said as he wiped laughter-filled tears from his eyes. "I was worried you had committed a sin that might affect your position as a missionary!"

Noticing my distress, he sought to comfort me. "I can see this was obviously difficult for you and I appreciate and admire your honesty," he said. "But everything is fine, Elder Wilder. The problem has been taken care of, and at minimal cost." Then he smiled again and tried unsuccessfully to contain his laughter.

The assertive side of me wanted to stand up and declare, "Really...?! You can't stop laughing? I wish I had known, Bishop, that breaking a pipe and throwing away thousands of gallons of water was going to be such a one-man comedy routine before I condemned myself to three days in my own private hell!" But what came out of my mouth was much more tactful.

"Thank you, Bishop," I said resignedly as I felt like a thousand pounds had been lifted off my back.

After this long and painstaking process of repentance through the proper channel, I finally felt forgiveness. God's mercy had overcome my foolishness once again, and I was grateful.

I walked out, closed the door, and heard Bishop break out into a chuckle again. Wallowing in my self-inflicted humiliation, I found myself standing face to face with a thoroughly amused mission companion.

"Feel better?" he asked me with a smile.

"Yes," I said. "I suppose I do."

CHAPTER 19

FRANCES
(FREE ONE)

Apopka, Florida | *September 5, 2004*

A mere twenty-four days had passed since Charley, and I found myself in the middle of my second hurricane, Hurricane Frances—a slow-moving behemoth dumping monsoon rains all over the state. President Sorensen seemed to learn a couple of important lessons from the first storm and by the time this one rolled around, he had indentured us off to a local Red Cross shelter at Apopka High School. The massive haven was housing hundreds of evacuated people, including a large population of homeless folks.

Desirous to serve and eager to make a good impression, the six of us missionaries immediately made ourselves available to the will of the supervisors. Quickly catching on that we were willing to do just about anything asked of us in the realm of service, the overseers of the shelter tempered our enthusiastic spirits by submitting us to every job imaginable. For nearly five full days now, we had been cleaning up vomit, mopping floors, working in the kitchen, checking people in, distributing blankets, escorting elderly people to the bathroom, scrubbing overflowing toilets, and more. The combination of those responsibilities—along with twelve-hour shifts for nearly a week—left me and several other elders violently ill as a result of life in unhealthily crowded conditions. The consolation prize for our suffering? Unlimited Uncrustables, which became our manna in the wilderness.

I was privileged to share the escapade with three of my favorite missionaries: Elders Warren, Gaertner, and Olsen. Gaertner had replaced Elder Rasmussen, whose twenty-four-month mission had come to an end. Rasmussen's shoes would not be easy to fill, but as Olsen had done in the wake of Larsen, Elder Gaertner proved that he was up to the task.

Best Kept Secret

While we were quarantined in the hurricane shelter the days had been long and challenging, and I looked forward to when we would be freed from our squalid prison and released from the labors that had taxed my body to its limits.

As Elder Beckstead (my new companion who had replaced García) was cleaning up vomit, I was getting nauseous while taking care of an overflowing toilet and feeling as though the whole room was spinning. Elder Warren, cleaning in an adjacent stall, started singing the pirate's life song but had changed the words: "Yo-ho, yo-ho, a missionary's life for me!" Even in my desperate condition, I had to chuckle.

"You'll love it," I said in a Russian accent, mimicking my older brother Josh. "It is the best two years of your life!" We all laughed hysterically, knowing that the downside of the missionary life was the Church's "best kept secret." As I sucked in air through my mouth after my outburst, I caught a powerful whiff of the previous tenants' donation to the mix—and I ended up contributing my own offering up to the porcelain throne.

Elder Warren and I had grown even closer to one another since our disastrous water-pipe mishap during Charley. Although we weren't direct companions and never dwelled together, we did have opportunities to go on exchanges with each other—a "companion swap" during which we would spend a day with one another, sometimes even overnight. One time, while visiting my apartment, he saw a picture of my sister and me on my desk.

"Dude," he said with ogling eyes, "is that your sister?!" He picked up the picture and pointed at Katie.

"Yes," I responded, knowing what was coming next.

"Can I write her?" he asked gleefully.

"Bro, she's fifteen. Ugh. Absolutely not."

Regardless of Elder Warren's intentions with my sister, I couldn't contain my fondness for my youthful friend. I was drawn to his kindness, compassion, and innocent demeanor. I was his district leader and overseer, and he humbly submitted to my counsel and treated me with respect. I didn't want to let him down...but I certainly didn't want him dating my adolescent sister.

When night arrived at the shelter, Warren and I attempted to sleep on a couple of couch cushions on the auditorium floor and struggled over possession of one very small blanket. We had just finished an exhausting day of service. As we rested, we were both staring up at the ceiling.

"Warren, it's hard to put this into words, but so much in my life is changing. I've been reading the New Testament every day and...I don't know, I just feel different. Like there's so much more than I already know. God is showing me things and opening my eyes. It's hard to explain. You should read the New Testament too. Read it...like a child. Put away all your preconceived notions about what you think is truth. Humble yourself, approach God with an empty cup, and let Him fill it. Come to God as a child would their Father and let Him teach you. That's what I'm trying to do...and it's the most amazing thing."

Elder Warren turned to look at me. I loved him, and I knew he loved me. He trusted me. "I will, Wilder. I will."

Eventually Warren drifted off—he had a knack for being able to sleep in the most uncomfortable of environments. I was not so lucky, not only due to the incommodious surroundings, but my mind contained endless thoughts of God's love that were piercing through me like arrows. Finding it impossible to sleep, I propped up my head with my hand and opened the Scriptures.

By now I had pored over the New Testament daily for more than two months, trying to deprive Benson of a win and disprove the evangelical "gospel of grace." I wanted to substantiate the Church's restored gospel using the Bible alone. In that time, I had read the New Testament in its entirety for the first time in my life. Though my testimony of the Church (and its five pillars) was never in question, I wanted the proper ammunition in case I was faced with a Pastor Bensonesque encounter again. I wanted to fight fire with fire, using what he used against me against others who made similar claims about the Church. While I hadn't come to any definite conclusions yet, in that time of study I was learning about one thing above all others: love.

When Erik told me "It's all about love" on the day we first met, I didn't understand the depth of his seemingly simple statement, but the words stuck to me like glue. And now I was beginning to get the first inklings of what he meant. God Himself was love, and to know God was to know love. To know Christ was to know God. The New Testament had taught me that love was the core of the gospel itself, and to love God and love my neighbor were the greatest of all the commandments. But what did that truly mean? What was love? I was still unraveling that mystery.

Bread of Life

My craving to fully fathom the meaning of love stirred within me a desire to read the New Testament again—and I found myself in the Gospel of John for the second time.

> Jesus said to her, "Everyone who drinks of this water will be thirsty again, but whoever drinks of the water that I will give him will never be thirsty again. The water that I will give him will become in him a spring of water welling up to eternal life." The woman said to him, "Sir, give me this water, so that I will not be thirsty or have to come here to draw water" (John 4:13-15).

Jesus' astonishing declaration to the Samaritan woman at the well awakened a cry within my soul as I pined for this same water to quench my unsatisfied thirst—"Sir, give me this water!" This was becoming a pattern now: Every time I read the Bible, it left me wanting more of what it was offering me. I would absorb every word and every phrase. I didn't want to stop, and so I continued.

> Then they said to him, "What must we do, to be doing the works of God?" Jesus answered them, "This is the work of

God, that you believe in him whom he has sent... For the bread of God is he who comes down from heaven and gives life to the world." They said to him, "Sir, give us this bread always."[55]

Jesus said to them, "I am the bread of life; whoever comes to me shall not hunger, and whoever believes in me shall never thirst...For this is the will of my Father, that everyone who looks on the Son and believes in him should have eternal life, and I will raise him up on the last day."[56]

"Truly, truly, I say to you, whoever believes has eternal life. I am the bread of life...I am the living bread that came down from heaven. If anyone eats of this bread, he will live forever. And the bread that I will give for the life of the world is my flesh."[57]

As my eyes scanned the pages, the culmination of years of seeking satisfaction through my religion rose to the surface, and I began to shed tears. Jesus had boldly pronounced, "I am the bread of life; whoever comes to me shall not hunger, and whoever believes in me shall never thirst." How could that be? How could He alone satisfy in such a way? Could the answer to filling the void that had plagued my life be...Jesus alone? It all seemed so simple. *Too* simple.

I instinctively knew there was a far deeper level to this love, and I yearned for what Jesus was offering. I hungered for the bread that would fill my soul and satisfy me eternally. But I didn't know how to partake of it, or even where to find it. I had spent my entire religious life trying to satiate the famine in my soul, but I was still left hungry. All I knew was that every time I read the Bible, something awakened within me.

"Heavenly Father," I pleaded, "give me this bread of life. Show me where to find it. I want so badly to have Thy love and grace. I know there's something more that I'm missing. Show me what I must do to have it. Point me to Thy truth."

CHAPTER 20

JEANNE
(GOD IS GRACIOUS)

Winter Garden, Florida | *September 26, 2004*

E rik and I arrived at the old wooden door and could hear the commotion emanating from behind it. It sounded like an epic battle from
Book of Mormon times was raging on the other side and about to burst
out. The door itself was flexing as if breathing. I tried to open it, but it
wouldn't budge. Erik grabbed the knob as if questioning my reluctance
and we pushed hard until the door relented just enough for us to squeeze
into the room. It then slammed shut with an angry thud. The force of the
wind, with all its rage, was incredible.

The howling sounded as though a speeding locomotive was approaching—the noise, due to a broken window, was deafening. We had to scream
at each other to be heard and could hardly hold ourselves up as we walked,
leaning heavily in surreal right angles to the floor as we headed to the
calmer center of room 315 on the third floor of the Edgewater Hotel.

Just then the large window beside me gave way—not in shards of
glass, but rather the entire windowpane. I watched it fly about seventy-
five feet, carried by the wind unbroken until it crashed into a parked car,
both denting the back door and breaking out one of its windows. All that
was left of the pane of glass was mere dust. This changed the trajectory of
the wind inside the room, and now entire storage boxes began hovering

and bouncing up off the floor unimpeded. One box—caught against the windowsill's top—opened, and several ties zoomed out of it and were now flying around in the air. Eventually the whole box was emptied of its contents and—along with the ties—was sucked out of the window and into the storm with the speed and ferocity of a deposit tube at the bank drive-up window.

Out of the corner of my eye, I caught a brief glimpse of a beautiful silver tie that I quickly recognized as being of immeasurable sentimental value: It was the tie I had worn the first day of my mission, a gift from Alicia that was a token and symbol of our love for each other and our mutual sacrifice to God. I had given the tie to Erik, just days earlier, as a contribution to his famous "missionary" quilt—a collection of ties from various missionaries to be made into a sprawling blanket as a remembrance of those who had served in the mission. It was the most cherished tie in my possession, the one I wanted to be immortalized in glory.

I gasped as I watched the tie dart through the open window. I wanted to cry, but the broken glass, water, and irrepressible wind embezzled that capacity. I glanced over at Erik and he at me. He then forcefully hiked to the empty window frame and searched for the whereabouts of the tie as water and wind pelted his face. His hair looked ready to leap right off his head.

Just then, with a steadfast determination combined with momentary superhuman strength, Erik headed to the door and yanked at it until he cracked it open, sliding his foot into the small opening until he could pry his body through. As soon as I realized the reckless plan that was coursing through his mind, I tried to stop him, but my attempt was futile. He flew down two flights of stairs and made his way out the front door into the horizontal rain and winds.

I could barely see Erik from the third-floor window through the sting of water hitting my face. He was leaning into the heavy winds and frantically hunting for my tie. The commotion was too heavy and the rain too thick, and eventually I lost sight of him. Moments passed by, and later, Erik reemerged from the storm looking much like a drowned rat, clutching a now badly wrinkled and wet silver tie and bearing a broad smile while looking up at me from the flooded street. I knew then and there that my tie would never be seen respectfully hanging from a neck again. As hard as it had been to part with, seeing it in its pitiful condition, I would no longer pang for it.

As I looked at Erik, time itself seemed to stop and something in my heart caused it to skip a beat. I was certain God had firmly planted my feet on a road that was leading me to the fullness of His love. However, I was conflicted by the fact that this hurricane marked the conclusion of my four-month tenure in Winter Garden. In two days' time, I would be transferred to a new home on the Florida coast. I had been promoted to be a zone leader—the youngest one in the mission—where I would be accountable for the spiritual and temporal oversight of twenty missionaries. As much as I coveted the leadership responsibilities, I didn't want to leave my lakeside home.

During the past weeks, I had experienced—even if in small, delicate glimpses—the love of God in a way that was reminiscent of what I experienced as a child. Every day as I read the Bible, I was overwhelmed by an indescribable love that was washing over me and transforming me ever so slowly. I was gently being reminded of the heart after God that had once dictated my very being. Slowly, it seemed, the void in my soul was being filled.

Erik finally returned to the bedroom and held up the scrunched tie with a broad grin on his face. I could only smile as I dropped all decorum and hugged him, sopping wet as he was. Even amid a 500-mile-wide vortex and 100-mile-per-hour gusts of wind that made us microscopic in proportion, for some reason, in this place, I felt safer than anywhere in the world.

"Are you okay?" I asked.

"Yeah, I'm fine!" he yelled as he stood with water dripping from head to toe.

"You're crazy, you know that?" I shouted in return while laughing.

Eventually, with the assistance of the seven other missionaries staying in the building along with the hotel staff, we managed to board up the windows and the room returned to normalcy.

"God sure has some interesting things in store for us tonight, doesn't He?" I exclaimed to Erik.

"He most certainly does."

A Complicated Friendship

These were exhilarating times. Not only because I was experiencing my third hurricane in the span of six weeks, but because Erik and I were just now developing the friendship I had yearned for since before I even met him, but this hadn't come without complications. From our initial awkward encounter in the hotel restaurant nearly three months ago, it appeared that we were destined to face relational obstacles.

Initially, I had somewhat of a disdain for Erik based on his lackadaisical attitude about keeping the standards of the Church—the way he dressed, his outward shortage of reverence, his lack of church attendance, and from time to time, he would even drink a glass of iced tea![58] Shamefully, I withheld myself from loving him because of his personal blemishes.

But as time went by, I observed him from a safe distance and started to see past his warts. Erik was never overly concerned about riches, possessions, fashion, or worldly matters. He loved and served others, and he seemed far more interested in the needs of his fellow man than those of himself. I saw how selfless he was with the missionaries, and even though there were dozens of them clamoring for his attention, he was careful to invest equally into each individual relationship—even in those whom he knew were attempting to expose him as a fraud.

After intentionally keeping my distance for a time, I found myself drawn to Erik—even yearning for his favor. Cautiously, I began to instigate an alliance with him. But there was a problem: Erik had been avoiding me at every turn. I didn't notice this at first because I had essentially been doing the same thing to him. But once I started shadowing him, I found it almost impossible to gain his attention, and this discouraged me. Observing his interactions with other missionaries only led to frustration and even jealousy. In the few exchanges we had, he would make seemingly offhand spiritual comments that, for some reason, wedged themselves in my heart. "You know that God rejoices more in the one sheep who is lost and found than the ninety-nine who are never lost, right?" he once said. He would impart random nuggets of wisdom, then abandon me. It was almost as if he was preparing me for something by testing me, but my patience was running thin.

One day, feeling hopeless after having failed to garner Erik's attention, I confronted him at my breaking point.

"Erik, why do you hate me?" I erupted with tears in my eyes.

His face crumpled, and he wrapped me in his arms.

"Oh, Kid, I don't hate you! How could you say that? I love you. In fact, you are my favorite missionary. But most importantly, you need to know that God loves you."

In that moment, everything changed. My confession had triggered an avalanche within Erik, and nothing could stop it. Instantaneously, seemingly impenetrable barriers were knocked down. After that encounter, Erik reciprocated my advances of amity toward him and, after months of distance, we began building a friendship that blossomed quickly. Erik had become someone I could trust. Through him I felt God's love, and this caused me to love him in return. He began teaching me simple biblical truths and planting gospel principles in my heart. I wanted to learn from him but was annoyed when, rather than give me direct answers to my probing questions, he would simply encourage me to read the Bible so that God could reveal Himself to me.

What's in a Name?

Admittedly, I had selfishly coveted an opportunity to spend a few days in isolation at Erik's hotel, a designated shelter during the storm. Because I would soon be transferred from Winter Garden, I knew this would be my last chance—possibly of my entire mission—to finally ask the burning question that had been left unanswered for far too long.

By divine providence, Erik and I ended up doing a work shift together several hours late into the evening. Toward the end of the watch we were both getting tired and our eyes were burning. Needing a few moments of precious rest, we found the only unoccupied room down the west hall of the building that was reserved for the busy staff and missionaries who were on duty.

We entered room 208, leaving the door slightly ajar so we could hear any distresses in the building. The small chamber was beautifully decorated. An antique bed with a white metal frame and gold trim sat to the left against the wall, and directly adjacent to it was a white dresser with an attached mirror. The floors were highly polished wood, and bright red pipes ran along the ceiling.

The room was dark, and ominous clouds filled the gloomy sky outside. The storm had sustained high-powered winds now for more than eighteen hours, and the howling sound it caused had gone from something to fear to something strangely comforting.

Erik sat in the chair on the opposite side of the room and I settled down in my wrinkly clothes on top of the blankets on the bed. For a moment I just rested there, looking up at the ceiling and focusing on the red pipes. So much in my life was changing, and it was all happening so fast. The Word of God and gospel of Christ were penetrating me, gradually opening my eyes to something I had never seen and didn't fully understand. All while God's love was pouring deep into my heart.

After a bit of hesitation, I spoke. "Erik, I don't get you. I feel like we've become such good friends over the last couple of weeks, and I know God has used you to help me see things I didn't see before. You've become one of my best friends. But there's something I don't understand. Why are you inactive? Why don't you have a proper testimony of the Church like I do? Why do you only tell me to read from the Bible?"

Erik smiled as he put up his hand and jokingly turned away to deflect my barrage of questions.

"Micah, please know that I love you," he said softly. "And please know that I love Christ. This has been a tough journey for me…learning to completely surrender to God and turn away from manmade desires and dreams." He paused as he leaned forward in his chair.

"You have to understand that my relationship with the Church is complicated. At the time I was being courted to join, I had more than a strong reason to believe that I was being led there—but not to be a witness of its truthfulness as many may have hoped, but rather as a medium for me to fulfill my purpose for God. The best way I can describe it is like a watchman, on guard, ready and waiting for the people and signs God would place in my life, and then report what I have seen. When I saw you that day in the restaurant for the first time, so many recollections came instantly to my mind as I shockingly realized…Micah, *you* are my purpose. Although I was confused and torn for a time about why I was led to the Church, it all makes sense now. I was waiting for you, and once I realized you were real, at first I was frightened.

"As for the Church, I didn't necessarily *want* to be there, but it's where I felt I *needed* to be. But right from the beginning, I started to suspect—and then realize—that Jesus wasn't the center of it, but rather, He was being used as a vehicle for submission to the Church and its leaders, as if submission to the Church itself were submission to God. And as God was working through me and displaying gifts of the Spirit, I was scrutinized seemingly by the highest levels of the Church. In fact, they explicitly forbade me from using what God has graciously bestowed upon me, even after I was given the 'priesthood.'

"Micah, I have always had faith in the Bible and in Jesus all of my life. But I felt like I was being asked to compromise my faith by putting a line of authority in between me and God, and I couldn't do that. I can't do that. God is bigger than this Church. He is bigger than any church or earthly authority, Micah. Go straight to the Bible to find the truth. Your authority is all in Christ."

Erik's response should have shocked me, but for some enigmatic reason, it didn't. While I recognized there were serious implications to his confession and thus I should have been concerned, I was too caught up in mustering the faith to leap off the cliff and ask him the question that was weighing on my mind. After all, I had waited for this moment for many years, and something unspoken revealed to me that perhaps, just perhaps, God would finally unveil to me the answer to life's most burning question, returning me to the intimacy I once shared with Him as a child. This might be my last hope.

Suppressing the tremendous fear that this moment would join the chorus of disappointing failures in my life, I took a deep breath and leapt headfirst off the precipice.

"Erik, who am I?" I blurted out, fearing that he might find the question foolish.

There was a long pause. I couldn't believe I had done it, but it was too late to take it back. I closed my eyes, waiting with angst, praying to God fervently in my heart. As the seconds ticked by, I slowly opened my eyes and glanced at Erik. He had no visible reaction to my query. Perhaps my suspicions had been accurate. I was humiliated.

Erik's voice then broke the awkward silence.

"Micah," he said slowly, "there is something I have wanted to tell you for a long time. From the moment I first saw you, actually."

My heart perked up. Could this be the revelation I was waiting for?

Erik hesitated for a moment, then continued. "You know, I do sort of know you by another name…in a sense, God knows you by another name."

My eyes widened and my heart pulsed in my chest. Erik paused again, then turned his gaze directly toward me.

"David…David is your true name," he said. "Which means 'beloved.'"

The unfathomable force of that name came crashing into me like a wrecking ball and I was instantly paralyzed, unable to speak. Countless memories from my youth surfaced in my mind. The void that had plagued my life for so long somehow, in an instant, vented its hidden contents.

As I laid there in silence, Erik arose from the chair, walked over to the antique dresser, and slowly opened one of the drawers. He retrieved a white envelope bearing a handwritten inscription, "To David." He handed it to me and looked me in the eyes. I held the envelope tight with both of my hands.

"Micah, this is your true purpose. You have a specific responsibility in life. By the time your mission is over, you will be on the path to fulfilling your calling by recognizing your namesake and knowing what it is like to be made in the likeness of God. You, through a band of ministers of the gospel, must help bring God's Word to the world, and by doing so work to unite the body of Christ in preparation for the second coming of our Lord Jesus Christ. In this letter, you will learn more when the time is right. Don't open it until your mission is complete. Then you will see and understand that your true mission is just beginning. But first, God must release you from bondage."

I remained there in silence while clutching the envelope in my shaking hands. Release me from bondage? What was he talking about? I now had more unanswered questions than ever racing through my mind, but I didn't have the strength to vocalize them. I had so much to process. But despite the level of my uncertainty, one thing I knew for sure: everything that had been seeded by God within me quickened as it came alive.

I knew my life would never be the same.

PART 3

A GREAT REVELATION

CHAPTER 21

FULFILLING ALL RIGHTEOUSNESS

President folded his arms with a disgruntled frown on his face. I had elected not to verbally respond to what I had interpreted as a rhetorical question, and his disapproval was apparent.

"Elder Wilder, as your priesthood leader in the Church, I must tell you that I do not feel this path is the one that God would lead you on," he said as he took it upon himself to invoke the biggest cache in his armory: his spiritual authority. "I believe you are being deceived in your actions. The only way to true eternal happiness is by the established order God has outlined through this Church by His chosen prophets in these last days."

Normally when given such a commanding line by a superior, I would be expected to submit to the priesthood authority and repent hastily (as I had been trained to do since birth), lest I wanted to lose everything I had worked for—most discernibly my exaltation. Up until recently, I probably would have done just that. But not now. Not after the truth had opened my eyes and removed my blindness.

As I prepared to articulate my newly discovered liberation from man-made intercession and total dependence on Christ, I reminisced on what Erik had declared to me that critical night during Hurricane Jeanne: he wouldn't compromise his faith by placing an earthly line of authority between himself and God. Initially I had disregarded his statement, but by now his concerns had been validated in my mind through God's Word. This man-centered hierarchy *was* using Jesus as the vehicle for submission to the highest levels of the Church, and a personal relationship with Christ—independent of my religious headship—was deemed inappropriate, if not impossible.

Now, for the first time in my life, I was determined to *not* rely on a priesthood leader or a burning in my bosom to establish the truth. The Word of God itself had become a lamp to my feet and a light to my path, guiding me to green pastures and still waters, and through it I had come to a personal and saving relationship with Christ. I had taken upon myself the full armor of God and was submitting everything to the authority of God's Word alone by holding fast to what passed the test (as the Bereans had done)[59] and rejecting what did not.

"President, no matter what you or anyone else in this Church may tell me, I know that I am following the Savior Jesus Christ. There is no one on Earth that can come between Christ and me, and I will submit to His Word, above all things. I have found His truth, I know His voice, and now I am following the Good Shepherd alone—not man. And He is the one who has called me to walk this path. I will obey."

President was stunned by my retort to the exercising of his authoritative muscles, which, in my mind, had gone from an Arnold Schwarzenegger-sized threat to a rooster bluffing me by ruffling his feathers.

"What about authority, Elder Wilder?" he pleaded. "Don't you believe that God has established the true priesthood authority through the Prophet Joseph Smith? Don't you believe in the line of authority that runs from Christ down through the Prophet and to me?"

I could read between the proverbial lines (of authority), and it was obvious President was attempting to validate and maintain his spiritual stewardship over me by reminding me of the priesthood chain of command that started with Christ and extended to him as Christ's earthly representative. I was expected to acquiesce to the Church's claim that this man stood directly between me and my salvation, sitting in judgment over my eternal soul. By stating I had direct access to God through Christ and His Word, I was defying—even threatening—the established order of the Church's priesthood hierarchy, all the way to the coattails of the Prophet himself. After all, if I could have a personal and direct relationship with Christ, what need was there for a prophet? (a fact Pastor Shaw had pointed out). My confidence and security were now in God's Word, which emboldened me.

"As First Peter says, Christians have been given the royal priesthood—to all who believe!" I exclaimed. "I believe that anyone who is part of the body of Christ holds authority by faith in Jesus. Now that I have found Him, I need nothing else but to trust in Him alone. My authority is in my faith in the Lord, and in knowing that He died for my sins."

As the shock of what I said hit him, President grimaced and squeezed back in his seat as if he were slamming on the brakes from the passenger side of the car to avoid a collision.

"Elder Wilder!" he bellowed. "Christ has established His Church to the earth for a *reason*. And He gave the keys of authority to the Prophet Joseph Smith to perform ordinances such as baptism. Do you not believe it is important to be baptized by the proper authority into the proper church?"

"President, I believe that *anyone* who is a Christ follower can perform water baptism as long as they do so in the name of Jesus Christ, as the Bible instructs. And it doesn't matter what church or what person in that church baptizes you. Water baptism isn't to join a church or to be saved; it is a public witness of one's faith in Christ and a symbol of becoming a new creation in Him. It represents the death to our old self and our resurrection into newness of life through the Spirit—just as Christ was buried and then rose from the grave. More so, I believe true spiritual baptism is not about being dipped in physical water, but immersion into the Word of God, who is Jesus Himself. And once the Spirit of God has given that baptism, no man can take it away from you."

There was no question that I was not a theologian and President would have little respect for my expressing any theological prowess, but I had spent a substantial amount of time pondering the complicated subject of baptism on my mission because it was a source of much discussion with prospective converts. After all, we were constantly telling investigators that our Church had the only true method and authority to baptize anyone in a way that would be acknowledged by God. We were proclaiming that salvation came exclusively through our institution.

So, without influence from the outside world—either Christian or Mormon—I had taken what Pastor Benson and Erik advised to heart, and I had been using the Bible alone to understand fundamental doctrinal truths, attempting to align my beliefs with God's Word by approaching it through the eyes of a child.

Baptism

Since my baptism at the age of eight, I had always believed that the sacred ordinance of being submerged in earthly water was a necessary part of my salvation and good standing with God. To me, it was an essential covenantal act that was renewed each week during the sacrament as I partook of the leavened bread and water at church. But as God seemed to have been doing with every aspect of my faith, He was rewiring my brain and recording His truth directly onto my heart through His Word.

The more that I read the Scriptures, the more I began to see baptism in a different light. I wondered, *Could baptism be more of a picture—an allegory—than an actual ordinance?* When Jesus said that His baptism fulfilled all righteousness, what did that really mean in the simplest of terms? Was it possible that when Jesus was demonstrating all righteousness in the River Jordan, He wasn't showing us *how* to be baptized, but rather, *what* baptism represented? If so, maybe baptism wasn't as much of a physical act as it was a picture of our righteousness—from justification, through sanctification, to ultimate glorification. I couldn't help but notice the not-so-hidden theme in His baptism.

As Jesus descended into the water, He was symbolizing His death, and subsequently our spiritual death to the world and ourselves when we receive Him by faith. This is our moment of justification, when Christ's righteousness is imputed on us. Then He rose from the water—the grave—and the Spirit of God descended upon Him. This is the process of sanctification that begins when we are raised into newness of life and the Holy Spirit indwells us, working in and through us to fulfill our purpose as disciples—which, as I had come to learn, was chiefly to take up our cross and fulfill the Great Commission. Then, lastly, the Father in heaven proclaimed, "This is my beloved Son," symbolizing our moment of adoption as children of God, when we will be glorified with Him in heaven and receive our promised inheritance as joint heirs with Christ. What an amazing depiction of God's love! That was how I saw it—in the simplest terms anyway.

Communion

Ironically, I also couldn't help but feel that there *was* an intrinsic connection between baptism and the sacrament, but not in the way I had always been taught. It didn't take long to wonder if, in a sense, the sacrament—or communion—was a renewing of the covenants I had made at baptism. But I now understood the covenant to be something so much more.

As the disciples partook of the unleavened bread and wine at the Last Supper in the upper room, they were commanded to do so in remembrance of Christ's body and blood, which represented the new covenant of grace. They were, essentially, taking upon themselves Christ's very name by committing to remember Him and the sacrifice He would make for their sins. But to remember Him meant more than to simply think about or reflect on what He did, it was to *act* on it. And as Jesus commanded them before He ascended to the Father, "Go into all the world and proclaim the gospel to the whole creation,"[60] He was commissioning them to do something about His love: tell others! So maybe *that* was the true meaning of the sacrament: Remembering what Christ had done by sharing His love and gospel with the world.

After all, if we profess to know and follow Jesus but we don't tell others, aren't we taking His name upon us in vain? And if we partake of the bread and fruit of the vine but don't tell others about Christ's unfailing love, what good does it do? Why would God save and redeem us through His unfathomable love only for us to selfishly keep that love within ourselves? Instead, He has commissioned us to go out and tell the world of His great love, thereby making disciples who then go forth and make other disciples. When Paul instructed believers to "examine" themselves,[61] he might have been encouraging them to actually do what they were promising to do by taking the sacrament: Remember Christ by proclaiming His death until He comes, acting on their faith in Him.

In a sense, I understood the Church's well-touted mantra from James that "faith without works is dead"—Christ's call to faith is one of action (after all, I had been a firsthand witness to many Christians who didn't share their faith with me when given the opportunity). But the works that are part of the Christian walk are vastly different from the man-made ordinances in the temple, or even the physical ordinances of water baptism and the sacrament. The good works as a Christian are to love our neighbor, and the greatest form of love (*agape*) for others is laying down our lives for them—being spiritually crucified with Christ and pointing them to the hope and salvation found in Him alone, no matter the cost. Therefore, good works are not the root of salvation, but the fruit of it.

The Church

"Elder Wilder, this is foolish and wrong," President said brazenly. "You are diminishing the power and importance of the priesthood. The priesthood is found only in this, the Lord's Church. Do you not believe that the priesthood was restored as Joseph Smith said it was?"

Without having to even think about what I was going to say, the reply was welling up in me as the Holy Spirit prompted me to witness with passion and confidence.

"I have come to learn recently, through the book of Hebrews, that the priesthood of the old covenant—along with all of its ceremonial rites and rituals—was fulfilled by Christ's finished work on the cross when He died for our sins. We no longer need the priesthood of the old law to mediate for us. We only need Jesus Christ, who is now our eternal High Priest."

I was mildly surprised as the incriminatory words flowed so clearly from me. It was evident that God was fulfilling His promise,[62] giving me a mouth and wisdom that was beyond my cognizant understanding as the truths of God's Word were brought to the forefront of my mind.

President, either unable or unwilling to contradict what I was saying, moved on in his line of questioning.

"Well, what of the Church, Elder Wilder? You said it doesn't matter what church we go to. But what about Christ's true Church that He established while He was on the earth? Do you believe Christ established a church?"

The dam had burst and there was no stopping the flow of living water cascading from me by God's grace.

"Christ did establish a church, but not in the way I was always taught and believed," I said. "The church is not a physical entity or organization. It is a living, breathing organism—a spiritual house, built by living stones, with Jesus Himself as the chief cornerstone. And those living stones are not brick and mortar, they are people—individuals who have been saved by their faith in Christ's atoning work. Through the gospel, the church was built as the apostles went out and proclaimed the message of the Son of God. The church, quite simply, is the all-encompassing group of Christians from around the world who have been saved by Jesus, working in unity to build the spiritual kingdom of God. It can't be limited to a certain organization or group. The church is the believers. All of them."

"So you don't think it's necessary to belong to the true Church of Christ and receive all the proper ordinances to be saved in God's kingdom, then?" President asked curtly.

"President, I believe that the Son of God died on a cross for me, and that by grace alone I have been saved. There is nothing you, or I, or anybody else can do that can add to what Christ did for us to earn salvation. Eternal life comes in and through Jesus Christ alone, not a church. As Jesus said in John 6:47, 'Truly, truly, I say to you, whoever believes has eternal life.'"

President scoffed at my profession, then sat forward in his seat and peered harshly into my eyes.

"You think all you have to do is believe, and that's it?" he queried. "You think God will let you into His kingdom by faith alone? That sounds kind of simple, don't you think?"

"Yes, President. It *is* simple. That's the point. But learning it has been the most difficult and painful process of my life."

CHAPTER 22

IT'S NOT FAIR

Palm Bay, Florida | *August 8, 2005*

L et's go!" I said anxiously as I stood waiting by the car while Elders Bingham, Santos, and Young dawdled far behind.

Today was perhaps the most anticipated day of the week for a missionary: preparation day. This sacred half-day "off" each Monday morning afforded us the only authorized time each week to go grocery shopping, do laundry, enjoy tame recreational activities, and most importantly, communicate with the outside world through emails and handwritten letters. It was hardly a day of rest, but the break from door-to-door rejection combined with the anticipation of hearing from family and friends made it worth the wait.

The four of us, donning our trademarked and world-renowned white shirts and ties, headed out to the Palm Bay Public Library to use the free community computers as had become our custom over the last few months. We savored each opportunity to sit down, open our email, and see what glorious news abounded from the outside world. It was also a chance for us to update our loved ones on the exciting happenings of missionary life.

Personally, I had grown to relish my weekly appointments to convey to my family the marvelous things God had been doing in me. Over the last year or so, I found myself slowly imparting tidbits to my parents, siblings, and most openly to Alicia concerning the transformation that was occurring in my heart and the discoveries I was unearthing in the New Testament. After all, I had uncovered a treasure, a stunning wealth of answers in the Bible, and I was compelled to share this good news to those I loved most.

As we entered the library, we passed the entryway display of newly released books, and I noticed a popular anti-Mormon selection that had been making its rounds, sitting front and center, and directly next to it, a film titled *I Am David*. I laughed. Glancing over my shoulder to affirm the coast was clear, I pilfered the nefarious book and concealed it in a corner bookshelf, eliminating any opportunity for the locals to discover it. I felt slightly guilty for doing this, but I justified myself by thinking that I was protecting the world from the toxic influence of apostates who had left the Church.

After my passive-aggressive act of community service, I strolled over to the computers and sat down, eager to read all the updates from the home front. I logged onto my missionary email account, opened my inbox, and scanned the bold, unread subject lines. Jackpot! My family members had written me. Mom, Dad, Matt, Katie…Jessica. Jessica?! I knew only one Jessica—my long-lost middle-school girlfriend from Indiana. Why would she be writing me? I hadn't communicated with her in years. Her subject title immediately captured my attention: "Very Sad News," it read.

Curious, I opened her message first and began to read it. "I don't know if I am the first one to give you this news, and if I am, I am terribly sorry to be the one to have to do this…" My inquisitiveness quickly turned to panic as I skimmed down the letter until my eyes landed upon these life-altering words: "Schuyler and his mother were killed in a car crash."

The moment I saw the haunting words, I felt as if I had been bludgeoned in the chest with a hammer. I couldn't breathe. I reread the harrowing sentence two or three times to make sure my eyes hadn't deceived me, but they hadn't. As my mind tried to process the anguish that was overflowing from my heart, the floodgates opened and I began to wail in the quiet of the library. As I sobbed I fell to the floor, burying my face from the scrutinizing view of the public eye.

Elder Young had no clue as to the source of my pain, but it was obvious that I was in desperate need of consolation, so he knelt next to me and placed his arm on my shoulder. It must have been clear to him that whatever I was experiencing was beyond the comfort of words, and so for the next twenty minutes, he simply sat next to me in silence with his hand gently rubbing my back.

Eventually I built up enough strength to climb back into my chair, and with quaking hands, I wrote my family a short email.

> I thought I would write a short letter to all of you. Upon hearing of the death of my dear brother Schuyler and his mother, I have not been able to stop crying. My heart aches and I need your prayers. It is hard to lose a best friend...I'm sorry I cannot say much...I do and will always love you.[63]

I sluggardly stood up and walked away from the computer, headed to a quiet corner of the library, sat on the floor, and began to weep again. I was in the middle of a nightmare, and no matter what I did, I couldn't wake up. My best friend had been killed at age twenty. My mind recalled every memory, every amount of joy, every time we laughed together, fought each other, forgave and hugged each other; every disappointment, jealousy, passion, and pride found in true brotherhood and friendship that could have been shared. I couldn't process that it had all come to an abrupt end.

"Why, God?" I lamented out loud. Elder Bingham, sympathizing with my distress, approached me with concern.

"Are you okay, Wilder?" he asked.

"No, Bingham. No, I'm not," I said through my wails.

With the gracious assistance of my missionary friends, I was escorted back to the car. Not a word was spoken on the somber drive home. Although none of my roommates knew the details of what had instigated my emotional breakdown, they knew enough to comprehend the brokenness of my heart was well beyond their ability to mend with words.

We arrived back at the house and I dove straight to my room, slammed the door behind me, and hit the bed face-first, weeping into my sheets. I couldn't accept what had happened. I was angry, confused, and grief-stricken beyond anything I thought I could ever bear. "Why, God!" I cried out. "Why would this happen? It's not fair!" I screamed while pounding my fists into the mattress.

Schuyler had always been somewhat of an enigma to me. A unique person with an amazing heart, he had made some foolish life decisions. After my family and I departed Indiana and moved to Utah, Schuyler began a reckless and destructive path of drug addiction and alcoholism, which eventually landed him in the hospital with a near-fatal overdose. Immediately before my two-year mission, the last thing I was impressed to do was to visit him, and I was relentless in trying to convert him to the Church. I wanted him to be freed from the bondage of addiction that was so blatantly consuming him like a disease. Though Schuyler had not accepted the restored gospel of the Church, he had made commendable strides in cleaning up his life.

As I lay on my bed, I suddenly remembered a letter that Schuyler had written me just months earlier. I wiped my eyes and stood up, making my way down the hallway to my desk, where I kept all my letters from family and friends in one sacred notebook. I sorted through the pages and finally found what I was looking for. I pulled it out, sauntered back to my bed, and fell on my back. I held up the letter and began to read.

> Micah,
>
> How are you? I hope things are going well in Florida. It's been almost a year and a half since I saw you last when you came to stay with me and my mom. Time has gone so fast. I'm sorry I have not written in such a long time. Have you talked to Ryan at all? He has probably done a better job of keeping in touch than I have. I know he misses you.
>
> …For the first time in my life I feel like I'm truly happy. I got to the point in my life when I felt like I was at the end of my rope. I had gotten so involved in drugs and alcohol my life was hanging by a thread; literally, as I almost lost my life when I OD'd. Because of my heavy involvement in drugs I had a miserable season at U of I and ended up quitting school my sophomore year. I could see that my life was in shambles. After that I realized I needed to make some serious changes in my life.

I thought about the time you came to Muncie and spent the week at my house just before you left on your Mormon mission. I remember leaving you home at night so I could go out and smoke pot and get drunk with my friends. Every time I saw you, I felt guilty for the things I was doing in my life. To be honest, I was a little jealous because of how dedicated you were to God and your church and how happy you seemed to be at the time.

But Micah, as lost as I was at the time, I cannot deny the influence that you had on me, and those missionaries that came to the house a few times. Those guys were cool. You taught me and showed me that God loved me and cared for me, though I didn't really even understand who God was at the time. I didn't even believe in Him. But after you left for your mission, though I had a lot of doubts about the Mormon religion, I started praying a little bit. I didn't know if God was listening, but I had hope that maybe He was.

I eventually gathered up enough strength to go to rehab and clean up my life. It was there that I started praying to God more and more and I even started reading the Bible a little bit. I feel like God gave me strength when I needed it the most. After a long battle with my addictions, I have now been clean for 6 weeks or so. I must admit that though I have no desire to be Mormon like you are, I do desire to be close to God like you are. I have been trying to read the Bible and understand what it's all about. I think I'm coming along. Ashley has been helping me a lot.

I don't really know all that much yet, I do believe this: God loves me. He has rescued me from myself. And I believe that Jesus died for me and that He forgives all the terrible things I have done. At least I hope He did, or else what hope is there for people like me? I hope your mission trip is going well. We will have to get together when you get back home and swing off the rope into the river just like the good ole days. I'll never forget that. You are a true friend, Micah, and I would not be

where I am today without you. You will always be stud #1.
Talk to you later.

Schuyler[64]

Believe and Confess

I slowly put the letter down beside me and closed my eyes. My heart-ache gradually morphed into hope as I realized that God had done something amazing in Schuyler's life. Perhaps there was a valuable lesson to be learned by this tragic experience. "God, whatever it is You want me to learn from this, teach me," I petitioned. "Help me to see Your truth, and let me know that my friend did not die outside of Your love, nor in vain. Give me comfort, God."

As I prayed, the Holy Spirit moved in my heart to turn to the Bible for answers. I reached down next to my bed, picked up God's Word, and randomly flipped to a passage and began reading in the book of Romans:

> If you confess with your mouth that Jesus is Lord and believe
> in your heart that God raised him from the dead, you will
> be saved. For with the heart one believes and is justified, and
> with the mouth one confesses and is saved...For "everyone
> who calls on the name of the Lord will be saved" (Romans
> 10:9-10,13).

Time after time, the power and beauty of the Word of God had impacted me with such ineffaceable force—and this time was no different. God was unmistakably giving me an answer to my plea, but could it really be that simple? Everyone who calls upon the name of the Lord will be saved? According to Schuyler's letter, he *had* called upon the name of the Lord and confessed Jesus before his death, much like the thief on the cross who had implored Christ, "Remember me when you come into your kingdom."[65] Would God grant a hopeless and desperate sinner like Schuyler—who had seemingly repented and turned to God in the last hour—the same eternal life as me, a faithful steward who had dedicated my life to the Church? That wasn't fair, was it? Wasn't I *more* deserving of God's love?

As missionaries, we plainly taught our investigators the justness of God: "Is it fair that if someone who is righteous and faithful their whole life, performs the correct works and ordinances, and follows the commandments perfectly be given the same reward as someone who lives in sin their whole life and then repents on their deathbed? Of course not! That wouldn't be fair. For that reason, God has established three kingdoms[66] in heaven."

I wanted to believe that God had redeemed Schuyler—but selfishly, I didn't want to accept that he could be given the same reward as me. After all, hadn't I earned my right into the highest kingdom of God? Hadn't I worked tirelessly to show God I was worthy of His forgiveness? Schuyler had seemingly rejected Mormonism but now confessed Christ. What then was his fate? One of the lower kingdoms?

I was torn and confused by the passage in Romans. On the surface, it appeared to be a direct contradiction to Matthew 7, which I had often used as a missionary to disprove the idea that salvation was as simple as many Christians were erroneously proclaiming.

In trying to reconcile God's Word, I flipped back to the Gospel of Matthew and began to read, like a detective solving a case.

> Not everyone who says to me, "Lord, Lord," will enter the kingdom of heaven, but the one who does the will of my Father who is in heaven. On that day many will say to me, "Lord, Lord, did we not prophesy in your name, and cast out demons in your name, and do many mighty works in your name?" And then will I declare to them, "I never knew you; depart from me, you workers of lawlessness" (Matthew 7:21-23).

Every time I had read this scripture, I had interpreted Jesus as rejecting those who would come to Him professing faith alone—hence "Lord, Lord"—but not fulfilling the works He was requiring. But this time I was seeing these words in a different and startling light, as it seemed I rarely sought to actually *finish* the passage. Curiously, it never mentioned that those calling upon His name were doing so in faith. In fact, it seemed to indicate they *weren't* calling upon Christ's name in faith, but instead, were coming to Him claiming they had done something worthy of being saved: "Have we not...prophesied, cast out demons, done many works...?" These individuals were approaching Jesus seeking justification by their actions without professing true faith and trust in Christ Himself.

So who would be saved? Who would Christ *truly* know? Those who did the will of the Father! But what is the will of the Father? And then, in a striking epiphany, I remembered the compelling passage that had penetrated my heart while I sat alone reading my Bible during Hurricane Frances. I had read all this before!

I frantically flipped through the pages of my Bible and zeroed in on John 6, tracing the verses with my finger until I found the treasure I was seeking: "For this is the will of my Father, that everyone who looks on the Son and believes in him should have eternal life, and I will raise him up on the last day" (John 6:40).

I was dumbfounded. The very will of God was…to believe in Jesus? Therefore, those who came to Jesus with true faith, believing in Him alone for their salvation, were fulfilling the will of God and would be granted eternal life. Matthew 7 didn't contradict Romans 10—they perfectly complemented one another!

Tax Collector

Even though I had scoffed at the simple concept of grace in the past, I now was beginning to realize that maybe *I* was the one that had it wrong all along. I felt ashamed. Perhaps I had been like the Pharisee in Luke 18, foolishly boasting in my righteousness before God—approaching Him in arrogance, saying, "Lord, Lord, have I not…"—when I should have been like the lowly tax collector, beating my breast and humbly proclaiming, "God, be merciful to me, a sinner!"[67] After all, Jesus declared him as the one justified, not the other. Was I more like the proud Pharisee?

Then a dim light came on in the far corner of my muddled mind: Maybe God's love and mercy *weren't* fair, as illustrated by the parables of the workers in the vineyard,[68] the prodigal son, the ten pieces of silver, the lost sheep[69]—and now most painfully by my best friend Schuyler's death. As the light grew brighter, I was beginning to see that that was to my benefit, because perhaps I was no worthier of salvation than Schuyler. How absurd it was for me to have been offended by God's mercy toward the undeserving! I, too, was a pitiful, sinful wretch whose only hope was to call upon a merciful God to save me. That's what I had been missing all along. I was equally as guilty as anyone, deserving of God's wrath. God didn't love me *because* of my righteousness; He loved me *despite* my wretchedness.

In a strange twist of fate, Schuyler, my dearest friend, the once-hopeless sinner in the eyes of many and my longtime religious antithesis, had seemingly found his way quite instinctually and rather innocently into the queue for salvation ahead of me. The only course of action for me was to swallow my pride and heed my friend's example—to recognize that I, too, was a hopeless sinner, and trust that Jesus could rescue me. I needed to be the tax collector.

As I pondered these hard truths, I realized this was never about determining my friend's salvation; that was in God's hands and out of my control. Rather, it was about me working out my own salvation with fear and trembling, a process I had been in now for many years.

With hope filling my heart, I sat up at the edge of my bed and contemplated how much Jesus had done for me and all the sufferings He had endured because of me. I turned to a passage in the Old Testament:

> Surely he has borne our griefs and carried our sorrows...But he was pierced for our transgressions; he was crushed for our iniquities; upon him was the chastisement that brought us peace, and with his wounds we are healed (Isaiah 53:4-5).

In a manner of speaking, I was somewhat right from the beginning. It's not fair. But not for the selfish reasons I had originally considered. It's not fair because He who was guiltless died for the guilty. It's not fair because He who knew no sin was made sin for us so that in Him we might be made righteous. It's not fair because the innocent, blameless, perfect, and holy one of Israel took our stripes, and by His wounds we are healed. That's not fair to Him. But that's why—for the world—it's good news.

CHAPTER 23

LOVE ELDERS

Palm Bay, Florida | *October 11, 2005*

Elders, I am humbled and grateful for this opportunity to share with you what is in my heart. What we're going to talk about today is the most driving force in the universe. This simple truth has—and is—transforming the very core of who I am, day after day," I choked out while fighting back tears. "It's the trait and attribute that defines the followers of Jesus, is part of God's nature Himself, and is the very reason why Christ died on the cross. Elders, today we are going to talk about the power of love."

Standing at the head of a large conference table with twenty-two missionaries listening intently to my every word, I was in my element. I had been a zone leader now for well over a year and I was a seasoned veteran of missionary leadership. Being the longest-standing zone leader in the mission, I had gained the respect and admiration of my peers. I had delivered dozens of these bimonthly trainings, but I never grew tired of the opportunity to convey to my missionary brethren what God was teaching me through His Word.

I was now steamrolling through the New Testament for the tenth time, and God's Word was slowly healing my broken heart in the aftermath of Schuyler's passing. The lessons I learned from his tragic death were becoming clearer and more focused. Through every verse, every chapter, and every book, I felt like an abundance of spiritual riches were unfolding before my very eyes. The more I read, the more I longed for what the Bible was feeding me. In fact, by now I had ceased my study of the Book of Mormon and other Church-specific materials, using the entirety of my morning study hours to read the New Testament alone. I so desperately wanted others to come to know the love that was being revealed to me. I relished these opportunities.

"If we are to fully grasp the power of love, we must first define it. What, then, is love?" I asked rhetorically. "First Corinthians 13:4-7 says, 'Love is patient and kind; love does not envy or boast; it is not arrogant or rude. It does not insist on its own way; it is not irritable or resentful; it does not rejoice at wrongdoing, but rejoices with the truth. Love bears all things, believes all things, hopes all things, endures all things.'

"The first and greatest commandment is to love God with all your heart and with all your soul and with all your mind. And the second is like unto it: love your neighbor as yourself. On these two commandments hang all the law and the prophets. We are to love God, but how? First, by loving others!

"Elders, we are called to love one another as Christ has loved us. But how do we love one another? We follow the example of Jesus Himself. We visit the sick and afflicted, we help the poor, feed the hungry, care for the orphans and the widows. We strengthen the weak, serve others, sacrifice for each other, and we put others' needs above our own. We are to be kind, gentle, and compassionate."

I paused while trying to contain my emotions. Running my hands along the edge of the table, I closed my eyes to suppress the tears. But as soon as I opened them, a flood of salty water drowned my notes.

"The apostle John says, 'In this the love of God was made manifest among us, that God sent his only Son into the world, so that we might live through him...Beloved, if God so loved us, we also ought to love one another.'"[70]

I took a moment to compose myself, my mind travelling at the speed of light and recalling the memories that had buried themselves in my heart over the course of my mission.

"I am coming to know the extent of this love that surpasses all understanding. I am being changed by this very love. I am now loving God because He first loved me. Every time I read the Bible, I am reminded of this love. My prayer—above everything else—is that we all come unto this Man, this Jesus of Nazareth, He who is the Messiah, that we may become His disciples and find our strength in Him. Let us all love and serve, with faith in Jesus Christ, fixing our eyes on Him. Amen."

The Love Crusade

Change was inescapable. I had been in Palm Bay for six months now, and with transfers only days away, the odds I would stay for another six-week stint were slim to none. God had done so much in my life over the course of my time here and I didn't want to leave the people I had come to love so much. This was a painful process we had to endure again and again, and was one of the most difficult aspects of missionary life. Leaving family, friends, and our old life for two years was hard enough, but to do it countless times with new family and friends was emotionally devastating.

As I was wiping the tears from my eyes, Elder Warren mauled me with his lanky arms and bear-hugged me with force. "Love elders unite!" he hollered with gusto. "I love you so much, Wilder!"

"I know, Warren. I love you too."

Over the past few months, Elder Warren and others had affectionately designated me as the trailblazer of the "love movement," as it had widely become known in the mission. The crusade had been born out of the "love zones"—zones where I had been the designated leader—with the nickname "love elder" given to the missionaries who were carrying on the vision of love and faith as the central components to missionary work. Inadvertently, all of this had brought forth an underground reformation in the mission.

Throughout the course of my thirteen-month tenure as a zone leader, I had made a concerted effort to allow the principles revealed to me in the New Testament be the mainspring for my leadership. I underscored the very truths I myself was learning in the Bible, and it was causing a noticeable and tangible impact on my approach to missionary work. I focused on loving God, loving and serving others, and building true faith on the foundation of Jesus Christ. What God was teaching me through His Word I was then teaching others, who, in turn, were teaching still others. As one torch lit another, the flames went on to spread like wildfire.

The unpredictable rise of the love movement was not without its complications, however. As the number of underground love devotees increased, the tension was mounting between President and myself. The more that I publicly emphasized to the missionaries the biblical foundation of faith in Jesus Christ and loving God and neighbor and the less I said about numbers, the more President subtly doused my message by accentuating obedience to Church leaders and faithfulness to the "standards of excellence"—a Church-wide series of benchmarks used to measure the progress of missionaries based on their reported weekly numbers.

President had his own dedicated following as well. These loyal disciples who strictly adhered to the rewards-based standards of excellence were coldly labeled "number Nazis" by us in hushed tones. The division between us and the escalating faction of antithetical insurgents was becoming spiritually brackish, tearing the mission apart and leaving a gulf that was increasingly unnavigable.

By the time the chasm had grown to massive proportions, President—in an obvious panic—changed his tactics. He went on an all-out assault against the individual members of the love movement rebellion, summoning them into his office and grilling them intensely. Battering them into submission, he compelled them into promising that they would follow his absolute orders with blind faith. Some were even forbidden from reading the Bible. (I was getting reports on these situations through the "elder network.") I was certain that Sorensen would eventually be coming after me, desiring to cut off the head of the snake and effectively end the movement. For weeks, I jumped each time the phone rang, but President never reached out to me even once with the same demands. I could only assume that God had intervened on my behalf time and again.

Please Stand Up

As seemingly merciful with me as President had been, I knew that his patience was probably wearing thin, no doubt on account of my increasing boldness to openly proclaim the love message.

In fact, only weeks earlier at zone conference, I—as the zone leader—went up to the pulpit to report on the success of my zone over the past six-week period. Generally speaking, this exercise was an opportunity to report on the number of baptisms a zone had achieved. Tradition dictated that the zone leader would invite all the missionaries who had baptized an investigator during the course of the transfer to stand up and be publicly recognized by their peers. This custom reeked of self-righteousness, and I couldn't ignore what Jesus had said in Matthew 6:1: "Beware of practicing your righteousness before other people in order to be seen by them, for then you will have no reward from your Father who is in heaven." God had been convicting me of my hypocrisy and changing my man-centered heart.

"We have had a wonderful and successful transfer in the Palm Bay zone," I said, looking out at my missionary peers. "God has been teaching us so much and we are growing together. Every good work that is done in our zone is not because of us, but because of God. And every baptism is not our baptism, but the Lord's." I paused, knowing what was expected of me, but I couldn't stomach it, so I did something that no missionary had ever done before. "So, instead of recognizing individual missionaries, I am going to ask the entire zone to stand up."

There was confusion in the room as a low rumble of chatter rippled its way through the chapel. One by one, the twenty or so missionaries in our zone slowly stood up, uncertain of what to think.

"Nobody should get individual recognition for the work that is God's. It is only in His strength that we can do what we do. In fact, let's all stand up," I instructed while motioning for everyone in the room to rise to their feet, including President. I glanced at him, and he looked slightly discomposed.

"We are all nothing, yet we know that with God, all things are possible. Nobody but God should be glorified for the lives that change because of Jesus Christ. So, we all stand together, and recognize God as the one who has transformed hearts and worked miracles, not ourselves."

I was afraid to even look at President's response, but I didn't have to. I could feel the glare from his eyes on the back of my neck. But it didn't matter. I was done being a Pharisee. I was a love elder.

CHAPTER 24

WILMA
(RESOLUTE PROTECTION)

Stuart, Florida | *October 24, 2005*

W hat was that!" I said as I laughed nervously trying to hold the camera steady while pointing it out the window. It looked like a crash-landing UFO! I ran to the larger bedroom window and looked out. Winds were gusting at well over 100 miles per hour, and all sorts of unidentified flying objects were soaring past us violently like we were in the middle of *War of the Worlds.*

As I strained to see through the torrential rain, I identified what had flown by us at our second-story level: a fourteen-foot-wide trampoline. It had been picked up from our neighbor's yard, lifted over a seven-foot-tall fence, and hurled into a palm tree, chopping it in half and mangling it. I couldn't believe it! In less than a week's time in my new area, I was now experiencing the *fourth* hurricane of my mission, all in the span of fourteen months. Was God out to get me? He seemed to be coming after me faster than I could run away.

After nearly six months in Palm Bay living in the same house, I had been transferred to the coastal community of Stuart. Our humble abode was located on the second floor of a very ugly yet fortified two-story cement block apartment building with tiny split windows. We were located directly on the edge of the waterway that led out into the bay, and beyond that, just a short distance away, was the vast barrenness of the Atlantic Ocean.

The fact we were even in our apartment while a powerful Category 3 hurricane pummeled us flabbergasted me. Being an involuntary weather-worn expert of hurricane survival, I was experienced enough to know that President's standard M.O.—in the past, anyway—had been to evacuate all the missionaries who had even the slightest possibility of being in the wake of the storm. Reports had said that Wilma was the most powerful storm ever recorded in the Atlantic Basin,[71] and our tiny town of Stuart was more than in the wake: it was predicted to be ground zero.

Ironically, I had first heard about the coming tempest from Erik, my now-best friend and closest confidant. "You know that there's a hurricane headed directly for you, right?" he called and asked.

"Uh, no. I mean, we've seen people putting boards on their windows. But we don't have access to news outlets. Is it going to be bad?"

"Well, at one point it was a Category 5 storm, although it looks like it's slowed down a bit. But it's still projected to make landfall on the west coast of Florida as a Category 3, with 120-miles-per-hour winds. You didn't know anything about this? President never called you?" he asked in disbelief.

"No. Should I call him?" I questioned in a slight panic.

"Yes, you should. Let me know what he says."

I called President, expressed my concern for the missionaries in our zone, and was met with a reassurance that everything would be fine. "Just remain in your apartment, Elder, and have the other missionaries do the same," he casually instructed. Feeling abandoned and apparently left for dead, I submitted to President's request. Perhaps the hurricane would take care of me so my commander wouldn't feel threatened by me anymore.

Number Nazis

Circumstances and poor decisions beyond my control had me smack-dab in the middle of the beastly storm. Our power had already gone out and the phone lines were down. Elder Jensen (my new companion) and I were in awe of the sheer force of the terrible winds as we hunkered down in the confines of our room while trying to document the historic event with our HI-8 video camcorder.

"I can't believe this is happening, Wilder! This is crazy!" said Jensen, a shorter, medium-built elder who was balding at only twenty years old.

"I think this is the worst one I've seen," I replied. "And I've seen a lot!"

In our short time as companions, Jensen and I had become a dynamic duo. Initially, I was slightly apprehensive about the prospective pairing, given that he had a solid reputation for being overly strict and (to my knowledge) was not a documented love elder. The first couple days together there was a slight bit of tension between the two of us, as we didn't quite see eye-to-eye in our approach to missionary work. I was squarely to blame for our lack of harmony, for I was prideful and judgmental toward him. But somehow—in less than a week—we had seemingly become unified. God had softened my heart and showed me the solution to our discord: love him, submit to him, and show him the magnificent things I was learning in the Bible.

"Wilder, I have somewhat of a confession," he said while avoiding eye contact with me. "When President said we were going to be companions, he made it very clear that I was to be your superior, even though you have been a zone leader for far longer." He paused and looked at me with brokenness in his eyes. "He also said he was pairing me with you so I could help you focus again on the standards of excellence. He said he was worried about you and he hoped that I would rub off on you."

Elder Jensen then gazed downward and shook his head. "Honestly, I think being with you has had the opposite effect. I think *you've* rubbed off on *me*," he admitted with a chuckle.

Now that he felt freed from his guilt, Jensen became animated. "I feel so…alive, Elder. I'm so passionate about loving and serving others in a way that I haven't been on my entire mission. You've helped light a fire in me. I'm sorry for being a jerk to you at first. I love you so much, Wilder."

A smile crept across my face. "Dude…I love you too. I'm sorry for the way I treated you. I judged you before I knew you. You're an amazing missionary, and I am grateful to be here with you. Bring it in!" I said while hugging him.

Jensen's heartfelt confession, as moving as it had been, was still privately demeaning and hurtful—not because of anything he had done, but because of President's seemingly deliberate underhandedness in trying to reform me by using my companion as an undercover agent. Honestly, I never intended to be at odds with President Sorensen. It was my nature to love and respect him, and concerning my actions, he never gave me any indication that what I was doing was wrong—at least not directly. Curiously, he chose to counter the blaze in my wake by crushing the embers that radiated from my fire, but never went directly to the source. So I had maintained my love-centered course.

As the storm continued to batter down upon us, our cell phone suddenly rang. Glancing at the caller ID, I could see it was the assistants—President's elite pair of missionary aides who had climbed the leadership ladder to the highest rung (and perhaps a position that would have been my destiny had I not launched the love movement).

"Hello?" I answered.

"Elder Wilder, how's it going?" Elder Kimball asked. It was hard to hear him due to the creaking of the roof and the whistling of the wind.

"Well, okay, I guess. We are in the middle of a major hurricane," I replied, trying to convey how imprudent it was that we were left here in the first place. "The power just went out, and a few seconds ago a tree nearly broke through the bedroom…and something very big just flew past the window. It…"

"Wow, sounds exciting," he said matter-of-factly while cutting me off. "Elder, do you have the weekly numbers ready to report for your zone?"

"What?" I blurted out almost inaudibly. Was this a joke? Here I was, along with sixteen other missionaries in an area that was supposed to be evacuated, all alone and trapped in our homes with no power or water as ferocious winds and rain raged all around us…and he wants the numbers report?

"Uh, no Elder, I, uh…don't at the moment. We are in the middle of a hurricane and I'm worried about the safety of the missionaries whom I cannot contact. Have you heard from them? The phone lines are down."

"Well, just call me when you get the info!"

No pleasantries, no good luck, and no goodbye.

I turned and saw Jensen staring at me. "He didn't just…"

"Yes. Yes, he did," I said.

Love Like Jesus

The hurricane continued its steady progress and eventually the winds died down and an eerie calm settled over us. Elder Jensen and I, curious about the unnatural tranquility, slowly made our way outside and gazed in astonishment at the unexpected sight. No, the storm was not over. Rather, the eye was directly above us, and the unnerving stillness sent a chill down my spine. We knew it was just a matter of time before the west eyewall would hit and the worst of the tempest would rear its ugly face. We went back inside and braced ourselves.

As I laid on my bed staring at the ceiling, I was transported back to the life-changing revelation that I received while in the heart of another formidable gale. The name David, which had brought back long-forgotten recollections of my youth, had instigated an impassioned vigor for Jesus and had solidified my commitment to keep barreling through the New Testament—although this time, I couldn't get David off my mind. So I opened my Bible to 1 Samuel and read about my childhood hero:

> ...the soul of Jonathan was knit to the soul of David, and Jonathan loved him as his own soul...Then Jonathan made a covenant with David, because he loved him as his own soul. And Jonathan stripped himself of the robe that was on him and gave it to David, and his armor, and even his sword and his bow and his belt (1 Samuel 18:1,3-4).

Reading the famed story of the Bible's greatest friendship, I was astounded by Jonathan's deep love and selflessness toward David. The son of Saul had even sacrificed his own heirship to the throne in order to support David as the chosen king of Israel, laying down his inheritance for his beloved best friend. This was akin to the agape love that Pastor Benson had described. Contemplating this unparalleled companionship teleported me back to the moments when I saw my reflection in the White River and imagined my own Jonathan in the swirling water. I could only pray that I, too, would encounter the caliber of sacrificial comradeship that David knew.

The storm finally passed, the sun crept through the clouds, and the ocean breeze brought a much-needed sense of normalcy. But as Jensen and I headed outside to survey the damage, the serenity was short-lived. People in the surrounding neighborhoods slowly began to emerge from their homes, shocked at the extensive damage done by Hurricane Wilma. Large branches had pierced roofs, palm trees had been uprooted, streetlights were lying in the street, and road signs were just plain missing. Wires hung haphazardly from some of the telephone poles and the litter from roofs, buildings, and trees was strewn about. After only a quick assessment, I knew by impulse what we had to do. I turned to my companion and set in motion a plan that had formulated out of the past few hurricanes.

"I think we need to commission all the missionaries in the zone to do nothing but assist others in helping clean up their yards and homes from the storm. Tell them not to worry about numbers until all the power and services are restored. Have them wear their casual clothes, walk the streets, and help however they can. Elder, it's time to love like Jesus tells us to love."

"Absolutely! Let's do it," he responded in agreement.

The love movement was alive and well.

CHAPTER 25

STANDARDS OF EXCELLENCE

Stuart, Florida | *October 27, 2005*

During the first three days after Wilma had decimated the area, the elders of the zone enthusiastically obeyed our orders and were working beyond exhaustion, on pure adrenalin, without so much as a complaint. Elder Jensen and I had dug in alongside and were leading the charge. We hadn't sported our white shirts and ties since before the hurricane, and I was almost starting to feel like a civilian again.

Today, however, Jensen and I (still without warm water to shower) dressed ourselves in our finest missionary apparel as we were summoned to attend the once-a-transfer zone leader conference; an instructional gathering of all the zone leaders from across the mission in an intimate forum with President, who would—by divine inspiration—impart direction for missionary work.

The predetermined topic for today's gathering, as had been delivered to us by the assistants, was the standards of excellence. This revelatory program had been instituted directly from God through an Apostle via a worldwide teleconference less than a year ago, and was essentially this: each week, a pair of missionaries had a series of benchmarks and goals they were required to meet, which could be measured by predetermined numbers. As directed by God Himself through the leadership of His Church, we were mandated to teach fifteen lessons per week, each of us contact ten people per day, and institute three challenges for baptism each week. If we blindly and obediently followed the demands of the regimented system, then we would be honored and recognized in front of our peers in a special rewards ceremony. If we did not, we would be chastised by our leadership and debased by our comrades.

The unfortunate and immediately detrimental side-effect of this newly implemented system was that missionaries were now incentivized to accomplish missionary work either by (1) a fear of punishment or (2) a desire for rewards and man-given glory, expecting to be blessed by God for strict obedience to their priesthood leader, regardless of their motivation. Naturally, the result was that they were attempting to do the right things but for the wrong reasons. The element of following the Spirit, which promoted faith and love, had been removed from the equation. The focus was on the *what* and not the *why*.

Admittedly, I myself had been as guilty as anyone of impure motives at the inception of the program, shamefully seeking for the honor of my leaders above my servitude to God and genuine love for others. For a short time, I was more focused on the flesh rather than the Spirit. In those moments of weakness, I would talk to people on the street not because I wanted to love them like Christ and share truth with them, but because I coveted the accolades that came from fulfilling my obligation to speak to them. Over time, the more I immersed myself in the Bible, the more the program became a thorn in my side and I found myself between a rock and a hard place: the rock being Jesus, and the hard place—more and more—the Church. At times, I felt I was serving two different masters.

Fortunately, by God's grace, I had spent much of the last year undergoing a necessary heart transplant. God had been painfully convicting, disciplining, and rebuilding me through His Word by reminding me of my duty to love my neighbor. I had been a noisy gong for too long, proclaiming to know and follow Christ with my lips but not truly loving others. Now, having become acquainted with a far greater incentive than any earthly rewards my Church was offering or any punishment they could impose, I wanted what drove me—the love of Christ—to also motivate my protégés. Today was my opportunity to impart that love.

Treasures in Heaven

Sitting in a large half-circle with President and his assistants at the head of the table, the meeting commenced with a leading question. "How do you feel about the standards of excellence, and how have you seen that commandment bless your zone?" Sorensen asked the captive audience.

As soon as his query fell on my ears, my knee started bouncing nervously. I had formulated quite an opinion on the matter based on my careful observation of the program over the course of the year, but I was uncertain as to how much I could—or should—vocalize. One lesson I had learned was that whenever President posed an inquiry like this, it wasn't really up for debate. The unspoken expectation for each zone leader was to confirm and affirm. After all, the divine decree came straight down from the apostleship of the Church, so there was no room for debate, as our Church adage said: "When the Prophet speaks, the thinking is done."[72] It was from God; no questions asked.

One by one, the zone leaders eagerly voiced their unwavering endorsement of the system. "Oh President, it's marvelous! We have a testimony of this program, and we have seen great blessings in our zone!" Bleh. I could hardly stomach the predictable and regurgitated responses, so I quickly tuned them out, knowing I had ample time to prepare my retort. I was to be the penultimate testimony, with Jensen the last.

Paying no attention to the droning robots in the background, I was praying feverishly for strength and wisdom to convey my complicated thoughts in a sincere manner, desirous to avoid any appearance of defiance. After all, I had never issued any decree to disobey President, nor was I trying to tear down the system that the leadership had put into place. I was simply attempting to plant it on a solid foundation. For that reason, I had worked extra hard as a zone leader trying to help the missionaries complete the benchmarks of the program, but with the proper incentive—fulfilling them according to their love for Jesus and not for temporal rewards or the glory of man.

Eventually, each zone leader shared their unoriginal thoughts and, ready or not, it was my turn. My knee was bouncing so strenuously it smacked the bottom of the table more than once. President looked at me and reeled me in with his eyes like a tractor beam.

"Elder Wilder, how do you feel about the standards of excellence? You have been a zone leader for a long time. How have you seen obedience to this program bless your zone?"

I didn't know exactly what was going to spill out of my mouth, so I spoke in a soft and hesitant voice.

"Well, I want to be honest about how I feel, President."

"And I want you to be honest with me. That is why we are here," he responded.

"Well, I don't think it has been good for my zone, or for me person-ally," I revealed slowly. The words rang out and buzzed in everybody's ears. I could see several missionaries turning their eyes toward the reactions of their peers with gaping mouths held open. President looked irritated and his face began to redden.

"The problem, I have noticed, is that people are so focused on blind obedience, and the rewards from that obedience, that they are losing sight of why we are supposed to be doing what we are doing. We are called as representatives of Jesus Christ Himself, yet so many of the missionaries don't know Christ and His love. Before they can go out and try to con-vert people, shouldn't they first be converted to what the Bible teaches? Shouldn't we teach them the love that comes from true discipleship in Christ? If not, aren't they just clanging cymbals?"

My candor most likely took President by surprise, and he sat motion-less while gathering his thoughts. Finally, he spoke.

"Elder Wilder, when we are given instruction from our leaders, we must obey. Do you not sustain the Prophet and the Twelve Apostles as the mouthpieces of God on the earth, the ones authorized to speak God's will?"

His pointed question was more difficult to answer than it ever had been, because only recently had I begun to struggle with sustaining the men I had always believed to be everything President had just claimed. I was starting to see an ever-growing number of contradictions between what was being revealed to me in the Bible and what my Church lead-ers taught, and it was creating an uncertainty in my mind that I could no longer ignore. Regardless, I was still holding fast to a testimony of the Church as God's kingdom on Earth. I thought all that was needed was a course correction in certain areas, and I really, *really* wanted to be accepted as the one to gently deliver that correction. But now was not the time to confess ambivalent faith in the Church's leadership.

"Yes, but that's not the issue. There is no problem with fulfilling the requirements and standards they have set for us. But first the missionaries must be built on the foundation of Jesus Christ, and His love, before we can expect them to be effective witnesses for Him. If not, we need to evaluate why we're here."

President stood up and walked slowly toward me with slightly jerky movements, glaring at me with a firm look on his face.

"So, Elder Wilder, you're telling me—and all these young men—that if they don't have the love of Christ, they shouldn't be missionaries?" he said, sweeping his hand around the room at all the elders as if they should be offended that I had leveled such an insult against them.

"I'm saying that if we teach these missionaries the love of Christ, then they will be motivated by that love to serve God with a pure heart. Then, I believe, they will do their work because they love, not because they fear or want some plaque to brag about after they return home. So many young men are being pressed into service out of obedience to the Church and not out of a genuine love for God. Why aren't we teaching the new missionaries who come into the mission the reason why we do what we do? Don't you think they would work even harder, being motivated by God's love?"

I reached down and retrieved my missionary quad from my backpack and opened my Bible.

"President, I want to read a passage that has been heavy on my heart. I think this explains what I'm trying to say. 'Thus, when you give to the needy, sound no trumpet before you, as the hypocrites do in the synagogues and in the streets, that they may be praised by others. Truly, I say to you, they have received their reward...Do not lay up for yourselves treasures on earth, where moth and rust destroy and where thieves break in and steal, but lay up for yourselves treasures in heaven.'"[73]

I set the Scriptures down on the table in front me, ashamed to have to admit that I had once been guilty of what Jesus was condemning. "I don't want my motivation for missionary work to be public rewards from the Church. If it is, why am I even here?"

President shook his head in frustration while pacing back and forth. "So, all the missionaries who aren't as spiritual and Christlike as you should just go home! Is that what you're saying?" he exclaimed with glowering sarcasm. I was growing irritated by President's line of questions, and my ability to stay calm and not raise my voice was running thin.

"No!" I replied rather loudly. "But are we to wander around all day, aimlessly talking to people just because we are told to? Because if we reach a certain number, we will be rewarded, and we've done our duty to God? If we don't truly love them in our hearts, then what good are we doing? Christ Himself said that the world would know His disciples because they would have love, one to another. So, if we don't have true love, are we Christ's disciples?" My emotions were surfacing and I was on the verge of tears.

"Are you presuming to judge others, Elder Wilder?" President asked harshly. "Who are you to say who is a disciple?"

"President, I am nobody. I can only tell you this because of my personal experience. Because for a time I was motivated by fear, or rewards, and not love. In that time, I don't think I really helped anybody. But I am learning, day by day. I wish I knew at the beginning of my mission what I know now, and because of that, I want to instill that same love and faith in others. Now when I go out and talk to people, I do it because I want them to know the love of Christ. Even if it were just about me, President, I can only tell you that putting this standard on me makes it easy to do the right thing for the wrong reason. I don't want to do that. And I believe there are many other missionaries who feel the same way."

President glanced around the room as the missionaries suddenly shirked, looking to their left and right in a panicked wave. He then returned his gaze to me for a moment without responding—then unexpectedly returned to his seat and sat down.

The room was dead silent as everyone's attention was now turned to the last of the Knights of the Round Table, Elder Jensen. Tension filled the air, as nobody knew how he would react or what he was going to say. Even *I* had no idea. We had been companions for only a little over a week, and while I knew how he felt in his heart about this topic, I didn't know whether he had the guts to let the cat out of the bag.

Although I didn't want him to be disrespectful, I was hoping he would not be afraid to be honest, and that he, too, would begin testing our leaders against the Word of God. I waited anxiously as President turned to him snappishly.

"Elder Jensen, how do *you* feel about what Elder Wilder has said?" he asked, no doubt with the assumption that Jensen would fall in line and dispute me. (After all, that's why he had paired us together in the first place—Jensen was a secret weapon meant to disarm me.)

"Well, President," he began with hesitation, "I have to say that I agree with Elder Wilder." I don't think I believed what I heard. I don't think anybody did, including President. There was a hush over the whole room. Jensen looked at me with the slightest of a nervous smile, and I back at him.

"I feel that too many missionaries are fulfilling these expectations because they are obligated to by their leaders, not because of a genuine love. Rather than think, *I'm going to make a difference is someone's life*, they are thinking, *I'll make sure to get ten contacts because I have to.* Where is Christ in that? Is that how He would want His disciples to be? Love is the motivator for works, and I feel if we can help everyone understand that love and faith, then they will be better missionaries."

By the time Jensen finished, I was baring my teeth and brimming with pride. He had not sold out Christ; rather, he had stood strong with me in solidarity over Christ's message. President, however, was in a mild state of shock. Knowing that the meeting could not end on such a sour note, Sorensen fished for support.

"Does anyone else agree with Elder Wilder about the direction of this mission?" he asked daringly. President was now an auctioneer, but no one who had been watching the volley so far dared to flinch or they might accidently buy something that they were not willing to pay for. No one wanted to be associated with my now-condemned companion and me. A long and uncomfortable silence followed.

Elder Kimball, who had so callously called me in the middle of the storm seeking report numbers, finally spoke up.

"I think we need to have more faith in our Church leaders and the direction they give us. Let's support President and the standards of excellence, and God will bless us all for it."

There seemed to be a communal agreement throughout the room as the elders nodded in response to Kimball's statement. I, however, could not hide my disappointment, for many of these missionaries were at one time numbered among the love elder collective. My heart broke upon seeing them betray the very teachings of Jesus that I had worked so hard to share with them. But I still loved them, and knew that I, too, had denied God's Word so many times before, so who was I to judge?

As we left the meeting, I put my arm around Elder Jensen.

"Why did you say what you said?" I asked.

"Because it's all about love, *isn't it?*" he answered, smiling from ear to ear.

"Yes," I replied while grasping my cross through my shirt. "Yes, it is."

CHAPTER 26

BANISHED
TO PATMOS

Stuart, Florida | *October 31, 2005*

W ilder, it's for you," Elder Jensen said while handing me the phone. His fretful eyes and ever-so-subtle pout gave me cause for concern.

"Hello, this is Elder Wilder!" I stated with vigor, trying to hide the distress in my voice.

"Elder, how are you?" The familiar voice immediately put me on guard and sent my heart racing.

"I'm doing just fine, President Sorensen. How are you?" I looked at my companion with a scowl, irritated that he didn't clue me in as to the identity of the very important person on the other end of the line.

"Elder, I just told your companion what I am about to tell you. We have...well, we have a rather special assignment for you and Elder Jensen. Because you are both so experienced in the mission, this is a unique opportunity where your expertise will be needed."

I glanced over at Jensen again, my eyebrows scrunching as I gave him a *what's up?* gesture. He shrugged his shoulders and motioned for me to pay attention.

"Elder, we are opening two new mission areas over on the Gulf of Mexico. They used to be incorporated within the Jacksonville Mission, but with the recent change in stake boundaries, they are now part of the Orlando Mission. We want you to go and be a leader by opening one of these areas. Elder Jensen will be taking over the adjacent area. You will have to start from scratch, but we have great faith in you, Elder Wilder."

I was baffled—and skeptical. Why would President be taking Elder Jensen *and* me both away from this area? We were the zone leaders! Removing an entire companionship from a region was ironically referred to as a "whitewash," and the more the gears turned in my head, the more I suspected this dubious move was a coverup. Before I could fully decode the suspicious circumstances, President continued.

"Elder, we feel that due to the nature of the situation and with so much responsibility already being placed on your shoulders, both you and Elder Jensen will no longer be serving as zone leaders. Elder Wilder, you are relieved from duty."

Although President had spoken softly, he was indeed carrying a big stick. I didn't know what to say. A crushing dread encompassed me, and instantly I felt sick to my stomach. I didn't want to swallow the pill that President had just forced down my throat, and I found myself choking on it while gasping for air. My breaths became short and heavy as I shook my head and fought back tears. The sting of betrayal paralyzed me and I was at a loss for words. Eventually, I managed to force out an insincere response.

"Well, President, it sounds like an adventure!"

"You will need to arrange a ride and be there tomorrow afternoon. Good luck, Elder Wilder; I will talk to you soon to see how things are in the new area."

"Thanks, President. Talk to you later."

I hung up the phone and sat down with my head in my hands. Elder Jensen, in a display of brotherly compassion, sat next to me and placed his hand gently on my shoulder. "How could this be?" I asked rhetorically. I had been a zone leader nearly my entire mission. I had put so much of my heart into loving and serving my missionary colleagues, using the leadership position I had been granted to communicate the life-changing gospel I was learning from the Bible.

For well over a year, I had been riding the proverbial leadership bike, charging forward with the wind in my face while leading a throng of missionaries. In an attempt to sabotage me, President had stealthily thrust his stick into my spokes, sending me headfirst off my bike and skidding down the road on my face. In an instant I had lost all my influence over the missionaries. My reward was that I was left with nothing more than a mouthful of pavement. I was crushed.

Though President probably thought he was clever enough to disguise the "special assignment" as a reward, I could see through the facade. The expanding of these two geographical areas gave him his much-needed opportunity to quarantine the elders he presumed to be a plague to the mission, especially those in influential leadership positions like myself. It was apparent I had made the top of his blacklist, so he stripped me of my authority in an effort to eliminate my influence on other missionaries and kill the love movement. At last, President had severed what he perceived to be the head of the snake.

The following day, after packing my meager belongings (which could still could be stuffed into two suitcases), Erik gave Jensen and me a ride in his old green pickup truck. We headed to my place of banishment—Beverly Hills, Florida, a small retirement community located in the heart of Citrus Country, eighty miles northwest of Orlando bordering the Gulf of Mexico and forty-five minutes from the nearest missionaries. It was, without a doubt, the most remote area in the entire mission.

After a three-and-a-half-hour drive, we arrived at my new home. The low-rent house was nestled on a street with huge willow trees lining the median. The white house with red brick trim had a small driveway and a large yard on both sides. Around back was a beautiful citrus tree that was perfectly visible through the rear window. This, most likely, was going to be my home for the remaining three months of my mission.

I unloaded my effects from the truck and gave Erik a hug. "I love you, Kid," he said. "God still has a lot to do in your life. I know you are troubled, and I feel impressed to remind you of the parable of the wedding feast[74] in the Gospel of Luke. Don't seat yourself in the honored position, but rather in the lowest place, so that the host might come and place you in a higher seat. If you exalt yourself, you will be humbled. But if you humble yourself, you will be exalted. Be humble and patient, Micah. Seek God's glory, not man's."

The Lowest Place
Beverly Hills, Florida
January 12, 2006

My first eleven weeks in Beverly Hills had been a tumultuous time for me, filled with growing pains of the heart. My pride had taken a major blow, and God was using my time in isolation to humble me and turn my heart to focus on Christ and not the adulation of men. After spending the greater part of my mission on the top of the leadership totem pole—and having garnered the respect and adoration of my missionary peers—I had been cast down to the bottom of the missionary ranks, sitting indeed at the lowest place of the missionary table.

Though President never outright admitted the reasons behind my untimely relegation, most of the love elders who knew me personally could read between the lines. The circumstances surrounding my down-grading affected the morale of those who were—until now—well-seated in the love movement. Without their leader, many were completely disheartened. (Not to mention they were also afraid they would be singled out next.) Among the missionaries who didn't know me personally and had never taken part in the love crusade, ugly rumors started circulating that I had committed a grave sin. "Elder Wilder got demoted! Did you hear why?!"

Having been stripped of my authority and my reputation tarnished due to the false claims being stirred up by the number Nazis, I—like the apostle John—had been banished to my own personal Patmos,[75] far from the missionary epicenter and beyond the reaches of influence. In President's eyes, everything must have appeared to be under control. After all, how could I possibly inflict any further damage on the mission or infect others with the love epidemic?

Although it may have appeared on the surface that the love campaign had largely died out as a direct result of my expulsion, the theme that watered the seeds—read the Bible like a child—had already fallen on good soil in the hearts of a small band of brave surviving love elders. One of them, who had been exiled to the bordering area, was the sometimes-irreverent Elder Bingham. He had lived with me for nearly six months during the spiritual great awakening in Palm Bay, and we had developed a deep and sincere brotherly affection for one another. I was candid with him regarding the changes that were taking place in my life, and he was receptive to the message of the gospel.

Most significantly, God was continuing to work in the heart of my closest and truest missionary friend, Elder Warren, who was planting seeds of his own by zealously challenging others to read the Bible like a child. Although I hadn't seen him for almost three months, we had been corresponding through letters, which had greatly encouraged me to continue to be faithful to whatever God was requiring of me.

Once I had been humbled to the core by my fall from honor (and eventually came to the point of completely swallowing my pride), it became apparent to me that my mission had never been about me teaching the other missionaries. Rather, it had always been about God teaching me to trust Him alone. I started to understand that my banishment to Patmos, just like my separation from Erik, was a time of learning and preparation so that God could bring me to the place of honor by His grace, in His timing, and by His choosing—and not by my own doing. And here, in this isolated area on the Gulf Coast of Florida, I was learning to be content with whatever conditions the world handed to me and place all my hope in the eternal riches granted through my adoption into Christ's family.

My time of seclusion had the unexpected side effect of allowing me to devotedly pore over the Bible every day, unhindered. Although I was reading the New Testament for the twelfth time spanning eighteen months, I still found myself enamored by God's Word. I craved it. However, I also found myself facing a growing mystery, struggling to formulate a clear picture of exactly what I had ascertained throughout my mission experience—or the repercussions of what it all meant.

Sitting at the edge of my bed while enjoying a few precious moments of privacy while Elder Lucas was performing his long daily rituals in the bathroom, I was determined to solve the conundrum that had beleaguered me for so long. What did this all mean?

I tore a blank sheet of paper out of my notebook and began to draft a doctrinal manifesto, point by point, praying that God would help me see a full picture of what He had been trying to teach me.

- God Himself is love (1 John 4:9-10,16).

- The greatest commandments are to love God and love your neighbor (Matthew 22:37; Luke 10:27; Galatians 5:14).

- Eternal life is freely given to all who believe (John 3:16,18,36; 5:24; 6:35,40,47,51; Acts 10:34; 16:31; Romans 3:22-26; 4:5; 6:23; 10:9-13; Ephesians 2:8-9).

- The righteous are justified by faith and not by works of the law (Romans 5:1; Galatians 2:16; 3:6-11,24; Philippians 3:9; Titus 3:7).

- The true church is the body of Christ, and all who have taken upon themselves the name of Jesus Christ by faith are members of it (1 Corinthians 12:12-27; Romans 12:4-5; Ephesians 2:19-22; 4:11-16; 5:29-30; Colossians 3:15).

- Nothing in this world or beyond can separate us from the love of God in Christ Jesus (John 10:28-30; Romans 8:38-39; Ephesians 1:13-14).

- Jesus is the way, the truth, and the life, and nobody can get to heaven without Him (John 14:6; Acts 4:11-12).

- The very will and work of God is to believe in Jesus Christ (John 6:29,40).

- Jesus is the bread of life, offers living water, and He is the most valuable treasure that we can ever have (Matthew 13:44; Luke 12:33; John 4:10; 6:35; 7:38-39).

- It's all about love (John 3:16; 1 Corinthians 13:8-13; Romans 13:8-10; 1 John 3:16).

I sat in silence, gazing at the list and scanning each point repeatedly while attempting to make sense of its deeper meaning. I flashed back to what Pastor Benson had challenged me to do a year and a half ago: "Read the Bible *like a child.*" Examining this list through the eyes of a child and removing my religious lenses, it all seemed so simple. So clear. So beautiful. Could having the guarantee of my good standing with God be as simple as professing true faith in Jesus? Could placing all my trust in Jesus alone bring me salvation? Could I have eternal life independent of the Church?

Something didn't make sense, though. I was desperately trying to reconcile what I had been taught in the Bible with what I had learned throughout my religious life, but there was a glaring disconnect. It almost seemed like the gospel I was reading in the New Testament was *different* than the gospel of the Church.

I shook my head while setting the paper down on the bed next to me and pounded the mattress with my fist, letting out a frustrated grunt. I *had* to be missing something. I didn't understand yet how the pieces fit together.

"God, give me the answers!" I shouted. I suspected that God was hiding something from me, deliberately holding His hand over my eyes to keep me back from a great revelation that would reveal a masterful portrait. I could sense I was at the conclusion of a long and tiring race but had not quite crossed the finish line, and I was striving, with all that I had, to make it to the end. I felt like I was so close to the truth…so close to finally having the gaping hole in my heart filled once and for all. The admonishment "Read the Bible like a child" kept going through my mind.

Show Me

I did the only thing I could do—which I had done time and again. I opened the Word of God in search of answers.

"God, please show me the fullness of Your truth. Don't hold back. God, I'm ready!" I cried out as I opened my Bible to the passage where I had left off the night before, Hebrews 7. The delicate pages were torn and tattered and I began to read with hope in my heart.

> This makes Jesus the guarantor of a better covenant…but he holds his priesthood permanently, because he continues forever. Consequently, he is able to save to the uttermost those who draw near to God through him, since he always lives to make intercession for them…He has no need, like those high priests, to offer sacrifices daily, first for his own sins and then for those of the people, since he did this once for all when he offered up himself. For the law appoints men in their

weakness as high priests, but the word of the oath, which came later than the law, appoints a Son who has been made perfect forever.[76]

After I concluded chapter 7, I was intrigued. Something was stirring in my mind. I pressed on to chapter 8.

As it is, Christ has obtained a ministry that is as much more excellent than the old as the covenant he mediates is better, since it is enacted on better promises...In speaking of a new covenant, he makes the first one obsolete. And what is becoming obsolete and growing old is ready to vanish away.[77]

Not yet satisfied and enthralled beyond measure, I continued reading in chapter 9.

According to this arrangement, gifts and sacrifices are offered that cannot perfect the conscience of the worshiper...how much more will the blood of Christ, who through the eternal Spirit offered himself without blemish to God, purify our conscience from dead works to serve the living God.

...For Christ has entered, not into holy places made with hands, which are copies of the true things, but into heaven itself, now to appear in the presence of God on our behalf... But as it is, he has appeared once for all at the end of the ages to put away sin by the sacrifice of himself.[78]

And finally, chapter 10.

Since the law has but a shadow of the good things to come instead of the true form of these realities, it can never, by the same sacrifices that are continually offered every year, make perfect those who draw near...He does away with the first in order to establish the second. And by that will we have been sanctified through the offering of the body of Jesus Christ once for all...For by a single offering he has perfected for all time those who are being sanctified...

Therefore, brothers, since we have confidence to enter the holy places by the blood of Jesus, by the new and living way that he opened for us through the curtain, that is, through his flesh, and since we have a great priest over the house of God, let us draw near with a true heart in full assurance of faith, with our hearts sprinkled clean from an evil conscience and our bodies washed with pure water.[79]

I set my Bible down on my nightstand and flopped down on my bed, closing my eyes. A cold sweat began to form on my forehead as I strained to fully comprehend what I had just read, even though I knew quite well that there was no explaining it away. I had studied these passages before—multiple times, in fact—but for some reason, this time something clicked within my heart. I was stunned.

In trying to decipher what God had laid out before me, I ripped out another page from my notebook and began to write a list of what had been newly revealed to me through God's Word:

- Jesus is the only one who holds the Melchizedek priesthood (Psalm 110:4; Hebrews 7:2-3,8,24).

- Jesus is the only high priest and mediator between God and man (1 Timothy 2:5; Hebrews 2:17; 4:14; 7:25-27; 8:1-2).

- Every element of the law was a type and shadow of the reality—Jesus is the reality (Hebrews 8:5,13; 9:23-24; 10:1).

- Only the blood of Jesus Christ can cleanse us from sin, and we can be forgiven directly through Christ, without an earthly man as our mediator (Matthew 11:28; 26:28; John 14:6; Romans 4:5-7; Ephesians 1:7; Colossians 1:20; 1 Timothy 2:5; Hebrews 4:14-16; 9:14-15,22; 13:12; 1 John 1:7; Revelation 7:14).

- The law and all its ceremonial rituals were fulfilled in and by Christ (Matthew 5:17-18; Romans 10:4; Galatians 3:23-25; Hebrews 9:11-16; 10:10-14).

- The role of the high priest was to offer sacrifices on behalf of the people. Jesus made the ultimate and final sacrifice of Himself (Colossians 2:14; Hebrews 9:24-26; 1 Peter 2:24).

- The earthly temple was a place to perform the ordinances of the law. Once Jesus offered Himself, He became the temple (Matthew 12:6; John 2:21; Colossians 1:19; 2:9; Hebrews 10:19-20).

- The institution of the new covenant nullified the old covenant (Romans 7:1-6; 8:2-4; 13:8-10; Galatians 3:10-14; Hebrews 8:6-7,13; 10:10).

- The blood of Jesus, shed on the cross, is sufficient to cleanse mankind from sin and perfect us (Isaiah 53:5; Romans 3:23-25; 5:9; Ephesians 1:7; 2:12-13; Hebrews 9:14,22,28; 10:14; 1 Peter 1:18-19; 2:24; 1 John 1:7; 2:1-2; Revelation 1:5; 12:11).

I sat dumbfounded as I stared at the list, my unstable hands trying to hold still as my eyes began to fill with tears. Among the hundreds of passages of Scripture I had read over the past year and a half, these were the most devastating. But how could I be upset? I had entreated God to open my eyes, and He didn't hold back on fulfilling His end of the bargain. I had received my own revelation on Patmos.

All You Need

This is what I could see for the first time in my life with astounding and undeniable clarity: The express purpose of each component of the law—priesthood, priests, high priests, offerings, temples, prophets—was to point to Jesus, the good thing to come. Each element was a physical representation, a shadow of sorts, of the true spiritual reality that was revealed in Christ 2,000 years ago.

Miraculously, Jesus was both the high priest and the offering, humbly submitting His own life as a ransom for the sins of the world. Through His perfect and finished work of atonement, Jesus fulfilled the law on our behalf by nailing our debts to the cross. In doing so, He instituted a new and better covenant—forgiveness through faith in His name. No longer would mankind be bound by the old system of works-based righteousness, but reconciled to God through the ultimate and final sacrifice of His Son. The age of human mediators ended with Christ's death, and Jesus alone is now our only advocate with the Father. Therefore, I didn't need this Church's priesthood, high priests, temples, or prophets. God's Word was shouting from its pages: Jesus is all you need! He is sufficient!

This epiphany had me both excited and terrified. Benson's pointed words from long ago had come back to pummel me in the face: "You boldly testify of the restoration of Joseph Smith, yet it seems as though Joseph Smith 'restored' everything that Jesus Christ fulfilled." I collapsed from the weight of this revelation and fell to the floor, my eyes spilling tears. I wanted to deny it all, but I knew that I could not outrun forever what had been chasing me for two years.

The very foundation of the Church—the priesthood and its works—had been eternally fulfilled by the Son of God. The Melchizedek priesthood that I claimed to hold was invalid, and the hardest pill to swallow was that I was blaspheming God by professing to have that which I now knew only Christ could possess. God had explicitly answered my petition, mercifully opening my eyes to see that the very organization that held the name of Jesus Christ, claiming to be His one true Church and kingdom on the earth, was in fact built on the unstable foundation of man-made sand. With that spiritual awakening, the whole Church and four of its pillars came crashing down, washed away by the living waters, and I painstakingly accepted that the Church to which I had given my life to was not what it claimed to be.

"God, if this is true, help me to have the faith to follow Your way. Father, I'm scared, but I am ready."

With my hands trembling, I picked up the phone and called the only person with whom I could confide this startling doctrinal revelation.

"Hey Kid, what's up?"

"Erik, I don't think the Church is true. I don't know what to do. Help me!"

CHAPTER 27

IT'S ALL
ABOUT LOVE

Beverly Hills, Florida | *January 15, 2006*

L ast night, I was in bed looking up to heaven. I closed my eyes and
reached up to God with all my might, desiring nothing but to worship Him. To serve Him. To be close to Him. So badly, Erik..." I paused
with the receiver held tight to my ear while struggling to suppress my emotions. "I would have given anything at that moment to love God with all
my heart, and to be certain that He loves me and forgives me for everything I have done. But most times, lately, God feels so distant and out of
reach. Sometimes, I want to give up because it seems hopeless."

"Micah, I love you," Erik said, "but you can't see the forest through the
trees. The truth is right in front of your eyes. But every day, you pass up
opportunities to both love and worship God. You're missing the whole
picture, Kid!"

"What do you mean, Erik? You obviously don't understand what I am
trying to say!" I struck back. "My greatest desire, more than *anything*, is to
be with Christ and worship Him. I want nothing more than to sit at His
feet and serve Him forever. That's all. I'm trying as hard as I can! Is that so
wrong?" I hollered.

Although I couldn't see Erik, I could imagine him shaking his head at
my obstinate pride.

"Of course not, but you're still learning, Micah. It's so simple," he said gently, perhaps to soften the blows that were hitting their mark on my prideful heart. "But you don't show your love for Jesus by reaching your hands up toward heaven, but by reaching your heart out toward others in love. What does the scripture say? 'For I was hungry and you gave me food, I was thirsty and you gave me drink, I was a stranger and you welcomed me...as you did it to one of the least of these my brothers, you did it to me.'[80] You still don't quite understand *true* love."

His declaration cut me to the core, and I knew he was right. I couldn't restrain my increasing vexation. "Erik, how then can I learn this 'true' love?" I blurted.

"Micah, to even have the capacity to truly love others, you must first come to know of God's love for you, which is Christ—to come to know God's purpose for Christ, and Christ's purpose for us. You need to surrender your flesh to the Spirit. You need to submit your heart and become a living sacrifice to God. Give yourself up and turn to Jesus! Only then can God's love truly work in and through you."

Erik's words haunted me. I had countless questions building up inside of me, but before I could vocalize any of them, he continued.

"I know the seeds have been planted in you, but God needs to make them grow. You need to work out your own salvation in fear and trembling, becoming properly trained for the race God is calling you to run. This is a race you will have to run on your own; no one can fulfill it for you.

"Right now, the final wisdom I can give to you is to trust in God's incredible love for you. Trust that Jesus died for your sins. Trust that He will forgive you if you ask Him. Doubt anything or anyone that does not confirm that simple truth. Return to the heart you once had as a child... be just like David and find confidence in God's great mercy toward you. And once you find the love you are seeking, learn to impute that love onto others."

My God, My God

Only days had passed since God's Word had confronted me in a way my mind could no longer reason away, and the religious shelf that I never knew existed was so stressed that it was reaching its breaking point. From the inception of my journey, the simple challenge to read the Bible like a child had indeed struck its mark, forever altering my trajectory—although for some time I had tried to justify the disparities. Even so, despite my ignorance, the Word had still activated within me as it slowly opened my eyes, even while I was not yet putting everything into practice.

Soon after that process had begun came the first inkling that what I was learning really did contradict what I had been taught all my life. That notion had now grown into an enormous certainty. The weight of carrying these incompatible dogmas—which was now growing exponentially—was becoming more than I could bear, and in trying to serve two masters, I was not only incredibly confused, I was conflicted beyond measure. Most recently, the revelation through Hebrews had recalibrated my internal discord and left me dreadfully uncertain as to my future.

Late hours now into my fourth sleepless night in a row, I tossed and turned while Elder Lucas was sawing logs. Not only was I facing the distressing reality that my faith to the organization that I had dedicated my life to had been fully compromised, but I was also confronting the despicableness of my sin, which was winding me up in a web, binding me to the stake, and deriding me day after day. The enemy was both cruel and relentless in taunting me, reminding me of all my countless past and present transgressions that were now simply fuel for the fires of hell. The turmoil raging about me had become insufferable and was reaching a breaking point. While a lifetime of sins repeatedly convicted me in my mind, I was finding it hard to believe—no matter how vigorously I attempted to push the bad thoughts away—that God could ever forgive and love someone like me.

Adding fuel to the fire was my phone conversation with Erik. I had reached out to him for comfort, but our exchange only served to escalate my frustration and hopelessness. Perhaps I was a lost cause. No matter what I did, it didn't seem to be enough. I couldn't comprehend what it meant to truly *know* God's love. Even after reading the New Testament twelve times, enduring four hurricanes, encountering two Christian ministers, and conversing with a sometimes wise, sometimes mysterious but always devoted friend, I still had not stumbled upon the missing piece for which I had been searching. My guilty conscience was insatiable. I was working *out* my salvation—no longer *for* my salvation—but I hadn't arrived at my ultimate destination: lasting forgiveness. After all, how could God love a wretch like me? I was already consumed with studying and reading His Word. What more could I do?

In a last-ditch effort to ease the torment inside of me, I fumbled in the darkness for my Bible on the nightstand. With the help of a small reading light, I opened its pages to Romans chapter 7. I had come to identity with Paul's lament of the flesh as my own weakness was bearing down upon me with each passing day.

> I know that nothing good dwells in me, that is, in my flesh. For I have the desire to do what is right, but not the ability to carry it out. For I do not do the good I want, but the evil I do not want is what I keep on doing…Wretched man that I am! Who will deliver me from this body of death?[81]

Reading Paul's forthright confession finally hit the nail on the head and convicted me. I suddenly became cognizant that for most of my religious life, at the very time I was endeavoring to draw near to God, I had unknowingly blasphemed Christ and opposed Him, just as Saul of Tarsus had 2,000 years ago as he naively went about fighting against the very God he claimed to serve. Not only had I been mirroring Saul's ignorance with exactness (just as Pastor Shaw had tried to point out), but the damage my ignorance had inflicted—in a sense—was even more severe.

After beginning to read the Bible and finally putting what I was learning into action, I had unintentionally blurred the lines between two incompatible worlds by attempting to mix the law and grace, thereby placing new wine in old wineskins.[82] For months now, my heart had been proclaiming the biblical Christ, professing the biblical Christ, and believing wholeheartedly in the biblical Christ, all the while masked in a clean-cut outer skin, the camouflage of an organization I now knew avowed an *extra*biblical Christ. I truly was a wolf in sheep's clothing, and—as Pastor Benson insinuated—an enemy of the cross! I knew what I deserved: death and hell.

"My God!" I cried out in fear. Nausea crept into the pit of my stomach and a wave of emotion rose from my toes through my neck, where it began to set my ears ablaze. I was scared to death! I recognized that in trying to right myself with God, I had instead further condemned myself by even more effectively polluting the message of Christ. As I realized what I had done, I became mortified, and the fear of God grew within me into a second even more conquering wave from head to toe.

"God, please, can You ever forgive me? Is there even something worth saving in me?" I said as I mourned in the darkness. "How could You ever love such a pitiful and flawed creature like me? Is that why You won't answer me—because of what I have done to You? I'm so sorry! Do not abandon me!" I called out to God with all my might, lamenting with grief.

Crippled with despair, I recalled what Jesus had declared on the cross just before He gave up His spirit. Quoting the psalmist, He said, "My God, my God, why have you forsaken me?"[83] For an infinitesimal speck of time, I felt like I understood what Christ must have undergone as He begged for His Father's comfort in His paramount trial. This recollection further drove me into a downward spiral. After all, if God had abandoned Christ on the cross—who was perfect—surely He had forsaken me, too, a derisible and sinful wretch.

Seeking comfort in my affliction, I lifted my Bible as I recalled a passage from memory that had wedged itself in the crevices of my heart:

> Formerly I was a blasphemer, persecutor, and insolent opponent. But I received mercy because I had acted ignorantly in unbelief, and the grace of our Lord overflowed for me with the faith and love that are in Christ Jesus. The saying is trustworthy and deserving of full acceptance, that Christ Jesus came into the world to save sinners...[84]

Tears streamed down the sides of my face as I blurted out the rest of the passage: "of whom I am the foremost"! I closed my eyes. My frustration had finally boiled over, and I had reached the end of my fraying religious rope. In pure, unbearable exasperation, I called out the pinnacle of all expletives into the empty air and broke down into tears, weeping into my pillow so as not to wake my companion.

I Would Die for You

For the next few minutes, I wafted in and out of sleep. As I lay there feeling despondent, I began to hear a voice, at first a mere whisper, subtly sounding as if someone was having a conversation outside. It grew in volume and evolved to speaking in a calm, steady, and deliberate manner as it continued toward me. When it reached me, it encompassed me from all directions, enveloping me.

"Don't you think that I can see you struggling and that I can feel your pain? I know every time you've reached up to Me. I've heard your cries every time you called upon My name in the middle of the night. My child, whose face do you think I was looking into when I was hanging on the cross? With all the beatings, whose life do you think was passing before My eyes as I paid your cost, telling you, 'I love you and I would die for you so that you can live'?"

As I listened, I sensed a peace that was far beyond any definition offered by the human tongue. Strangely, I had heard the voice speaking, yet not from anyone or like anything I ever heard before. Even though it filled my head and overpowered all other thoughts, I was convinced it did not quake a single air molecule in the room. Rather than entering into my ears, it imprinted itself on me as an effervescence of love all around me that was beyond comprehension, smothering me with a thick and elastic tenderness that transcended any possibility of human origin.

I was so shocked that I held my breath lest I create a ripple that might pop whatever bubble my mind had fallen into. More than anything, I did not want whatever was happening to me—the intense and overwhelming feeling of relief as love overcame me and poured itself into my heart—to come to an end.

As I lay there contemplating the vastness of the love that had been so extraordinarily conveyed to me, the magnitude of Christ's atonement exploded in my heart like a supernova, radiating far beyond my mortal vessel and bringing with it the desire to fall to my knees. The Holy Spirit then began painting a picture of perfect love before me, in mere seconds, that I had waited a lifetime to understand.

Jesus of Nazareth, the Son of God, after having been betrayed and falsely condemned, was dragged into the streets of Jerusalem, where He was brutally beaten, fiercely scourged, spat upon, and publicly scorned. The blameless and spotless Lamb of God cried in agony as a vicious crown of thorns was thrust onto His head and the Roman soldiers mocked Him, saying, "Behold, the King of the Jews!" And yet Jesus was the King of all kings and now sits triumphantly at the right hand of God. Through Him the vast universe and all its glory was created, and yet He was led to Calvary, where He was crucified on a tree formed by His own hands, nailed to it by the very people He came to redeem.

And there, on Golgotha's rocky hill, the very Word of God made flesh endured with incomparable humility the most excruciating and harrowing death the world has ever seen. God's immeasurable love for all mankind was on full, heartbreaking display as Jesus bore in His stricken body the sins, iniquities, and infirmities of the world. Bleeding the precious blood of eternal atonement on the cross, the Messiah paid—in full measure—the debt that we owed God because of our transgressions. But this priceless offering wasn't just a collective sacrifice. It was personal. It was intimate. It was for *me*.

The Savior of the world drank the cup of wrath that *I* deserved and freely poured out His soul to death *for me*. As my kingly substitute, He willingly took my place on the cross of Calvary and died on my behalf— a guilty sinner—all the while looking into my eyes and proclaiming His ineffable love for me. Jesus endured a transcendent passion that was driven by an infinite and intimate love that surpasses all knowledge and understanding. He suffered and died because He loved, and for the joy that was set before Him, Christ endured the cross—my salvation was that joy. How could anyone love me so much?!

God Is Love

Not since the innocence of my youth had I considered that God knew and loved me so personally and intimately, but this expression of love was infinitely greater than anything I had ever imagined. Although I was already familiar with the concepts in the Bible that outlined *a* love of Jesus (I had been witnessing of the only version of His love I knew), it was only in this metamorphic flash of grace that it was impressed on me with such an unparalleled intensity just how deep and wide and magnificent that love really was—a love that drove Christ to endure the unthinkable, and while suffering unspeakable pain, see my very face. This wasn't a romantic, familial, or brotherly love. This was a profound love that encompassed the very essence and nature of God Himself. This was the sacrificial *agape* love I had long been waiting for—the only love that could eternally satisfy. Truly, there is no greater expression of love!

Why had I not seen this before? The mud in my eyes was being washed away, the message of grace was permeating my blindness, and it was all becoming so vividly clear: Christ Himself was God's ultimate manifestation of love in the flesh, the indisputable evidence of His deep desire to reconcile mankind to Himself. Therefore, the only way to know God's love was through His Son Jesus.

With this understanding, the Holy Spirit perforated my doubt with irrefutable proof that God had *not* forsaken me in my hour of need as I had foolishly believed. He did love me—more than I could comprehend. And I had been engraved in the very palms of Jesus Himself as an eternal reminder of that everlasting love.

And as I contemplated Jesus' puzzling pronouncement "My God, my God," I wondered—with my new insight regarding God's wondrous love for mankind—if perhaps Jesus *wasn't* declaring His abandonment, as I had long been taught. Rather, it appeared that Jesus' statement was actually a direct response to the mocking of the chief priests as they sarcastically quoted Psalm 22: "He trusts in the LORD; let him deliver him."[85] Jesus, too, was quoting the messianic psalm, but maybe not to concur with His detractors; He was answering David's plea by proclaiming His messiahship! He was identifying Himself as the evidence that God had *not* forsaken His people. Later in the psalm we are told that "he has not hidden his face from him, but has heard, when he cried to him."[86] God did not forsake Christ, and God has not forsaken us—Jesus Himself on the cross attested to God's grand love for all mankind.

Humbled by the immensity of God's boundless grace toward me, I once again immersed myself in the Word of God:

> God is love, and whoever abides in love abides in God, and God abides in him…There is no fear in love, but perfect love casts out fear. For fear has to do with punishment, and whoever fears has not been perfected in love. We love because he first loved us (1 John 4:16,18-19).

Drowning in a sea of living waters, I suddenly became aware that my love for God should not be an endeavor to earn His grace and approval, nor should it result from a fear of punishment and hell. If fear was my motivation, then my impetus exposed a lesser, conditional love—a non-agape love. Rather, an authentic relationship with God is not rooted in fear, but in an unconditional trust in His perfect love in Christ! Therefore, our love for God is to be a natural response to the great love with which He first loved us—a reciprocation of an unworthy orphan loving their father because they know the depth of the father's love and forgiveness. After all, God *Himself* is love!

This sudden comprehension of God's incalculable love washed away my fear with a flood of confidence. I didn't need to fear His wrath. To His praise, the enormous sin debt I had accrued didn't have to be mine any-more—if I trusted in Christ's finished work on my behalf. I could now have the guarantee of my right standing with God. I could be called His child by adoption! And because of this love, I could have an eternal rest in Him that neither my religion nor the world could offer. The remedy to my perpetual dissatisfaction was so simple: Jesus!

The gaping hole that had plagued my life for so long was, in an instant, filled to the brim and was now magnified and overflowing with a desire to share this agape love of God with others and bring them also to the Lord's table to partake of His goodness and grace. Jesus alone had been the answer all along!

One of my favorite verses permeated my heart:

> Come to me, all who labor and are heavy laden, and I will give you rest. Take my yoke upon you, and learn from me, for I am gentle and lowly in heart, and you will find rest for your souls. For my yoke is easy, and my burden is light (Matthew 11:28-30).

With God's beautiful canvas laid out before me, I could see a master-piece so intricate and yet so simple a child could have painted it: God's love for us is Christ; Christ's love for us is the cross; our love for God is loving others; and loving others is to point them to God's love in Christ. Thus Shaw, Benson, and Erik were right from the beginning: It's all about *love*.

As tears of gratitude and joy saturated my pillow, the words spoken during a charismatic preacher's prayer slowly surfaced in my mind: "God, give him a great revelation as You did Your servant Paul." Pastor Shaw's prayer had been answered.

Overwhelmed by mental as well as physical exhaustion, I relaxed... and fell soundly asleep for the first time in days.

Reborn

When I awoke the next morning, I knew that my life had changed forever. And even though I was certain that the Spirit of God had reached out to me the previous night, I doubted how it had all transpired. Was it a vision? A dream? I didn't know with certitude because I was no longer convinced I was even awake during the incident. But it didn't matter. God's message had been delivered, and I was amazed at how it had so thoroughly altered my understanding of Him and His love. In one providential evening, everything I had read and learned over the past two years had come together in a whirlwind of spiritual clarification, and now I was left to absorb the aftermath.

What I now knew—and maybe what I had once glimpsed as a child—was that eternal life was not about a religion or a church, or a particular priesthood, or a modern-day prophet, or temples and saving ordinances; it also wasn't about my goodness, righteousness, works, or efforts. Rather—to God's glory—it was all so much simpler and purer. It was about a personal relationship with God by adoption through faith in His Son Jesus Christ. Amazingly, this was the prescription Benson had so fervently laid out before me as I stormed out of his office: approach God as a child, and through His Word, I would come to know His love. With that invitation long ago, a candle of the Lord had begun to smolder.

I recognized that for many years I had indeed been foolishly reaching up and pushing past Jesus, blinded to the fact that all I had to do was reach out like I once had as an innocent child on the banks of the White River (but this time, with a mature understanding of His love), approaching God as a son would a father, and trust in His unconditional mercy and forgiveness, just as David had done. And now that I could truly trust in God's love—no longer having to fear whether I had done enough to appease Him—I was called to love and worship God in a manner that would glorify Him. But how?

I recollected Jesus' encounter with the Samaritan woman in John chapter 4, and His exhortation to her that the true worshippers would worship the Father in spirit and in truth. But what did that mean? What was truth? Jesus said during His high priestly prayer, "Sanctify them in the truth; your word is truth."[87] Jesus also proclaimed to Thomas, "I am the way, and the truth, and the life."[88] This was all opening up to me and becoming so clear. The only offering I could make that would be pleasing to God, according to Paul in Romans 12, was to present my own body as a living sacrifice[89] by surrendering my worldly desires while spreading God's Word. My act of worship was not in going to a temple or any earthly building, or in the raising of my hands in the air. True spiritual worship is found in reaching out to others in love, fulfilling the will and work of God by sharing the gospel of Christ and bringing people to the salvation found in Jesus alone. Worship, then, is not about reaching up, but reaching out! Erik was right.

It all came together for me in such a rush and I did the only thing I could think to do. For the first time on my mission, I broke the rules and reached out to my mother by phone. I had to reveal to her what I had come to know: I was a hopeless sinner, it was my fault Jesus had died, and even if the Church poured the water from the entire Great Salt Lake upon me, they could not cleanse of my filthiness—only the blood of Jesus could wash away my sin. She didn't answer, so I left her an urgent message: "I just need my mom." To the woman who had given birth to me, who had compassion on me as the son of her womb, I had distilled the most significant moment of my life down into five simple words.

Uncertain of what to do or where to go, I parked myself at my desk and searched God's Word. By divine intervention, I found myself reading Isaiah chapter 55.

> Come, everyone who thirsts,
>   come to the waters;
> and he who has no money,
>   come, buy and eat!...

> Incline your ear, and come to me;
>   hear, that your soul may live;
> and I will make with you an everlasting covenant,
>   my steadfast, sure love for David.[90]

I now had the blessed assurance that everything I had yearned for in my life—forgiveness, grace, love, favor, purpose—I could have directly through Jesus Christ. I didn't have to wonder or fear if I was good enough for God. His love was enough for me. All I had to do, then, was put all my faith and hope in Christ alone, trusting that the same everlasting mercy that God showed His beloved yet fleshly servant David is the same forgiveness He has promised to me—and to all who trust in Christ. In that way, all mankind is akin to David of old—wretched sinners dependent on God's grace to cover our iniquity. Now I finally knew what it meant to be David: a picture of God's amazing love.

It was then that the final scales of blindness fell from my eyes as I realized the spirituality of the whole situation from the beginning of my journey to now. I felt compelled to accept the cleansing blood of Christ—to take the plunge into the spiritual baptism of God.

I ran into my bedroom, and better late than never, cried out to heaven, "God, I am broken, and I am a hopeless sinner. I have blasphemed You. I'm not worthy of Your love." I then laid down and planted myself flat on the floor with my arms stretched in the shape of the cross as I yielded myself in complete surrender.

"Please forgive me, just like You did Your servant Paul. I believe in You. I trust in Your mercy. I confess that Jesus is my only hope, and I put *all* my faith in Him alone. Rescue me!"

Following that moment, the candle was fully lit and I was a new creation, yet another light to the world. In a matter of minutes, I rose from the floor with a clean conscience for the first time in my life. I had been reborn!

PART 4

SET FREE

CHAPTER 28

PASSPORT
TO HEAVEN

Well, if ever there was an opportunity for turning back, the occasion had passed. Being forced to answer President's direct questions one by one had nudged me beyond the point of no return. Much like my journey over the past two years, I had been taking one small step at a time without realizing how far I'd come until I looked back at where I began, and by that time it was too late. God's work in my life was irrevocable.

President looked straight into my eyes with astonishment. The grilling had gone on for what seemed like hours now, and suddenly it came to a halt as if he was trying desperately to devise his next move. During the break in the interrogation, the passage delivered to me this morning in the Gospel of Luke came to mind.

"I'd like to read you something," I said.

"Certainly, Elder Wilder."

As I turned the pages in my missionary quad, President retrieved his Scriptures. "Where are you, Elder?" he asked.

"Luke 21."

He found his place as I began to read out loud. "They will lay their hands on you and persecute you, delivering you up to the synagogues and prisons, and you will be brought before kings and governors for my name's sake. This will be your opportunity to bear witness. Settle it therefore in your mind not to meditate beforehand how to answer, for I will give you a mouth and wisdom, which none of your adversaries will be able to withstand or contradict."[91]

After I concluded, President peered up at me, squinted his eyes, and nodded while tensing his lips. I couldn't interpret this peculiar expression, so I tried to ignore it as I kept talking.

"God led me to this scripture after you called me this morning. President, I knew this was going to happen," I said. "I am at peace. Do what you must."

The Faith Inquiry

President locked eyes on mine and refused to release me from his gaze. He then glanced down into his briefcase, subtly shook his head, then reached in and snatched a black notebook. As he cracked it open, he turned his attention back to me.

"Elder Wilder," he said slowly, "I'm going to ask you some questions." He paused to find his place in the notebook, using his finger as a guide until he found what he was looking for.

"You realize that as a missionary for the Church there are certain standards you must uphold, and certain beliefs you must profess to maintain this sacred and special calling." He hesitated for effect, perhaps giving me time to assess the bleakness of my situation and come to my senses. "If you cannot answer these basic doctrinal questions, it will certainly be difficult—well, *impossible*—for you to continue on as a missionary."

I involuntarily frowned and nodded knowingly. This was the moment I had been anticipating.

"I understand," I relented, my heart pounding harder and harder. Waiting for him to execute me was like being blindfolded and tied to a log as it is headed for the saw. As I contemplated my fate, distress and doubt consumed me and I feared for my life. The confidence that had pervaded me just moments ago had all but vanished.

President, still looking down at his notebook, began reading aloud the first question.

(1) "Do you sustain Gordon B. Hinckley as the Prophet and the only

one authorized by God to receive revelation for the kingdom of God on Earth?"

I could do nothing but stare at President and blink as I was frozen in fear. How was I going to answer a very complex question that—I rationalized—could not be resolved by a simple yes or no? I quickly considered my options for how I could respond without sentencing myself to death. And then, it hit me: If I could satisfy his query by giving a somewhat ambiguous reply, I might placate him without condemning myself in the process.

After careful thought, I spilled out my obfuscated answer.

"Well, I believe that he is the leader and head of *this* Church...and could very well receive revelation for its members," I said as I took a gulp of air.

President gazed at me with an uncomfortable grimace. "That's *not* what I'm asking, Elder Wilder," he retorted. He was nothing if not a wise old bird. He knew what I was attempting to do, and he was not going to fall for it as easily as I had hoped. He turned up the heat and grilled me.

"Do you believe that he is *the* Prophet of God and the *only* one with the keys to the kingdom of God on Earth?"

In my cowardice, I opted to ignore the first part of the question and respond to the second part, attempting to avoid a direct answer and prolong my survival.

"I believe he holds the keys for this Church, yes. But I believe there are many who can communicate with God and work for His kingdom."

President, growing more frustrated by my attempts to circumvent his question, became angry. "Elder Wilder!" he said fiercely. "*Yes* or *no!*"

As I sat in silence contemplating what I had just attempted to do, guilt and shame shrouded me. I was seeking to save myself by trying to avoid condemnation. As much as I professed with my mouth my devotion to the Lord Jesus, I—like Peter—had succumbed to the weakness of my flesh in my moment of trial and denied the Christ who had purchased me with His blood. Embarrassed of myself, I began to cry.

Sitting in disgrace, I quietly begged for God's forgiveness and pleaded with Him to supply me with the strength necessary to be His witness no matter the cost. My cross was indeed heavy to bear. But I knew that after everything I had said, and everything I had endured, and everything the

Word of God had taught me, there was no way I could turn back now. I pondered David's comforting words in Psalm 23:

> Even though I walk through the valley of the shadow of death,
>> I will fear no evil,
> for you are with me;
>> your rod and your staff,
>> they comfort me.[92]

By God's grace and strength, I was now resolute not to bargain on the truth to save myself. In the end, what would it profit me to gain the world but lose my soul? Determined to take up my cross and not deny Christ again, I realized there was no point in dragging this on any further. I finally divulged my concession and sealed my fate.

"No, President, I don't believe he is a prophet of God. Jesus is my prophet and He alone stands between me and Heavenly Father," I said softly. "As the scripture says, 'There is one God and one mediator between God and men, the man Christ Jesus.'"[93]

Even though my answer was given in a calm and resolved voice, President reacted like I had screamed at him while delivering a swift kick between his legs. His face turned beet red and his lips quivered, but he held fast to his controlled posture and tone.

"I see," he said with his irritation clearly evident. Obviously I was not going to be bagged all so easily as he perhaps had predetermined. He stoically read aloud the second question.

(2) "Do you believe that Joseph Smith was a prophet of God and that he saw God the Father and His Son Jesus Christ in the flesh as a fourteen-year-old boy?"

Throughout my upbringing, so much reverence had been placed on the man Joseph Smith by my Church leaders. I myself had loved and adored him with all my heart and I had sought to emulate his courage. I had passionately testified of what I believed to be his divine calling from God to bring truth to the earth. I had been ridiculed for defending his honor. Though I had always claimed not to worship him, I highly revered him as the great prophet of the last dispensation, often relating him to Jesus Christ—even down to his death for the Church.

In light of God's Word, however, I now knew that Joseph Smith was no longer the prophet and vessel of God I had believed him to be. I could no longer defend him, but I mourned for him. More so, I mourned for those who had been blinded by a false gospel of works and ordinances that Joseph Smith had used to place them in shackles. I could no longer testify of this man.

"I believe that at one time in his life he may have been inspired by God; I don't know for certain. Unfortunately, regardless of his intentions, he brought forth a gospel that contradicts the good news as revealed by Jesus and His apostles in the New Testament. Even the Bible says, 'If we or an angel from heaven should preach to you a gospel contrary to the one we preached to you, let him be accursed.'[94]

"He undid what Christ fulfilled by restoring the elements of the law that no longer have any bearing on our righteous standing before God. He has burdened an entire people with a man-made legalistic system of ordinances and works that can never save them. He instilled in people a mistrust of the Bible and proclaimed his own word as God's. I no longer believe that this man was a prophet or that he was visited by God and Christ in the flesh as he claimed."

My accuser began to sweat. His mouth was slightly agape and his forehead wrinkled.

"President, I no longer have the need to believe in or trust man for my salvation," I declared. "The foundation of my testimony is based solely on Jesus Christ. I have put every amount of faith and trust in Him alone and now know that He is all I need for salvation. Christ is enough for me."

President looked down wearily at his questions and, for some unknown reason, he chose to continue. I had divulged more than enough to incriminate myself, but President wouldn't yield.

(3) "Do you believe the Book of Mormon is the Word of God, and contains the fullness of the everlasting gospel?"

From the time I was a young child, the Church had instilled in me a love for and trust in the Book of Mormon. I was taught it was the keystone of our religion, contained the fullness of the gospel, was the most correct book on Earth, and that a man would get closer to God by reading and obeying it than anything else.[95] It was, without a doubt, placed on far higher spiritual ground than the Bible and was the supreme Scripture in Church canon. I had read the Book of Mormon at least four or five times before my mission and had gleaned from its words.

But now I knew it was not the Word of God, as my leaders had claimed. The clarity and simplicity of the everlasting gospel of Christ, as revealed in the Bible, had opened my eyes to the earth-shattering reality that the foundation of the Church was not Jesus Christ and His saving gospel, but rather was a counterfeit message built on man-inspired falsehoods that pointed to a different Jesus. The Book of Mormon was a part of that false foundation. The more I had read the Bible, the less essential the Book of Mormon had become.

"Honestly, I don't think we need the Book of Mormon. On the surface, it does seem to teach faith in Christ, yes—but I'm no longer certain if it's the *same* Christ," I asserted. "After reading the Bible for the past year and a half, it is clear to me that the Book of Mormon does not contain the fullness of the gospel. It contradicts the good news delivered in the Bible, which stands alone as the authority of God and witness of Christ. In the New Testament, we have the testimony of Jesus Himself and the gospel message given to us by the apostles, who were commissioned by the Lord to preach it. Everything must be tested against the message that was delivered once for all to the saints, and if it does not stand up to that test, it must be rejected."

President, rather than seeking to refute the claims I had made that so directly contradicted the teachings of the Church, simply breezed on to the next question without even making eye contact with me.

(4) "Do you believe the Church of Jesus Christ of Latter-day Saints is the only true and living Church upon the face of the earth?"

For as long as I could remember, I had been taught that the church whose name was inscribed in white letters on my nametag was Christ's solitary true organization on the face of the earth. But through the living Word of God, I had come to know that the Church was not what it claimed to be. I no longer was dependent on an earthly institution to have right standing with God. I could now have the assurance of the forgiveness of my sins through the blood of Christ, independent of any man or church.

"President, I know that I am saved by faith in Jesus Christ alone, and not through the Church. I have hope that if the Church holds fast to the Bible as its authority and rejects everything that does not align with the written Word, then it, too, can be part of the worldwide body of Christ. But as it stands now, it does not proclaim the saving gospel. Therefore, I must reject its claim as the true church of Christ."

Released from Bondage

Now that I had so unashamedly repudiated four of the five pillars of faith in the Church, President had no choice but to take swift action against me. He and I both knew the consequences that would follow, and although we sat across the table mere inches from each other, we were separated by a wide canyon, and the bridge between us had been burned from both ends. My inexorable execution was now a mere formality, and a reading of the equivalent of my Miranda rights was soon to follow.

"Elder, you do realize that because of your responses, there will be serious consequences. We cannot let this go undealt with," he stated as he closed the notebook with a loud thud. In that instant, the gavel slammed the table, judgment was pronounced, and I was found guilty of treason.

"Elder Wilder, do you have your temple recommend with you?" he asked.

"Yes, President, I do," I answered. I knew what would happen next, and I understood its ramifications. In the Church's eyes, I was relinquishing my eternal life.

"Would you give it to me?" he asked, holding out his hand.

I looked at him, froze for a second, and then gave a pained smile, knowing that this meant—without a shadow of a doubt—that my time as a missionary and a member of the Church had expired.

Reaching into my wallet, I pulled out the small card and stared at it. As I did, the meaning of what had just happened hit me quite unexpectedly. I thought back to the night of the hurricane when Erik gave me the letter and said something that confounded me for many months: "But first, God must release you from bondage." Until now, I had no idea that the bondage he was speaking of was symbolically encapsulated in a tiny business-sized card that I had carried in my pocket.

Prior to being freed in Christ, the Church held me captive by my sin. In order to attain God's forgiveness, I had to keep repenting of my sins to my religious leaders and fulfill whatever they required of me to find penitence. In this way I had been a slave to the Church. Through the liberating truth contained in God's Word, I had now been unshackled and freed from that bondage by Christ's blood. All that held me to this religion, then, was this small piece of paper that I now knew represented my indentured servitude to the Church.

With this understanding, I willingly placed the card in President's hand. I was giving up my dead works to serve the living God and I rejoiced in Jesus' proclamation: "The truth will set you free."[96] I was free indeed!

Although fear had won a number of the battles during this hearing, God's grace had won the war, and I now found myself overwhelmed by an all-encompassing peace. I didn't need a piece of paper to indicate my worthiness before God—Jesus Himself was my temple recommend, the champion of my righteousness. His blood made me worthy of life eternal. He was now my passport to heaven, and His promised grace was all I needed. It's all anyone needs. That's good news.

CHAPTER 29

NEHOR

President Sorensen leaned over to retrieve yet another notebook from his briefcase. *Good grief, how many notebooks does this man have?* Setting it on the table in front of me, I could see a phone number that was conveniently displayed on the topmost page.

"I will be calling your stake president[97] at home to inform him what is transpiring," he said. "We will then decide what is to be done with you."

My religious leadership in Utah was now being summoned, and I couldn't overlook the severity of the situation. I folded my hands and set them on the table, struggling to maintain a facade of bravery while my knee was vigorously springing up and down.

"I respect that you must do what you must, and I will do what I must," I replied, trying to convey confidence. "I hold nothing against you or anyone else."

President callously ignored my remarks, stood up, and exited the room without a response, closing the door securely behind him.

Sitting there left to my own devices, I contemplated the theme verse that I had carefully selected before I embarked on my two-year voyage. At the time I hadn't truly comprehended its meaning, but now the words had taken on a new and astonishing significance.

> I have been crucified with Christ. It is no longer I who live,
> but Christ who lives in me. And the life I now live in the flesh

I live by faith in the Son of God, who loved me and gave himself for me (Galatians 2:20).

It was a local custom that each missionary, prior to leaving home, would select a passage of Scripture to be engraved on a plaque that was displayed in the local chapel as a commemorative of those in service to the Church. The plaque was also adorned with a picture of the missionary and a flag designating the destination of their mission. My verse was quite an unusual selection for a young Latter-day Saint. Not only was I the only missionary I knew of who had chosen a passage from the New Testament (nearly all scriptures were from the Book of Mormon or Doctrine and Covenants), I had even picked an excerpt from the epistles of Paul.

Reciting the verse over and over in my mind, I found it humerous that I had set out into the Mormon mission field convinced that I would save the Christian world, never foreseeing that God—through the Christian world—was going to save me. And now, two years after hanging that foretelling sign on the wall, I was being crucified with Christ and surrendering all that I once considered as gain, with Christ now living and working in me. Although at the time I couldn't begin to fathom the true depth of this scriptural passage, I was now living out Paul's very declaration.

Not Ashamed

President was gone for only fifteen minutes or so, but in my current condition, it seemed like an eternity. Eventually, I could hear the quick rhythmic pattering of nervous heels coming back from down the hall until the sound ended abruptly just as the handle turned on the door. As the door opened, I couldn't help but notice the change that had come over President's face. For some reason, he seemed to have a look of renewed confidence and determination.

"Elder, your stake president would like to speak with you," he said as he grinned strangely at me, like he had just ratted me out to the principal and washed his hands of me. President handed me the phone and then ducked out of the room.

I shut my eyes for a moment as I struggled not to let fear overcome me. Though I had the consolation that this encounter would not be face to face, I had come to know this man personally over the years and his stern demeanor had intimidated me even when I was the most faithful of Church members. I took a deep breath and put the phone up to my ear.

"Hello?"

"Hello, Elder Wilder. How are you doing?" It was the very man himself who had issued my temple recommend and deemed me worthy to go on a mission.

"I'm doing okay, President Hansen."

"Elder Wilder, what's going on? It sounds like there are some problems and issues you have with the Church. Is there anything you'd like to say?" he asked.

"No, there is no problem. I'm just following Jesus Christ as instructed in the Bible. I am doing the right thing according to the Word of God," I said as calmly as I could while my shaking hands held the phone up to my ear.

"You think that you not needing the Church is the right thing?" he snapped. His words were ripe with sarcasm. I scrambled to affirm my defensive position.

"I have done nothing wrong. All I have done is witnessed of Christ and how He is all we need to be saved," I stated firmly. "I have put all my faith in Him and what He has done for me, and I am adhering to His Word, and not man. I'm saved by grace. Show me in the Bible where it says otherwise, and I will submit. Not you or anyone else can change that."

"Who has told you these things? I've heard it all before. You sound like a Baptist, Elder Wilder!" he barked. "What anti-Mormon literature did you read on your mission that caused you to lose your faith? You are very confused, young man."

"No, I think I'm the only one who isn't confused," I countered. "And if you consider the Bible anti-Mormon material, then yes, that's what I read!"

Evidently when I said that, I had poked a little too close to the hornets' nest.

"Well it sounds like you've been overtaken by a spirit!" he bellowed through the phone.

"You're right, the Spirit of God!" I refuted.

"No, Elder Wilder, the spirit of the devil! You are being deceived. Lucifer is very cunning."

The irony was that for so long, I had been called a devil by Christians because I was a Mormon, and now I was being called a devil by the Mormons because I was Christian. Everything in my life was flipping around and upside down at a dizzying pace. I had turned both cheeks now and had taken a hard slap on each.

"I've found the truth of the gospel in the Bible, and I can't deny what I know," I said.

"I've heard this before. I've seen it happen all too many times. You are lost to Satan, young man. There is no place in the mission field for a person like you, or even a place in this Church if you will not repent. You are on the path to outer darkness."

President Hansen's castigatory words cut me. Did he infer that I was possessed by Satan? Why wasn't he happy that I had found Christ? All I had been doing for the duration of this meeting—and for the last six months as a missionary—was testifying to the saving grace of Jesus Christ, proclaiming Him as the only way to eternal life. I was no longer seeking to work for my salvation and justify myself before God through the ordinances of the Church, but had found an eternal Sabbath rest in Christ. I had made Jesus the focus of everything I lived for and believed in, and now I was being condemned for it. My heart broke as it became clear there was no bridge that crossed the mighty chasm that had grown between the Church and me. For them, Jesus wasn't sufficient.

"If I am lost, sir, it is in the beauty of the grace that I have found in my Savior Jesus Christ. He is my Lord, and I am His servant. I can't change what I know I must do in my life," I said passionately. "I want to share with others what I have come to know, and that is the good news of Jesus Christ that has opened my eyes through the Word of God. I want to testify to the world of God's love. That is my purpose. That is my calling. I am not ashamed of the gospel!"

"Well, you're assuming quite a calling, aren't you? You need to humble yourself!" he retorted. "God has not called you to do *anything* outside of the Church. Your pride is blinding you from the truth."

I hadn't assumed any calling; I had only yielded myself to my responsibility as a follower of Christ: to fulfill the Great Commission by going out and making disciples of all nations. I had committed my life to be a witness of the gospel of Christ and knew that it was God who would now work through me—that by His grace I would walk in the good works that He had prepared for me. And these good works would not save me, but would result from my salvation.

"Do you not see what is happening?" Hansen continued. "You are who is described in Alma chapter 1. Maybe you should read it and you'll see that you are lost!"

I was astonished by his unwarranted attack; I was more than familiar with the story to which he was referring in the Book of Mormon: A young man, Nehor—an anti-Christ—was going about deceiving God's people by introducing priestcraft, teaching false doctrine, financially profiting from his religion, and establishing his own church. A murderer, he deceived many people and dragged their souls to hell. President Hansen's comparison was a strong and malicious one.

I wanted to defend myself, but I couldn't ignore the fact that I—just less than two years ago—had sat in the exact seat that Hansen and Sorensen now occupied. I was once face to face with a Christian man who was lovingly and boldly proclaiming the Word of God while I was embarrassingly left with no response. I had been Benson's adversary, unable to withstand or refute the wisdom that was revealed to him by the Spirit of God. My only recourse was to condemn him as a devil and anti-Christ (even if only in my head rather than verbally) because I couldn't contend with the Word of God.

Now, in an ironic twist of fate, I was sitting in Benson's seat, proclaiming the Word of God. And my once-allies-now-adversaries seemed to reveal that they also could not withstand or refute what the Bible said. God had given me a mouth and wisdom as promised, and it was evident that these men were also unable to contend with the Word and Spirit of God. The only recourse for my opponents was to label me an anti-Christ and devil.

"President, there's no use," I said. "There is nothing you can say to me that will change what I know through the Word of God. I'll never turn back. My faith is in Christ and no longer in man. My salvation is secure in Him."

President Hansen paused while awkward seconds ticked by. Then, in a harsh and punitive tone, he declared, "I've heard all I need to hear. Let me talk to President Sorensen again."

I didn't say a word as I stood, my legs barely having the strength to hold me up. I walked over to the door and opened it, scanning the passageway until I spotted President sitting at the end of the hall on the couch.

"He wants to talk to you again," I called out.

President came and retrieved the phone from my violently unsteady hands.

"I'll return shortly, Elder Wilder. Wait for me in the meeting room."

I closed the door behind me and sat, once again, all alone at the table. Time seemed to be stuck in place as I waited for President's inevitable return. I was uncertain as to how much more pressure I could handle, and I was being squeezed far beyond what I ever imagined my emotional limits to be. I put my head down and sobbed. "God, please keep giving me strength," I prayed. "I just want this to be over."

New Creation

I heard the door open down the hall and footsteps heading my way. President entered the room and looked more unyielding than ever.

As he took his seat, I said, "I'm not scared. I know Jesus is with me. I love Him with all my heart."

President was silent and contemplative, seemingly preoccupied in thought as he sat staring at me. Then his chest heaved and he let out an intense sigh.

"Elder Wilder, I remember you as a young boy in this mission. You had such a glow in your eyes. You were so passionate about the Church and what you were teaching." His gaze darted back and forth between my eyes, assessing me deeply. "You were so dedicated to the truth and helping others come to the knowledge of the restored gospel. And slowly, over the course of two years, you have changed. That light that I once saw in your eyes is now gone." He paused for a second and revealed a glimmer of empathy. "Your passion for the Church and for the restoration of the gospel has faded, Elder Wilder."

"Maybe I'm not passionate about the Church anymore," I said, "but now I'm passionate about the Lord Jesus Christ and His gospel. I'm passionate about people knowing the truth of God's love through His only Son. Christ is now my life."

He looked at me like a father losing his son, shaking his head in deep disappointment.

"I don't know what has happened to you, Elder. I started to see signs. For the last six months or so, every time you have given your testimony, all you have mentioned is Christ. It worried me a great deal. That's how I knew that something was wrong."

I couldn't believe what I had just heard. He was worried because my testimony was *only* in Jesus Christ?

"Even up until Tuesday," he continued, "I still had a fair amount of respect for you, despite the obvious change I was observing in your behavior. After that day, and the days following, I lost it all."

I was perplexed. What was he talking about? My public testimony of Christ alone was on Wednesday. Had he mixed up his days? What was he was referring to?

"What happened on Tuesday?" I asked.

"That's when I received a call from your fiancé's father."

"I knew it!" I blurted out. Luke 21 came to my mind: "You will be delivered up even by…relatives."[98] The scripture had just been confirmed to me with a devastating blow.

"He was so worried that you were leading his daughter away from Christ. Then he told me about your plans to marry outside of the temple. I didn't know what to think. And then your testimony at zone conference. What has happened?" he lamented. "You are not the young man that I once knew. You are so different now, and it breaks my heart to see you fall away like this."

I gazed at the ground, feeling like I should be offended by the accusations that had spilled from his mouth. But as his words looped in my mind, I realized that he was right. I shouldn't take umbrage. I praised God because of it—I *had* changed, because the gospel of Christ gave me newness of life: "Therefore, if anyone is in Christ, he is a new creation. The old has passed away; behold, the new has come" (2 Corinthians 5:17). I couldn't hide the change God had made in my heart because true faith was bound to bear fruit. It was obvious to President, to the entire mission, to my family, and to everyone who knew me that I was no longer the same starry-eyed religious boy that had entered the mission. I was a new man!

"You know what…you're right!" I exclaimed. "Something *has* changed within me. I have been washed, sanctified, and justified in the name of Jesus Christ. My life will never be the same!"

"You may think so, Elder Wilder. You may think so."

Is This the End?

An awkward silence followed, which left us both fidgeting. I couldn't hold back my next thought any longer. "I know you blame Erik."

"I blame myself!" he bellowed. "This is the most tragic thing that has happened to me as a mission president."

"President, you shouldn't be worried about me," I said, trying to comfort him. "I've never been closer to God in my life. No matter what it may seem to you, I am following Jesus. He is my Savior and King. He is the Messiah, and He is returning to Earth. The time is coming, and there is so much to prepare."

He shook his head in disagreement. "I am going to use my authority as your priesthood leader, Elder Wilder," he stated resolutely. "As your leader in God's holy priesthood, I am telling you that what you are doing is wrong. The path you are choosing is *not* of God. You are not following the right spirit…"

I was so stunned I interrupted him. "President, be careful what you say."

He shook my words off. "This is not the right path. You are being led astray by Satan…"

A second time I interrupted him. "President, I'm warning you to *stop* what you are saying. It's for your own good."

President ceased speaking and looked defeated. We both knew we had reached an impasse and there was no benefit, for either of us, in continuing with the inquisition.

"I'm not afraid of what you have to do," I declared. President brushed off my words and packed up his briefcase.

"I must contact the leaders of the Church and see what actions will be taken. It would be wise if you returned to your apartment and waited there for my call. Cancel all your appointments for the day. You are *not* in the mindset to teach the gospel, or to be a missionary of the Lord any further," he said in a scolding tone.

I smirked at the irony of his statement. I had given a two-hour confession and witness of Jesus Christ and His Word, and yet I was not in the mindset to teach the gospel? What, then, were his qualifications?

President, breaking tradition and formality, stood up without offering a closing prayer and headed straight to the door. I followed closely behind, praying to God for forgiveness for any animus I might have displayed, pleading with Him to fill me with love. I remembered Jesus' command: "I say to you, Love your enemies and pray for those who persecute you" (Matthew 5:44).

I stopped President before he reached the door, as Benson had done to me. "I love you, President," I said, embracing him with an extended hug. "I am grateful for what you have done for me these past two years."

"Elder Wilder," he said while patting my back, "we love you and are only trying to help you. I have faith you will come back to the fold."

CHAPTER 30

JESUS IS ENOUGH

Leesburg, Florida | *January 18, 2006*

The event that marked the completion of my two-year mission had arrived: my final zone conference.

Although the main purpose of a zone conference was to give the mission president the opportunity to direct or correct the course of the entire mission, for an elder who is about to go home, it is a final opportunity to leave a lasting and positive legacy on the impressionable younger missionaries. This was accomplished by sharing a departing testimony—a public witness of one's faith in the Church. Today, along with a handful of other elders, I would stand at the pulpit and impart what I had learned over the past two years.

As I entered the chapel, dozens of missionaries were greeting one another with joyous laughter and jubilant celebration. As much as I relished having the opportunity to see everyone that I had come to know over the course of my mission, there was only one person I wanted to reunite with: Elder Warren, whom I hadn't seen for nearly twelve weeks. It wasn't difficult to spot him from across the room—he was sporting the wide, hideous old maroon and white tie I had given him months earlier. (It was customary for missionaries to present ties to their friends as a gesture of love;

the uglier the tie, the greater the love. My fondness for Elder Warren was on full display as I had sought out and delivered up the most gruesome of ties imaginable.)

Warren glanced over and saw me eyeing him from afar and his face lit up. We both carefully made our way through the maze of missionaries greeting each other. Upon reaching him, I embraced him close, and he returned the brotherly goodwill. This would be our closing reunion as missionaries, with my completion date now just weeks away.

Warren had become such a significant part of my life (as I had hoped from the beginning), and my love for him was deepening with each passing week—our very souls felt like they were knit together in the love of God. Serving in such close proximity in Palm Bay, we had spent countless hours reading the New Testament while on exchanges, savoring the immeasurable love of God that was dripping from every word. I had been a firsthand witness to the powerful change that God was making in his life through the Bible, which he had been consuming daily for well over a year. I was convinced that he, too, was being washed by the water of the Word of God and it would only be a matter of time before he was born again in the Spirit.

A Proper Testimony

Candidly, these conferences were always boring and hopelessly monotonous. The mornings were filled with mundane talks by various leaders followed by training sessions on how to be a more effective missionary. After lunch, the coup de grâce was President's multi-hour sermon, often centered on obedience and the practical execution of missionary work.

The afternoon arrived slowly, and it was time for President to give his homily to the missionaries. He stood in front of all of us at the pulpit with all the decorum of a wise doctor ready to give an in-depth medical analysis. As always, he was wearing a suit and tie, his hair parted and slicked back, and his glasses hung at the edge of his nose. Before he spoke, he always paused for effect, as if to convey he had a level of knowledge and spirituality that we couldn't comprehend. At last, he began his long discourse.

"Elders and Sisters, we must be balanced missionaries. A true servant of God has a balance between Christlike attributes and practical skills that are attained through hard work. Not more of one than the other, but enough of both to be an effective minister of the restored gospel."

I had always found it difficult to stay focused on President's long and dogmatic sermons. Not only because he had the proclivity to drone on and on in a soft-spoken and emotionless voice, but especially today because I was still uncertain as to what I was going to share for my departing testimony.

"A balanced missionary cannot be too centered on love, because too much love might blind you from finding those who are prepared for the gospel," he decreed. "But most importantly, a balanced missionary has one trait above all others; this is the attribute that I, Heavenly Father, and the leaders of the Church would want you to have above all others: obedience." President then glared down at me, making certain I was absorbing his calculated words. It was obvious that my love crusade had not gone unnoticed.

I turned to Elder Bingham, who was sitting next to me, and the sour reaction plastered all over his face evidenced his inner turmoil. Being one of my closest and most trusted friends, he was one of the last surviving love elders. He was only weeks away from completing his mission, and today he would share his departing testimony as well.

Disappointed, I opened my Bible to 1 John 4 and put my finger on a passage for him to read: "Let us love one another, for love is from God, and whoever loves has been born of God and knows God," I whispered. "Anyone who does not love does not know God, because God is love."[99] I leaned my head on the pew in front of me in aguish as President continued.

"Elders and Sisters, it is imperative that as balanced missionaries we have a testimony of the work to which God has called us. We must have a testimony of Jesus Christ, and a belief that He is our Savior and Brother. But with one pillar alone, our testimony is not solid. A witness of Christ by itself is not a sufficient foundation, but just the beginning." He paused and glanced down at me again.

Was he so cavalierly saying that Jesus *wasn't* sufficient? His statement was completely antithetical to the singular truth that I had come to know through the reading of the New Testament for 568 consecutive days: Jesus *was* enough; He was the only pillar of testimony I needed.

I almost stood up with my torch in hand, wondering if his blasphemous words might cause a riot. I looked around to see how everyone else was reacting, expecting the righteous mob to be banging their cups on the table in defiance of him. Instead, the room was dead calm, paralyzed in reverential awe at President's wisdom. No one, besides Bingham sitting next to me, even so much as flinched.

"There are five components to a proper testimony of the gospel of Jesus Christ," President continued while holding out his hand with all five fingers raised. "When we have all five, our foundation is secure and our testimony complete.

"Along with a faith in Christ, you must have a testimony that Joseph Smith was a true prophet and that he did in fact see God the Father and His Son Jesus Christ. Third, you must have a testimony of the Book of Mormon as the word of God, that Joseph Smith translated it through the power of God, and that it contains a second witness of Christ. Fourth, you must believe that the current prophet of the Church, Gordon B. Hinckley, is a true prophet of God, just like Moses or Abraham, and that he holds all the priesthood keys on the earth today. And finally, you must believe that the Church of Jesus Christ of Latter-day Saints is the 'only true and living church upon the face of the whole earth,'[100] and that the priesthood power to perform eternal ordinances has been restored to the earth through this Church."

President hesitated and then fastened his eyes on mine. "So, Elders and Sisters, it is not a complete testimony unless you have *all five* of these components, for without all of them your testimony cannot stand. A testimony of Jesus Christ alone is not enough!"

President's words rang in my ears. I so desperately wanted to rise to my feet and call out this man for proclaiming a false gospel that was not built on the foundation of Jesus Christ. But this wasn't the time or the place to do that. In fact, I realized that God was giving me an opportunity to lovingly witness of Christ through my departing testimony. I didn't have to stir up an angry mob by calling out the false doctrines of the Church here and now. All I had to do was witness of the one pillar—the Rock—who had changed my life. I didn't need to proclaim what was wrong with the Church, only what was right with Jesus.

Good News

After President concluded his long-winded lecture, the time came for the departing missionaries to share their testimonies. It was obvious that President's oration was meant to impact those who were going to share their beliefs, coercing them to give a "proper" testimony. What he didn't know was that I was now committed to giving a *proper* testimony for the first time in my life.

One by one the veteran elders stood at the pulpit and imparted their final testimonies with heartfelt goodbyes. Following President's regimented guideline, they obediently witnessed of the five pillars of faith with fervor. As each one robotically regurgitated the same message, I prepared myself to testify of what God had done in the heart of a young shepherd boy.

As Elder Bingham finished his testimony and stepped down from the pulpit, it was now my time to stand in front of my peers and tell them—with confidence—that there was a Christian in their midst, I was that Christian, and Christ was responsible for that change in my life. This was my time to make less of myself so I could make more of Jesus.

I looked over at Elder Warren, smiled, and whispered, "I love you." Then I stood and slowly walked to the podium. I didn't know what I was going to say or how I was going to say it. I was terrified. I prayed that God would give me the words and strength to be a faithful witness of the love He had manifested to me through His Word.

Unable to control my emotions, I paused for a second, my shaking hands grasping ahold of each side of the pulpit as I peered out over the fifty or so missionaries in the audience, all of whose eyes were locked on me.

"I can only tell you how I feel, and what is in my heart," I said as tears gently dropped from my eyes. "All I can say is that the love of God changes people, and it has changed me in ways I didn't even know possible. It has made me a new person. For so long I was in darkness, and now I have found the light of the world, Jesus Christ. My life will never be the same."

Through my watery eyes, I looked out at the many people I had come to know and love on this most incredible journey, struggling to find the words to convey to them the magnitude of what the gospel had done in my life.

"I have fallen so many times. In brokenness, I have come face to face with my own sin and weakness, and yet Christ has picked me up and carried me in the safety of His merciful arms. As the Bible says, 'God so loved the world, that he gave his only Son, that whoever believes in him should not perish but have eternal life.'[101] Elders and Sisters, God loves us *so much*. He grants us eternal life through His Son Jesus Christ as a free gift by His amazing grace, even when we don't deserve it…even when we are unworthy. 'God shows his love for us in that while we were still sinners, Christ died for us.'"[102]

I looked down and gathered my thoughts, reflecting on the mercy God had shown to me throughout my life, which was now a testament to His vast love and forgiveness. God had saved me, as the most wretched of sinners, and now was calling me—as He does all His children—to preach His gospel. I looked up with a smile.

"Jesus Christ is the way, the truth, and the life. He is all we need for salvation, as He alone gave the ultimate and final sacrifice for our sins. For the first time in my life, I know that I am forgiven and redeemed because the blood of Christ has washed me clean. God has seen the depth of my sin and failure, and yet He has forgiven me through Christ. That's true and everlasting love!"

I realized at that moment why the Holy Spirit had encapsulated into a narrative—in the middle of the night as I desperately cried out to God—the picture of Christ on the cross dying for me on a personal level. That message was not just for me, but for everyone—not collectively, but intimately and individually. What He had demonstrated that fateful night when I was struggling to accept His forgiveness was the most significant revelation ever to take place in my life, and as I stood there in front of my peers, a passage came to mind: "What I tell you in the dark, say in the light, and what you hear whispered, proclaim on the housetops."[103] God was calling me to openly witness of the love He had exhibited to me personally and affectionately under the cover of night.

"In my time of greatest despair, finding it hard to believe that God could forgive me, I found comfort in the unfailing love of Christ. If you have ever had that same doubt, just ask yourself: Don't you think that when Christ was hanging on the cross, He saw your face? And don't you think He looked into your eyes as He suffered and said, 'I love you, and I would die for you so that you can live?'"

The puddle of salty discharge on the pulpit was slowly growing into a reservoir as I couldn't contain the power of God's love that had been expressed to me through the Holy Spirit.

"I know He saw each one of our faces on the cross, and because of His perfect and endless love, He paid the ultimate price for all of us. And all we have to do—all we *can* do—is receive that sacrifice by faith, trust in Christ alone, and we will have the guarantee of the forgiveness of our sins. That's good news.

"My dear friends, Christ waded through the horrible agonies of the atonement—*for us*. He drank that most bitter of cups and did not shrink—*for us*. He carried His own cross that was placed upon Him to Calvary, where He was crucified. Jesus gave the supreme sacrifice when He laid down His life for us and bought our salvation with His own blood. On the third day, He rose again—proof that He had conquered death itself. This is the greatest expression of love in the history of mankind. Compared to that, nothing else matters."

As I scanned the audience, I could see missionaries wiping tears from their eyes while unsuccessfully attempting to hide their emotions. I had long given up trying to conceal my own.

"The Lord is my shepherd; I shall not want. He makes me lie down in green pastures. He leads me beside still waters. He restores my soul… Surely goodness and mercy shall follow me all the days of my life."[104]

I looked at Warren and we connected for an intimate moment. "To my friends, I love you and I'll miss you. Never forget that Christ is everything that we need, and without Him we are nothing. I am not perfect, but through my faith in Him I am perfected by His righteousness, so I will always do my best to bring glory and honor to the King. I no longer have to wonder if I have done enough because I have been bought with a price. I testify that Jesus Christ is enough. He is everything. Amen."

After I took my seat, I saw President discretely hand a note to one of his assistants, Elder Kimball, who immediately went up to the pulpit and began to share his testimony. It seemed President was setting the meeting on a course correction as Kimball obediently and predictably bore witness of four of the pillars of faith, curiously omitting his profession of Jesus. One after another the missionaries made their way up the podium, each proclaiming the five (or sadly, four) testimonial pillars as instructed by President.

As I tuned out the predictable and repetitive testimonies, I was startled when Elder Warren stood up and made his way to the front of the room. Although he wasn't a departing elder, he must have been motivated to declare his witness. I waited with bated breath to see what he would proclaim.

"I'd like to bear my testimony," he said. "I know this is Christ's Church. I know that my Savior lives and loves me. I know the power of His atonement and forgiveness. I've been changed by it. I know the love of my Father in heaven and I strive every day to show that love to others." He paused, then glanced at President. "And…I know Joseph Smith is a true prophet of God. I say these things in the name of Jesus Christ, our Savior, amen."

As Elder Warren trudged his way back to his seat, he glanced in my direction, then tried to hide his face from me. His sorrowful eyes revealed his shame and my heart broke for him.

After the meeting concluded, I pushed my way through the sea of elders and made a beeline to Warren, wrapping him tight in my arms. "Warren, things are not easy for me right now," I said, fighting back tears. "No matter what, never forget that Jesus is enough. I love you."

"I love you too, Wilder. I'll always be the Sam to your Frodo."

CHAPTER 31

BREAKING
THE SEAL

I t's time to leave, Elder Lucas," I said, motioning for him to follow me. My companion was still seated on the couch, seemingly frozen in place as if he hadn't moved a muscle from when I had left him nearly two hours ago. He appeared hesitant, wondering why we were leaving without him being castigated first, but obediently followed anyway.

We exited the church and I marched toward the car. Lucas was trailing behind, looking back over his shoulder every few feet as if waiting to be called back to the interrogation room for his turn on the rack. As I neared my getaway vehicle, I paused, took a deep breath, and wondered if I would ever wake up from this unimagined dream.

"Is everything okay?" Lucas asked when he caught up with me.

I smiled and put my arm around him. "Everything's fine, Elder. I'm grateful for the time we've had together. You've been the perfect companion for me. I hope you know that no matter what happens, I love you."

"I love you too, Elder Wilder," he responded, bashfully glancing at the ground.

We climbed into the car and began the hour-long journey back to our modest home. As the world whizzed by, I contemplated President's poignant words: "For the last six months or so, every time you have given your testimony, all you have mentioned is Christ…That's how I knew that something was wrong." It saddened me that the very institution claiming to be Christ's earthly kingdom had condemned me, referred to me as an anti-Christ, threatened me with excommunication, and declared that my salvation was at stake—not based on any transgression or wrongdoing, but solely on my testimony of the sufficiency of Jesus Christ. Truly this was not the church of Christ as I once believed it to be. And now that I had been cast out, my future was destined to unravel outside of my religious heritage.

The question I had yet to answer was, What was I going to do? I couldn't foresee any outcome that ended with me completing the final three weeks of my mission; that was evident. I also had the threat of excommunication looming over my head. In my heart, I just wanted to run away and start my new life. There was no longer a place for me in the Church and I couldn't continue serving two masters. Why even return to my mission? I was in strife, and it must have been broadcast all over my face.

"Are you sure everything's okay?" Lucas asked.

"Elder Lucas, I can assure you this will all be over soon. I'm going to miss you so much. You've been such a good friend. I'm sorry to have put you through this. Things have changed in my life so much. I…"

I wanted to cry. My heart was broken for my friend, an innocent bystander, a child with no more guilt than a newborn fresh from his mother's womb. I never intended for him to be involved in the cataclysmic events that were taking place in my life, and I had no way of adequately explaining to him all of what was happening. What would I say? *By the way, Elder, I came out here to earn my salvation, but they are stripping me of that salvation because I received my salvation without earning it?* Looking into Lucas' frightened eyes, I could do nothing but pray for my friend as I considered my impending demise.

David, Jonathan, and Saul

We arrived at the house and I immediately went to my room, pulled off my tie, and collapsed on my bed. I gazed up at the ceiling and speculated about what fate God had laid out in front of me. "God, what do I do?" I cried out. "Where do I go?"

As I lay there, out of the corner of my eye I noticed the envelope Erik had handed me. In an instant, I realized that I had fulfilled the prerequisite for opening the document: my mission was over (though not in the way I would have ever anticipated). The long-awaited time to read the letter had finally arrived!

I flung myself off the bed and snatched up the letter, but then I hesitated. For nearly a year and a half I had anticipated breaking the seal—not just on the envelope, but on my life—to fully understand God's greater purpose for me. God had already done the unthinkable, revealing to me more than I could have ever fathomed since Erik imparted the letter to me, and I was slightly tentative about what more there was to be discovered.

I stared at the writing on the front of the envelope and ran my fingers over the name. "To David," it read in black ink. Just seeing that name brought countless reminiscences to my mind. I slowly peeled back the flap and pulled out the stack of pages. I unfolded them started to read.

My Beloved David,

My love for you goes beyond what we can know in this life. And the love of Christ Jesus surpasses all knowledge and understanding. It is He who died for us so that we could live. Upon your reading this letter, I must trust that you have completed your mission for the Church, that I suspect was cut short. I trust you have held fast to the truth and have passed the test that God has provided to come along with it that will forever mark the change in your course, and that which led you legitimately out of bondage.

For in here lies our mission: It is our duty to openly confess the Word of God, and to openly confess of the Son of God as the Savior of all who believe. This must be done in everything that we do. God knows that you are weak, but you trusted Him and set your fate into His hands. He sees that you have kept His Word; you have depended on Him and you have not denied Him, but have witnessed and testified of Him, in the face even of the threat of destruction. The Lord has given you a refuge in Him, and He will save you and deliver you from all who now pursue you.

The leadership of the LDS Church is as your Saul. God trained you (as David) through the LDS Church (as Saul), and you will now take part, among many, to train the end-time church. A portion of your calling is designed to bring the body of Christ together under one roof. You are to labor to tear down the walls that separate the faithful into denominations and bring unity within the bride of Christ, as one body made up of many different members, with one single purpose in Christ. This is all in preparation for His second coming.

David trusted God as the foundation. You shall do the same. He followed God's Word and trusted it. You shall do the same. You must test all things with the Word of God. David knew God would open doors for him and so was watchful for the opportunities that he trusted would befall him, as you will also. David committed himself to God's hands and recognized by design that God's battles were his battles. Even given the opportunity to kill Saul, David left Saul's fate in God's hands. He let the Lord be the judge...

God is seeking you, and unlike those around you who judge you from the outside, God sees what is on the heart. He is expecting that when you stumble in the flesh, you will get back up and go on with enough faith in Him that you will no longer accept a probationary period after repentance, but will instead trust God that within His mercy He has forgiven you instantaneously. Trust that God is all-loving, whose forgiveness knows no guilt. Trust in His deep well and do not allow your guilt to make you ineffective for Him...

Beloved, to simplify our relationship with God—that very complicated nature—understand that God and Jesus each have a life independent of each other, yet share a single Deity. And that Deity, which is the willing extension of the Father that will indwell all the children of God, began with Christ in the flesh on the day in which God called Him His Son.

Consider this: Jesus, the Son of Man, accomplished what no other man could. Through His sacrifice, He reconciled the flesh to the Spirit of God for the very first time, for all time, when overcoming the flesh on our behalf. He became the second Adam and the first-born of many to follow in His shadow, over all of creation. The first Adam was created in the image of God on the earth, and was to receive the likeness of God in the garden, where he later fell through disobedience, bringing sin and death into the world. (As you consider these things, don't unnecessarily concern yourself with the age of the physical earth as many do, which has created much division in the church—God has given us the age of the world. This mystery you will understand in greater detail over time.)

The reconciliation and restoration of man was the Christ, who was also overshadowed by the Spirit of God and given life in the flesh. He reconciled the flesh to the spirit, the image and likeness of God, and we are being prepared by Him to enter into the triune nature of God through adoption, and be one with Christ as Christ is one with the Father, and be brought to complete unity through the Holy Spirit.

So, in taking upon us the full image and likeness of God, which is the nature of Christ, we are to be all-faithful and all-loyal to Him and His purpose. That is what is asked of us. As Abraham was asked to lay his child upon the altar and lift a knife, we, too, will be ready to give up what is important to us, to put God first and therefore demonstrate our faith. Until that day when I will be taken from you for an earthly time, I shall continue to love, to serve, and to protect you. Peace be unto you in the name of Jesus Christ our Lord and Savior.[105]

Run

I sat in stunned silence, trying to process the enormity of what I had just consumed. The Davidic likenesses outlined in the first page were unfolding before my very eyes, and in good conscience I could not deny what God had been doing from the beginning—long before I was a missionary, and perhaps even from before I left the womb. I was flooded with a sense of purpose as I scanned the letter over and over. Admittedly, I wished the letter had more to say about David; but instead of revealing more about my childhood hero, it progressed to explaining a difficult postulation about the image and likeness of Christ (which I had no choice but to ignore for the time being, as my mind was already blown past its limits and incapable of comprehending what Erik was saying).

My immediate priority, then, was not deciphering Erik's doctrinal statements, but seeking the Lord's direction in light of my predicament. I set the letter down on my nightstand and picked up my Bible—the source for all my answers—and I turned to the story of David and Saul in 1 Samuel, praying for God to give me instruction for His will.

"Jonathan told David, 'Saul my father seeks to kill you. Therefore be on your guard in the morning. Stay in a secret place and hide yourself.'"[106] Jonathan then made arrangements for David to safely flee the city.

The parallels had manifested themselves with an alarming clarity: The Church I had served and loved with all my heart—which had groomed me and found great favor in me—was now the very entity, Saul, that would seek my destruction. The sagacious friend who had lovingly guided me to and through the Word of God, Jonathan, would help bring me safely to my refuge. And God had given me an answer as He had His servant David: RUN!

I immediately called Erik.

"Hello?"

"Erik, it's over," I said in a panic. "My mission is over. You need to come and get me."

"Whoa, Kid, slow down. What's going on?" he asked.

"Erik, everything we suspected is true. They are going to excommunicate me. There is no reason for me to stay anymore. We can talk when you get here." I stopped for a second, held my breath, then confessed, "Erik, I read the letter."

"Okay, Micah. I'm leaving right now. Stay strong."

I sat on the floor next to my bed and rested my head on my knees. Like a rain shower waiting to break through the dark clouds, tears burst from my eyes and I sobbed in the quiet of my bedroom. I was bearing a cross that was indeed heavy to bear in my weakness, but I trusted God with all my heart.

Gathering sufficient strength, I meandered into the study and plopped down at my desk. I hastily crammed all my notebooks and journals into my backpack—a meticulous compendium of all that had taken place over the course of my mission. Awaiting the arrival of my friend, I set my Bible down in front of me and, as I had hundreds of times previously, gently opened the tattered pages.

> Consider your calling, brothers: not many of you were wise according to worldly standards, not many were powerful, not many were of noble birth. But God chose what is foolish in the world to shame the wise; God chose what is weak in the world to shame the strong; God chose what is low and despised in the world, even things that are not, to bring to nothing things that are, so that no human being might boast in the presence of God (1 Corinthians 1:26-29).

Truest Friend

As the Word of God was washing over me, I heard the front door open and close. Without having to look up, I knew my beloved friend had arrived. I leapt out of my chair, ran across the room, and embraced him.

"Hey, Erik," I said, squeezing him tight. Jonathan had arrived to escort me to my refuge and safe place. I had finally found the face in the water from long ago.

"Hey, Kid," he responded, swallowing me in his grip.

I was prepared to flee to a new land and home like David, but there was a slight logistical snafu. Before I could leave, I had to figure out what to do with Lucas. I wanted him to be safe. Leaving him alone would be like leaving a starving puppy in the median of a busy highway. The only problem was I didn't know where to leave him—or with whom. I racked my mind, and there was only one other friend I could turn to who could help me: Elder Bingham.

I was confident I could confide in Bingham and he would be able to sympathize with the complexity of my situation. After all, he had never really landed solidly in the Church because he didn't fit the standard religious mold. A bodybuilder, he tended to be loud, brazen, and lacking basic propriety in his manners. He had a fierce temper and could swear like a sailor. On the surface, he could easily offend the unknowing person, but I was fortunate to have seen a side to him that most did not. Despite his rough exterior, he had shown himself to be loyal to a fault, dedicated in loving others, and surprisingly gentle.

Besides being a devoted friend, he was also the only person, by providence, who was geographically situated to help me. Due to his suspected status as a love elder, President had cast him out of the former mission boundaries to the adjacent area. My plan was to drop off Lucas at Bingham's missionary house and then beat a hasty retreat to the Edgewater Hotel.

I picked up the phone to call my ally in arms.

"Hello, this is Elder Bingham."

"Bingham!" I yelled.

"Wilder?!" he responded in confusion.

"Are you going to be home in an hour or so?"

"I'm not sure. Why, what's going on?" he asked. He must have noticed the urgency in my voice.

"There's no time to explain the details," I said. "But I'm getting thrown out. The Church, they're throwing me out."

"What do you mean they're throwing you out? Wilder, what's going on, man?" He sounded anxious.

"I don't have time to explain it all. But I need you to be home in an hour so we can drop off Lucas with you…then I'm leaving."

"You're leaving? Where are you going?"

I was at a loss for words. I knew it would be hard for him to understand what I was going through and how I had arrived at this point. I thought about the memories we had made, and how many times I had warned him that one day I would call upon his friendship in a time of need.

"Hey, remember when I used to ask you if you'd trust me, no matter what?" I asked.

"Yeah."

"Well, ole' buddy, this is one of those times. You're one of the only true friends I've got. I need you, man."

"All right Wilder, I'll be here," he replied.

"Thanks, Bingham. See you soon."

As I gathered my belongings, I glimpsed at Lucas, who was sitting in the living room with a terrified look on his face.

"Elder Lucas, we are going to take you to Belleview to drop you off with the elders there."

"Okay," he said, averting eye contact as he pawed at the ground with his foot.

"Everything will be fine, Luki-Bear. I promise." Lucas cracked a smile and I snagged a quick hug that ended with a fast tickle to the armpit.

Erik, Lucas, and I walked out of the house. As I sauntered toward Erik's pickup truck, I paused to look back at the place I had called home for the past three months. It was here, in this humble abode, that the greatest change of my life had taken place—my old self had died, crucified with Christ, and I had been raised into newness of life.

A small portion of me was sad to be leaving; but I rejoiced at the future that God had laid before me. My walk with Christ had begun, and my bags were packed for the journey. I didn't have all the answers, but I had faith that God was in charge of my destiny, and my life was squarely in the palms of His mighty hands.

CHAPTER 32

THE KISS
OF JUDAS

I looked behind me at Elder Lucas sitting in the back seat. He was staring out the window with a dazed look on his face.

"Do you still love me?" I asked, trying to get him to relax.

At first he hesitated to respond. Then he took a deep breath and spoke up. "Yes. I don't really understand what's going on, but I still love you." He cracked just a hint of a childlike smile, which made me laugh.

"Well, then, that's all that matters, isn't it?" I said as I patted his knee and then turned my attention to the road ahead.

The three of us remained eerily quiet for the remainder of the forty-five-minute drive to Belleview. As the miles passed by, I retrieved the gold cross from under my shirt and held it tight in my hand. Like the apostle Paul, I knew that I could not boast in anything or anyone except the cross of Jesus Christ, by which the world had been crucified to me and I to the world. To the praise of God, the message of the cross was no longer foolishness to me—it was the power of God for my salvation.[107]

Glancing down at the cross in my hand, I relived the moment when it was gifted to me by Erik eight months earlier. While standing outside of an ice cream parlor, I saw the unassuming but captivating gold cross hanging from his neck and I was immediately drawn to it—not so much to the item itself, but to what it represented. I was already undergoing my transformation at the time, and the symbol of the cross no longer repulsed me, but rather, gave me hope that through Jesus Christ I could be saved and forgiven.

"I want to wear that," I said while pointing at his necklace, knowing that it held priceless value to Erik.

"You do?" he responded with surprise. "It was hand-forged from gold that belonged to loved ones and gifted to me. I haven't taken this off my neck since I received it. When I joined the Church, I was strongly discouraged from wearing it. But I didn't remove it because of what it symbolizes."

Then, unexpectedly, Erik pulled the chain off from around his neck and slipped it over my head. "Take it; it's yours," he said graciously.

I looked down at the cross and held it firm in my hand. "Thank you. This will be a symbol of my faith and devotion to Christ." I never took it off from that day forward.

Delivered Up

From down the street I could see the unmistakably stocky body-builder frame of Elder Bingham, who was nervously kicking at something in the driveway. I exited the truck, grasped hold of his rigid frame, and hugged him tightly before I noticed that he was reserving himself—if not outright resisting me.

"What's going on?" he burst out. I took ahold of his shoulders and shook him gently. He was so inflexible.

"I'm leaving the mission. I think they're going to excommunicate me."

"What? Why? What did you do?"

What had I done? I was still trying to figure that out.

"Nothing. They just found out some stuff about what I believe and don't believe anymore. It all has to do with my new faith in Jesus Christ, and everything that I have discovered through reading the Bible. I can't explain it all now. There's no time. I have to get out of here."

Talking as we walked, we made our way inside his apartment. Bingham's companion, Elder Hatch, was there, and he threw me a dubious glance.

"Make sure you call President after I leave and tell him where I am.

Here is my number if he needs to reach me." I scribbled it on a piece of paper and handed it to Elder Bingham.

I turned to Lucas, who looked like a frightened puppy about to be dropped off at a kennel. My poor companion had experienced enough trauma for one day.

"Lucas, I love you so much. Everything is going be okay. I'm going to miss you, my friend," I said, hugging him and stealing one last tickle as he chuckled softly.

"I'm going to miss you too, Wilder," he replied.

"We should get going," Erik said from behind me.

I turned to Bingham and looked him in the eyes. I couldn't grasp what it was, but something was different about him. He seemed to be having a hard time maintaining eye contact with me and a troubled feeling started to creep up in my gut. Something besides Erik was prodding me to get out of there fast. The misgivings were eating me alive.

"I gotta do this. Do you understand? I gotta go." I embraced Bingham again. "I love you with all my heart. You have been a true friend. Just think back to everything we talked about in Palm Bay, and you'll understand what's going on."

After I released Bingham, he seemed reluctant to let me leave. "Wilder, just come talk to me for a second," he said. I was torn. I wanted to depart, but didn't want to deny a friend who was most likely confused and fearful. Against my conscience, I relented.

"Okay, man."

We headed outside toward the truck where Erik was waiting, but Bingham unexpectedly turned me around and led me in the opposite direction to the back of the house, apparently for privacy.

"Dude," he started, "just tell me what's going on."

"You trust me, right, Bingham?"

"Of course, Wilder," he said while eyeing the ground.

"Micah, we should go!" Erik cried out, as if he was expecting someone to swoop in on us at any moment and snatch me away. Despite the urgency in his voice, I ignored him, chalking his insistence up to paranoia. I knew I was safe. If there was any oncoming danger, my muscular amigo would have already warned me.

Bingham observed me looking at Erik, and quickly manipulated me around with his arm on my shoulder, turning me away.

"Wilder, just explain to me what's happening," he begged. I was caught between his supplications and Erik's pleas.

"Look, all I can tell you is that I know some things about the truth. Things aren't what you think they are...the Church, it's not what you think it is. I can only encourage you to continue to read the Bible and I pray that you will one day see what I see. Christ is all you need."

I was weary and finding it difficult to explain the situation. "But I feel good. I've never felt better. I'm following my destiny, you know?"

Bingham nodded, as though he didn't understand but was willing to believe. He still avoided eye contact with me, though he kept his arm tight around me as if to hold me in place.

"If you say so," he replied.

"I'm going to miss you, brother. I hope nothing changes our friendship..."

Right then Bingham took a quick glance behind me and I recognized a flash of regret and shame in his eyes that I had seen many times before, such as when he had let loose a string of profanities.

Confused, I turned around and immediately realized my foolishness as I plowed head-on into my very own betrayal. Though Bingham had not surrendered me with a holy kiss, he had ensnared me just long enough for another portion of the scripture to be fulfilled: "You will be delivered up even by...friends."[108] I was speechless.

There they stood, my valiant zone leaders, rushing in to save me from the destructive path that I was taking. I spun back around and looked at Bingham with so much anguish in my heart but not a word came out of my mouth—just a single tear from my eye. Of all people, I thought he was one person I could trust. I was shattered.

"What's going on, Elder Wilder?" Elder Carr asked.

"I'm leaving," I quipped as I walked toward the truck.

"Just wait, we can work this out," Carr pleaded, suddenly losing all sense of authority as his voice gained a few octaves. "There's no reason for you to leave," he cried.

"No reason for me to leave, huh?" I said tersely. By my count, everything

I had ever believed had been ripped out from beneath my feet—the very Church I had given my life to was not founded on the biblical gospel and in fact was opposed to God's Word; I was fallaciously accused of being possessed by Satan after testifying of Jesus; and people I thought were my friends had stabbed me in the back and betrayed me. I had no reason to leave? I had no reason to stay.

"There's nothing for me here anymore." I resumed walking to safety, but my liberators wouldn't give up that easily. Elder Carr grabbed hold of my arm.

I stopped, looked at him, then growled out, "Let go!" He looked at me fearfully. "I'm not staying, and you won't stop me!" I yelled.

I yanked my arm away from him and glanced threateningly at him. Promptly recognizing my recklessness, I calmed myself. I *had* to learn to respond in love and gentleness. Carr was not my enemy. He was a hostage, a man in desperate need of being rescued from bondage, as Christ had done for me.

"I have to do this, Elder. I know you don't understand, but I need to go. I've found Jesus, and I can only hope that you do too."

I turned around, walked to the truck, and never looked back.

CHAPTER 33

MORE THAN
A FRIEND

Winter Garden, Florida | *September 28, 2004*

I felt like I was walking out on thin emotional ice that was crackling under each step I made toward the truck.

"Ready to go?" Erik asked.

"Yeah, I think so," I said reluctantly as I looked back at the spectacular view over Lake Apopka while fabricating a smile.

I was going to miss this place so much. More than anything, I was going to miss Erik and the relationship we had developed during my four months in Winter Garden. I would have but a short hour to spend with my friend, and then we would be severed by seventy long miles. Far too soon I would be in a new place, and I knew that one wrong move would cause me to fall through that emotional ice and drown in my sappy sentiments.

I climbed into the truck, and Erik and I began our trek to Port Orange, where I would begin my tenure as a zone leader. There was an uneasy quiet for the first while or so as I leaned my head against the window and stared at the objects passing by as raindrops gently fell outside. I was struggling not to be angry at God for removing me from my home, especially because only two days had passed since Erik dropped the startling revelation of David on my life during Hurricane Jeanne. Just when I was beginning to get answers to my deepest questions, God was ripping me away and replanting me elsewhere. Eventually, I slipped through the ice and tears filled my eyes.

"What's wrong, Kid?" Erik asked as he put his hand on my shoulder and gently shook it.

"I don't want to leave," I moaned. "Why would God take me away when I was beginning to learn so much?"

"Maybe God wants you to learn the rest on your own, Micah," Erik said with a smile. "He has planted something deep within you that has been watered and now it must be allowed to grow. Over time, you will see that God has a purpose for you. But like David, God must groom you personally and teach you through His Word. Your life is destined to change in ways that you cannot imagine. You can't continue to depend on me, or anyone. You must instead find undying faith in Christ and His love through His Word, and come to know without any doubt in your mind that He will never leave your side."

As much as I didn't want to admit it, I knew he was right. God had displayed His faithfulness to me throughout my life, and even when I had abandoned Him, He never forsook me. I needed to trust Him.

"I hope you're writing everything down," Erik suddenly blurted out.

"What do you mean?" I asked, looking at him.

"One day you will have a story to tell the world. You need to record everything that happens to you on your mission because someday, you will look back and see what God has done in your life. You are being molded to become a light to the world. But you must always know and remember: it's not all about us. It's not about you, Micah. God's work has a purpose greater than us individually. Think of it like this: You are standing on the peak of the highest mountain in the dark of the night, holding up a bright lantern for the world to see. It doesn't matter who's holding it up because no one sees your face; they only see the light—Jesus is that light. As He increases, you must decrease."[109]

I was taken aback. I could hardly see anything about my life worth telling the world. "What?! That's impossible," I muttered. "Why would anyone want to listen to anything I have to say? What would I even tell people?"

"Micah, one day you will write a book and tell a personal story of God's love. And the book will be designed to reach people around the world.

What has happened and will happen to you will point them to the Word of God and the salvation that can be found only in Christ. You, like David, are to be a witness to the mercy and love of God."

I didn't say anything. I didn't know what to say. Had he gone mad? His postulation was absurd. I didn't know how to write a book. Besides, I didn't think I had a story to tell.

"Micah, what happens from here on out is up to God. But know this: You have my heart, and I would want nothing more than to see what God has planned for you to bear fruit. Be faithful to His will in your life and surrender your own. Someday, God will open your eyes and you will know that He has been avidly pursuing you the entire time. Take up your cross and follow Christ with all your heart."

As he finished his sentence, he reached into the console of the truck and retrieved a compact disk. "I want to play a song that I had planned to play for you when the time came," he said while inserting the CD in the player. "This song[110] encapsulates our relationship together in Christ. I love you, Micah, more than you'll ever know."

A Fiery Trial
January 20, 2006

Sitting in the passenger seat with rain pouring down washing all things new, I couldn't believe that—in a sense—I was running from my mission. The Church. My life. Seeking comfort, I opened my Bible and the Spirit of God led me to a stirring passage:

> Beloved, do not be surprised at the fiery trial when it comes upon you to test you, as though something strange were happening to you. But rejoice insofar as you share Christ's sufferings, that you may also rejoice and be glad when his glory is revealed. If you are insulted for the name of Christ, you are blessed, because the Spirit of glory and of God rests upon you (1 Peter 4:12-14).

"Erik, what's going to happen?" I asked.

"I don't know, Kid. But I do know that everything is going to be okay. One day, this will all be behind you."

I couldn't help but exude my uncertainty. "I know, Erik. Everything will be okay," I stated robotically.

I couldn't wait to start my new life. The rain outside was making everything fresh and clean, and I along with it. Jesus said, "If anyone thirsts, let him come to me and drink."[111] I had drunk of that water and within me had sprung water welling up to eternal life, birthing a new creation with a new life, new purpose, and now a new home.

Just then, the loud ring from Erik's cellphone startled me. "It's President," he said, handing me the phone like it was a hot potato. My heart started pounding. What was he going to say? What was *I* going to say?

"Erik, I don't know what to say!" I said in a panic, pushing the phone back at him.

"Just answer and have faith, Micah. It's all going to be okay." He was right. Of *course* he was right. I closed my eyes, said a prayer, then spoke hesitantly into the phone.

"Hello?"

"Elder Wilder, this is President Sorensen," he said in an authoritative voice.

"Hello, President."

"Tell me what's going on, Elder Wilder."

"Well, I'm leaving the mission. I have no reason to stay," I stated curtly.

"And what makes you think that, Elder? You need to think about what you are doing. We can work this out, but you need to come back," President pleaded.

"I have thought about it, President. This is what I must do. Even by your own acknowledgment, I can no longer continue. There is nothing left for me in the mission or in the Church. I am following Christ."

"That's not true, Elder Wilder. You are just confused and scared. We only want what's best for you. We are trying to help you. Why don't you come to the mission office so we can talk?"

"No...I will be at the hotel, President. If you want to talk to me, you can come there."

An unnerving silence filled the air.

"Okay, Elder Wilder," he relented. "I will call you later and arrange a time to come and speak with you. I will see you soon."

After thirty minutes of calm, my attention perked up as the truck bounced on brick streets and I saw familiar landmarks: The yellow caboose, the clock tower, and ahead to the right, my new home and refuge, the Edgewater Hotel. We pulled up to the front doors, and I felt as if I were returning home after a lifelong sabbatical.

I entered the building and ambled toward the antique Otis elevator with my backpack and small suitcase. As I did so, a dark-haired woman approached me.

"David?!" she exclaimed enthusiastically, hugging me without warning.

"Do…do I know you?"

Before I could figure out the identity of this mystery woman, Erik's phone rang. I glanced down at the caller ID. It was President. *Not again.*

"Hello, President Sorensen," I answered.

"Elder Wilder, I would like to talk to you face to face. I will be at the hotel in one hour." He hung up.

I tried not to let fear overcome me.

"Erik, I don't want to do this again," I said as we entered the elevator.

"I know, Kid. But be aware that he will tempt you," he warned with a serious tone.

"What do you mean he will tempt me?"

"He will offer you something that seems good, but it won't be. You must be careful what you do, Micah. Think about the story of David. Saul promised him safe passage, then tried to kill him. Though your physical life is not in danger, they will seek to excommunicate you to discredit you."

Terms of Surrender

Waiting for President to arrive felt like the longest hour of my life. I sat impatiently reading the Bible in the second-floor lobby. I wanted this all to be over. I was ready to move on, but I felt the weakness of my flesh mocking me, as it had earlier this morning. Thankfully, God's Word gave me encouragement.

> He said to me, "My grace is sufficient for you, for my power
> is made perfect in weakness." Therefore I will boast all the

more gladly of my weaknesses, so that the power of Christ may rest upon me. For the sake of Christ, then, I am content with weaknesses, insults, hardships, persecutions, and calamities. For when I am weak, then I am strong (2 Corinthians 12:9-10).

I was interrupted as the elevator door opened and out came President in his dark blue suit donning his briefcase at his side. He approached the table and sat down on the opposite end from me. Although his attire was identical to what he wore for our previous engagement, he did not exhibit the same confidence as before. Perhaps, like me, he wanted this whole ordeal to come to an end.

"Elder Wilder, how are you?" he said with a smile. His friendly behavior made it appear increasingly less like he was here to do battle and more like he wanted to negotiate terms of surrender. For the first time, I felt like I had the high ground.

"Elder, I have spent the last couple hours in prayer, as well as on the phone with the Brethren. We have decided on what would be the best course of action in your situation."

"Okay, I'm listening," I said without taking my eyes off him.

"We feel it would be best for you to return to your home in Utah to meet with and be released honorably by your stake president there. We can arrange for you to have a ticket to fly home tomorrow."

At first consideration, President's offer was enticing. I could go home and see my family, get an honorable discharge, and come back to Florida with a clean record. I wouldn't have to face the embarrassment of losing my friends and family, and no one would know the difference. But something didn't sit right. I remembered Erik's warning. Maybe this outwardly appealing offer was the temptation.

"Why can't you just release me here and now?" I questioned.

"Elder, you need to go home and be released properly by your stake president. He is here to help you." Perhaps President was sincere in his naivety, but I couldn't so easily forget Hansen's harshness toward me over the phone just hours earlier.

"President, how do I know that he will release me honorably? I don't want to deal with what I already did today. President Hansen doesn't want to help me; he wants to interrogate me…and excommunicate me."

"Elder Wilder, I can assure you that he won't interrogate you. He will simply release you from your missionary service and you can walk away. Your local leaders can then work with you to refortify your testimony."

I paused to consider his proposal. "Give me your *word* that nothing will happen. He will release me, and that's it."

"You have my word, Elder Wilder. Take some time to think about it. Let me know your decision in the morning."

He stood up and walked away. No prayer and no farewell. He had done his duty and relinquished himself of any further responsibility for me and clearly wanted to make a rapid exit.

Now I had a decision to make.

As personally beneficial as the offer appeared—with President's pledge that I would be given safe passage—I couldn't ignore the warning given to me by my dear friend. Wanting to settle the dissonance in my heart, I summoned Erik and disclosed everything President had proposed.

"I know you want this, Micah, and you think that returning to Utah and getting honorably released will keep you from the shame and disgrace you fear awaits you. But you have to decide who it is you are serving—man, or Christ. In John, it talks about people who believed Jesus, but because they were afraid of their authorities, they didn't openly confess their belief so they wouldn't be put to shame. They loved the praise of man more than the praise of God. Where do you stand? Going to Utah is a trap."

Wanting to justify taking up President on his offer, I pleaded, "I know, Erik. But he gave me his word that nothing would happen."

"It's your decision to make, Micah. Spend time in prayer and the Scriptures this evening," he urged.

I was internally conflicted. The more I deliberated over my quandary, the more I realized my pathetic cowardice. The only reason I wanted to return to Utah was to appease man and make a vain attempt to salvage my reputation. I was disappointed in myself. As I sat all alone, I searched the Scriptures for the passage Erik had referenced in the Gospel of John:

> Nevertheless, many even of the authorities believed in him, but for fear of the Pharisees they did not confess it, so that they would not be put out of the synagogue; for they loved the glory that comes from man more than the glory that comes from God (John 12:42-43).

God's Word convicted me, a two-edged sword that had once again discerned the thoughts and intents of my heart. Deep down, I knew I could not—and should not—return to Utah to save my standing among men; I was a fool for thinking I could. I knew where I stood with God, and that's all that mattered. But I was torn about my family. I had been on this voyage away from home and loved ones for nearly two years, and now I was going to tell them I wasn't ever coming back? That would break their hearts and crush their spirits—especially my parents. I didn't want to let them down.

Treason

I slipped away to an unoccupied hotel room to gather my thoughts. Alone in the silence, I fell to my knees and poured my heart out to God in prayer. "God, I need You so much right now. You have been my strong tower. Strengthen me as I prepare to tell my parents what You have done in my life. Soften their hearts toward me, God. Show them what You have shown me. Open their eyes."

The emotional weight of the day had nearly collapsed me, and I could barely find the strength to stand up. Falling on the bed, I began to consider the gravity of what was transpiring in my life. From the time I was a young child, I had been the most stalwart and faithful of Latter-day Saints. I was as Saul of Tarsus was in his zeal as a Jew—unparalleled. Every aspect of my life had been centered and built on my faithfulness to my religion. But as a result of my newfound testimony, I knew I could never have the things that had once mattered most to me. And in all I was bound to lose, I now faced the most terrifying prospect of my new faith: revealing it to my parents, and in particular, my father.

For years, my dad had showered me with love, praises, and validation throughout the many facets of life I pursued—music, academics, sports, art. He was the greatest father I could have ever hoped for. But now, I had committed the most abhorrent crime a son could carry out: treason. I had left the faith of my father, betrayed his trust, and given up my place as his religiously zealous son. I knew that the news about my transformation would shatter him to the core, and I feared his reprimand. I could only pray that he would show me the mercy I had seen him demonstrate time and again over the course of my youth.

One such instance, after a family vacation to Yosemite, my parents made a major financial sacrifice and bought a brand new raft for our family. As kids whose kingdom was the river, we became captains of our very own ship, sailing up and down the murky waterway with reckless abandon.

Just days into our newfound adventures, my older brothers—Matt and Josh—carelessly left the raft on the banks of the river overnight. Dad had already given them countless warnings to retrieve their ship and bring it home at the end of each day. Upon returning to the house at dusk, Father directly questioned if they had brought the raft home, and in response, they lied through their teeth: "Yes."

That night, a torrential downpour flooded the river and the surrounding forest, sending the raft careening down the violent rapids and out of our lives forever. Initially, my brothers tried to conceal the raft's fate from father, but eventually he found out about its demise. He was not happy.

With a belt in hand (something I'd never seen him do before), he chased my barefooted oldest brother out of the house and down the gravel driveway. Josh was screaming in fear and trying to bargain for his life, spewing out endless empty promises as he squealed for help from the only savior he knew—my grandmother, who lived upstairs. Hearing and being overcome by Josh's distress, she called out to my father, stopping him in his tracks and saying, "Don't you hurt my grandson!" My father's response, as he gave up and doubled over gasping for air, was, "I don't want to hurt him; I just want to catch him."

My present transgression was infinitely worse than leaving the raft down by the river. But maybe—just maybe—my father's reaction would be the same, and his mercy would overcome his wrath. Perhaps he, too, wouldn't want to hurt me, but simply catch me.

I finally mustered up the courage to call my parents and reveal my treachery to them. My hands were convulsing as I dialed their number. Dad answered.

"Hello?"

"Hey, Dad," I said somberly.

"Micah!" he exclaimed.

"Dad, I need to talk to you and Mom about what's going on."

"Hi, Son," my mother chimed in.

"Hi, Mom."

"We know what's going on, Son," Dad said. "I talked to your stake president for over an hour this afternoon. He is very concerned about you. He said you have the spirit of the devil in you…"

"Oh…" I mumbled. My heart started pulsating harder. Perhaps Dad had already picked out the proverbial belt for my chastisement.

"They want me to come home and be released. But I don't feel good about it. I think they're going to excommunicate me. I don't know what to do."

"Micah, you need to come home and get this straightened out," he said firmly. "Your stake president loves you and is trying to help you. He will give you an honorable release from your service and everything will be okay. Nothing will happen; he assured me of that—as did your mission president. He told me to encourage you to come home. They're not going to punish you. But you need to do the responsible thing and face this."

"I don't know, Dad…I just don't feel good about it."

"Micah, you have our word that if anything happens, you can go right back to Florida. You need to trust us, and you need to trust your Church leaders. They are only doing what's best for you."

I hesitated. To argue would be useless. Although I suspected ulterior motives behind the Church's petition for me to return to Utah, it would be difficult for my parents to understand. They trusted their leaders, as they should. As I once had.

"Dad, I will sleep on it tonight. If I come, it will be for you and Mom. Nothing and no one else. I…" I wanted to say more, but I couldn't find the words. "Goodnight, Mom and Dad. No matter what, know that I'm secure in Christ. I love you."

"Goodnight, Son. Your mother and I love you more than you know. Whatever happens, you'll always be our son. There is nothing you could do that would ever change that. We are going to get through this together."

CHAPTER 34

SALT-LAND

January 21, 2006

P resident, I've made my decision," I said with a slight tremor in my voice.

"And what decision have you made, Elder Wilder?"

"I will go back to Utah," I disclosed softly.

"I believe that is the right choice, Elder. You must understand that President Hansen only wants what's best for you. You can trust him, I assure you."

Internally I questioned whether he could be trusted, but I was far too tired with little heart to fight anymore.

"Your plane leaves at four o'clock this afternoon. The assistants will be by to pick you up around one thirty. We will see you at the airport, Elder Wilder."

"See you then, President."

I perfunctorily started to pack a bag that was far too small for a permanent move back to Utah. I had no intention of leaving behind the place of my rebirth. This fruitful garden land was my new home.

I tied my tie and stared at my reflection in the mirror. I was astounded to consider that nine days ago, I woke up thinking my life would continue in normalcy and the most frightening prospect of my future was revealing to my parents that I was going to take time off from college in Utah and

291

stay in Florida to work for a season. Now, just over one week later, I had renounced everything for which I had fervently fought my entire life. And as a result, I found myself condemned in the eyes of my religious authorities and I was on a path from which there was no return.

The knocking on the door pulled me out of my reflection.

"Micah, the assistants are here," Erik said through the door. "It's time to go."

"Okay. I'll be right out."

I retrieved my bag and looked at myself in the mirror one last time as a missionary for the Church. I nodded, then mouthed, "Here we go."

The Scarlet Letter

As I sat on the plane staring out the window, I could see the world below me, and it all seemed so distant…and small. I had found something so much greater and grander than anything the world and all its treasures could offer me, and my greatest desire now was to be a faithful witness of the bread of life that had satisfied me eternally.

I leaned forward and rested my head on the seat in front of me. I closed my eyes and said a prayer. "Father, I know I am weak and small, but Your love has given me the strength to stand for Christ. Once again, God, give me Your strength so I can be a witness of Jesus to my family and friends."

I then opened the Bible to a passage where the apostle Paul described his spiritual transformation—which was a perfect parallel of my own journey:

> Whatever gain I had, I counted as loss for the sake of Christ. Indeed, I count everything as loss because of the surpassing worth of knowing Christ Jesus my Lord. For his sake I have suffered the loss of all things and count them as rubbish, in order that I may gain Christ and be found in him, not having a righteousness of my own that comes from the law, but that which comes through faith in Christ (Philippians 3:7-9).

The plane touched down in Salt Lake City late that evening. A plethora of emotions were surging through me. I had no idea how everyone was going to react to what was transpiring. I had been slowly planting seeds of the gospel through my email correspondence with each of my family members, and I could only hope that God would sustain me as I faced my loved ones.

As I threaded my way through the crowds in the airport, I was trying hard not to make eye contact with anyone. It was hard enough to keep my fear and shame suppressed without having it pumped back up to the surface by the friendly and vigorous greetings and handshakes I was enduring from all directions: "Hey Elder…" "How's it going, Elder?" "Good to see you, Elder!" The muggings were coming from every angle from the Utahns who revered and imbued missionaries with a generous amount of celebrity status. Apparently, they could not see the Mormon equivalent of the scarlet letter on my forehead: a giant red *A* denoting that I was an apostate and had broken my covenants by cheating on the Church. If they would have known the embarrassment I was bringing upon my family, I doubt I would have been greeted with so much fanfare.

Making my way through the maze of well-wishers, I finally arrived at the escalator that would cede me down into the bowels of the airport, dumping me out with the rest of my burdens and returned baggage, which had been destined now to pile onto my parents in a proverbial heap. I knew my family would be waiting for me, and my heart was nervously beating like a drum, trying to push its way out of my chest. What was I going to say? My life had radically changed during the twenty-four months we had been apart. Micah Wilder—the son they knew and raised—was dead, and I wasn't certain how they would react to the new man who had been resurrected in place of the old.

While slowly descending, I silently chuckled, realizing that this approaching reunion was hardly the extravagant return I had been dreaming about for two years. I had fantasized about a grand homecoming and a hero's welcome from all my family and friends, who would celebrate my arrival as if I were a returning conqueror. Instead, this would be a quiet and uncelebrated return to my family. No hero's welcome. No awards. No medals of honor. No balloons. Just a vessel on a shameful return from absentia, uncertain as to my future in the world, but certain as to my future in Christ.

When I reached the bottom, a smile crept across my face when I saw that Mom, Dad, Katie, Matt, and his girlfriend, Nicole, were all there waiting for me. My nerves subsided upon seeing the smiles on their faces, and I ran to my mother and embraced her in my arms with tears flowing from my eyes.

"Oh, Son, it's so good to see you," she said as she hugged me tight. Her genuine love for me quickly surmounted my anguish.

"You too, Mom."

My dad approached me next, and with no belt in hand, embraced me with all the fatherly love I could have hoped for.

"I love you, Micah," he said tenderly while patting my back.

Matt and Katie followed, each taking their turns hugging me and welcoming me home. I didn't know what my parents had conveyed to them about why I was concluding my mission three weeks early, but for the moment, they greeted me in love, and the grace of each one of my family members alleviated much of the weight on my shoulders. I could finally breathe a sigh of relief after thirty-six hours of nonstop turmoil.

The Ambush

I seized my bag of worldly possessions and we headed to the car. As I was overtaking my father, he nonchalantly dropped an unexpected bomb on me.

"Micah, President Hansen wants to meet with you as soon as we get home. We will be heading to the stake center tonight."

I was stunned and stopped in my tracks, swinging around to face him and couldn't help but react with contemptuous scorn. My heart sank and my anguish returned.

"He wants to meet with us *this* late?"

Meeting with my religious authority was the *last* thing I wanted to do, and I had not anticipated, being that it was after nine o'clock at night, that he would want to see me right away. But his request was clear: I was to report to his office immediately. *Why so little patience? Why could I not be released in the morning?* And then it hit me: Tomorrow morning was Sunday, the traditional gathering time of the high council, the only ones authorized to conduct an official excommunication hearing at the request of the stake president. It seemed that whatever was being set in motion was on the fast track. It all started to add up: If President couldn't force my repentance tonight, tomorrow morning I would be dishonorably sent to the gallows. No matter how much my parents and others tried to console me that no harm would befall me, I couldn't shake the suspicion that this whole situation was a snare. It had to be.

As I mentally prepared myself for the ambush I knew was awaiting me, and despite the overwhelming stress of the situation that was playing out before me, I took solace in the fact my whole family would be present when I was released from my missionary service. It was a pride-filled Mormon family tradition. This time, I wouldn't face King Saul alone, and my family would serve as my armor and shield during the confrontation. I could count on their presence softening the blows from Hansen. They would be my first line of defense.

Matt, who was closest to my age, perceived my distress and put his arm around me and squeezed me in a halfhearted headlock, as if to show me that no matter what, he loved me. Though he himself was a returned missionary and a faithful member of the Church, his unconditional love overcame any judgment he may have held against me, and I was relieved to have him at my side.

However, as inseparable as Matt and I were, my sister gravitated toward me more than anyone else in the family. I had always been her friend and protector, and that had not changed one iota in the two years I had been gone. She was the family member I had confided in most about the change that was taking place in me, and I had imparted to her the single most important nugget of truth I could think of after having become born again: "Don't make Jesus part of your testimony. Make Jesus Himself your testimony." As I slowly peppered her with what I was learning from the Bible, she wisely took it upon herself to begin reading the New Testament. In many ways, she was already in the tender throes of her own metamorphosis, and I prayed God would open her eyes as He had mine. It was only a matter of time.

We exited the airport, and I noticed how, after nearly two straight years in the sunshine state, the January air was frigid and bitter. The six of us proceeded to the parking garage, and I followed my brother and his girlfriend to his car, along with my sister. My parents, who had driven separately, noticed that I was not following them to their vehicle, and my calculated decision to ride with my siblings in lieu of them left a crushing and painful disappointment registered on their faces.

Although I felt guilty about not joining them, I was not yet ready for any line of questioning that might have been brewing with them. I assumed they were probably chomping at the bit to get me alone before the meeting to ask what I planned to say to my religious authority. After all, if they did have reservations, I could hardly blame them, as the ramifications of my nonconformist testimony could be catastrophic for them, directly affecting their lives, careers, and reputations. However, as much as I sympathized with them, I needed a temporary sanctuary, and I naturally found that asylum with my siblings.

I didn't say much on the drive home. The past few hours had been exhausting, and the emotional and mental toll that had taken place in my heart and mind left me feeling broken and weak. As I contemplated meeting President Hansen, I remembered the passage that had calmed my heart when I was preparing to meet with Sorensen the day before: "Settle it therefore in your minds not to meditate beforehand how to answer, for I will give you a mouth and wisdom…"[112] As much as I attempted to heed the words of Scripture, I couldn't help but ponder what to say to the man who—just the day before—had maliciously referred to me as an anti-Christ. *I came here to be released and I'm asking you to release me,* I repeated to myself.

As we approached our destination, I called my dad to solidify our plans. "Are we all just going to meet at the stake center? Or are we meeting you at the house?" I asked. Dad seemed a little hesitant to respond and he stumbled over his words.

"Actually, uh, Matt and Katie won't be going with us. They will need to drop you off with us at the house." At that moment the car might or might not have kept moving, but the brakes in my head brought everything to a screeching halt as I slid sideways, blocking the road in an act of mental abstention. In an instant, I had lost my armor and my shield. I felt helpless.

Up to this point, everything had been preceded by fear; however, what my father had just said did not foster fear; rather, it brought immediate disappointment and even anger. I now knew that what I was facing was premeditated—everything I had suspected from the night before was true. My own naïve father had been made to lead me into a trap, making me the proverbial scapegoat whose mission would end with Hansen tossing me off a cliff in fear that I would return and reinfect the sheep with my sin. How could I have been so stupid?

"What do you mean they're not coming!" I blurted out. "Why can't they come?"

"I don't know, Son. President Hansen called me just a few minutes ago and requested that your siblings not be present for the releasing."

It *was* an ambush! Even my parents, as innocent as they were, were about to play into the hands of the deceivers and deliver their own flesh and blood up to Saul. Thus far, those outlined in Luke 21:16 were being crossed off the list one by one like clockwork: "You will be delivered up even by parents." I felt sick to my stomach.

Hated for Christ

It was unnervingly dark outside as we arrived at the place I had once called home. I climbed out of the car onto the snow, which crunched under my feet. The sound of my steps was amplified as it echoed through the ravine. It was bitter cold to boot.

I gazed at the world around me. From almost every window of the house, which was perched high on a bluff, it was possible to see spectacular views of the towering mountains. But the connections and feelings I once had for this place were washed away by a violent torrent of my painful present reality. The land I had once presumed to be the pinnacle of God's connection to man on the earth now appeared heavily parched, frightfully dark, and lifeless. This was no longer my home. This was not the life I was going to live, and I could now see past the grand illusion. Utah was a waterless and desolate place, a salt-land where countless people were unknowingly living under spiritual bondage, blinded by the god of this world.

As I contemplated the spiritual destitution around me, God filled my heart with a brokenness for those in darkness. More than anything, I wanted the people of this land—and of the entire world—to know of the righteousness of God revealed in Jesus Christ. I pondered Paul's stirring words concerning his people, the Jews:

> Brothers, my heart's desire and prayer to God for them is that
> they may be saved. For I bear them witness that they have
> a zeal for God, but not according to knowledge. For, being
> ignorant of the righteousness of God, and seeking to estab-
> lish their own, they did not submit to God's righteousness.
> For Christ is the end of the law for righteousness to everyone
> who believes (Romans 10:1-4).

Although my heart was softened toward the spiritually blind of my former community, I was still wrestling with feelings of resentment for my
parents. Frustrated, I hopped into the back of their SUV, where at first
we sat in silence. Then my mom turned on the dome light, spun around,
and with a gentle smile on her face, asked, "Would you like us to pray
before we leave?"

"Sure," I retorted while avoiding eye contact.

"Mike, would you like to say it?" she asked Dad.

He prayed, but I was far too consumed with my own thoughts to listen to a word he said. My mind was set on David, who had been faithful
to God even in times of trial. I thought about how he must have felt as he
faced Goliath, then Saul, then all his enemies rising in a tsunami against
him that seemed to have no end. I knew that my life was not in physical
danger like David's had been, but I was facing a relative Saul of my own.
I wanted the faith that David had—a faith that fully trusted in the Lord
for deliverance.

While lost in my thoughts and fighting a growing sense of antipathy,
Jesus' words pierced my stubborn heart:

> Blessed are those who are persecuted for righteousness' sake,
> for theirs is the kingdom of heaven. Blessed are you when
> others revile you and persecute you and utter all kinds of evil
> against you falsely on my account. Rejoice and be glad, for
> your reward is great in heaven, for so they persecuted the
> prophets who were before you (Matthew 5:10-12).

God's Word convicted me. I knew I needed to stop wallowing in my
self-pity. To be committed to Christ was to be hated for Christ. If I had
been willing to suffer for the word of man, how much more willing should

I be to suffer for the Word of God? As a disciple of Jesus, I was called to rejoice in persecution for His sake and allow Him to work through me. Besides, as Charbel had shown me long ago when I sat in the pew at Calvary Baptist Church, people all over the world endured unspeakable horrors for their faith in Jesus. My cost, in comparison, seemed rather insignificant.

I came to my senses long enough to know that harboring hostility toward my parents was not going to make things any easier for me or them.

"Mom and Dad, I don't feel good about doing this, but I want you to know that I have faith that God will be with me no matter what."

My father sighed and turned to me. "Micah, everything will be fine," he said. "There is nothing to worry about. President promised us that he was simply going to release you and that they won't question you about your beliefs. Trust him."

CHAPTER 35

RELEASED

Alpine, Utah | *January 21, 2006*

After an awkwardly silent but brief five-minute drive, we pulled into the eerily empty parking lot of the church as the clock struck ten. I opened the car door and stepped out into the freezing mountain air. Looking up at the clear sky dotted with striking celestial bodies, I supplicated God in my heart: *I need You once again, Father. Give me strength in my weakness and help me testify of Your love.* I could only hope this meeting would be the closing episode of my two-year rite of passage from childhood to adulthood.

My parents bravely headed toward the towering edifice ahead of me and I dutifully shadowed them. Their eagerness was evidence that ignorance truly was bliss.

As we climbed the stairs to the side door and entered the building, my mother turned to me and gently slid her arm around me. "We're here for you, Son," she whispered.

"I know, Mom."

We cautiously strolled through the dark entryway and made our way around the corner. President Hansen popped out at us unexpectedly, as if he had been shrouding himself there in the shadows all along.

"Hello, Brother Wilder," he said with a broad smile while shaking my father's hand. "Good to see you."

Stake President Hansen was a seasoned man, probably in his late six-ties, and even though it was very late, he was dressed for the occasion over which he was about to preside. He was tall and thin, wore glasses, and had on a black suit. His appearance was nearly identical to that of President Sorensen the day before, sans the nametag.

After greeting my parents, he looked at me and leered in a most bizarre and unwelcoming way. "Hello, Elder Wilder. Good to see you," he said as he vice-gripped my hand.

"You too," I replied disingenuously.

President Hansen escorted us to his office, and we sat down across from him at his large mahogany desk. I glanced around the room, taking note of the enormous painting depicting the First Vision of Joseph Smith, and directly behind Hansen, centered over his chair, an opulent picture of the three highest leaders of the Church.

I then turned my attention to the man in front of me. Before the inter-rogation had even begun, I could already sense a root of bitterness welling up inside of me. I prayed to God that He would fill me with love. Love is what had saved me, and love is what could save this man.

"So, Elder Wilder, does the Spirit speak Spanish?" he asked, seem-ingly jokingly, perhaps fostering for my parents the illusion of a friendly atmosphere.

"Much better than I do," I responded with feigned amusement.

"Michael," he said turning toward my dad, "would you please open us in prayer and invite the Spirit of the Lord to be here with us tonight?"

As my father began his prolonged King James English prayer, I directly petitioned God for strength so that His vessel would not be broken, no matter the cost before me. I understood that at this time, my physical life was not in danger because of my profession of faith (in contrast to the many Christians around the world who did encounter physical persecu-tion), but I was facing a loss I was afraid to incur.

House upon the Sand

When my dad concluded his prayer, President promptly began the interview.

"So, Elder Wilder, how was your mission?" he asked.

What? How was my mission? *I could write a book about that,* I thought to myself. But I conceded to give a simple answer.

"Good, President. I learned a lot."

"And what did you learn, Elder Wilder?"

This was it. Now was my God-given opportunity to witness of the gospel—not just to this religious man, but to my parents, whom I loved with all my heart. Perhaps this would be the defining hour for the Spirit to trim my wick and elevate the mantle in preparation for lighting the path to their salvation as well.

"Well, I suppose more than anything, I've learned that God's love and mercy are so much deeper than I ever knew. I now know, with unwavering certainty, that Christ died for my sins and that by His grace I have been saved and forgiven. I know where I stand with God, and I know that if I die right now, I will be with Him—not because of what I've done for God, but because of what He has done for me." I was fighting back a growing emotion that was welling up within me. "Jesus Christ is the only way to eternal life. I love Him. I know Him. I want to live for Him. I know that now more than ever."

Hansen gazed at me with emotionless eyes while slowly nodding his head (but certainly not in agreement). Based on our conversation from the day before, he most likely already knew the gist of what I would say. He must have been using the time to assess my weaknesses and plan his next move.

"Well, Elder Wilder," he said softly yet provocatively, "thank you for sharing your testimony with me. As your priesthood leader, I feel inspired to share *my* testimony of the restored gospel with you." He paused for a moment and took off his glasses, folding his arms across his chest while leaning forward and resting them on the desk.

"You know," he began quietly, "a testimony of the truth is perhaps our most valued possession as members of Christ's Church. And so, I would like to share my testimony with you about this great work of the restoration," he said while increasing the volume of his voice. "I know, Elder Wilder, that (1) the boy Joseph Smith went into the woods looking for answers, and in his sincere desire to know the truth, was visited by God the Father and His Son Jesus Christ." Our eyes were fixed on each other as his voice became increasingly authoritative and louder, his nostrils flaring as he spoke. "He did see them, and they did speak to him!" he shouted. "I *know* he did, for the Spirit of God has witnessed it to me!"

His words were unexpectedly harsh and punitive.

"Young man, Joseph Smith *was* a prophet of God. (2) He restored Christ's true Church to the earth, including the priesthood authority that is necessary to administer the proper ordinances of salvation—an authority found only in *this* Church. Elder Wilder, eternal life—exaltation in the highest kingdom—can be found through no other organization!"

Hansen was progressively getting more boisterous as he testified of each point, pausing just long enough each time to see how I was reacting. I was vigilant not to provide any feedback to his brooding exhibition and continued to look at him calmly as he blasted me with the same sulfurous fires of hell that I had discharged on Benson. He was a living testimony to the blindness that once held me captive.

As I listened, I could see with crystal clarity the stark and disturbing contrast between the gospel I once followed and the gospel as revealed in Scripture—and the testimonies that accompanied each. This man wasn't testifying of the good news of God's promised grace and mercy in Christ. Rather, he was proclaiming a complicated belief system rooted in the testimony of a man and an established earthly authority that kept one perpetually jumping through hoops—a gospel of performance, obedience, laws, and works. A false gospel.

With each word that Hansen spoke, his frustration seemed to grow exponentially. By now he was discharging his testimony with derision.

"(3) He was led by the angel Moroni to the gold plates by which he translated the Book of Mormon, the most correct and true book on Earth, and the fullness of the everlasting gospel. I testify that a man will get nearer to God through this book than through any other book, including the Bible!" he yelled while holding up the Book of Mormon in his right hand.

It was apparent that Hansen's blatant declaration about the supremacy of the Book of Mormon over the Bible was an attempt to illicit a reaction from me. I suppose he expected me to bow down at his religious authority and humbly recant everything that I had said earlier, but I didn't take the bait. Instead, I sat motionless and offered no visible response.

"(4) Today, we have a living prophet who leads God's kingdom and Church. He is the very mouthpiece of God and the *only one* with the authority to receive revelation for the world. He is the one true prophet and high priest on the earth!" he said with roaring anger as he shot his last silver bullet directly at my heart in a final, futile attempt to get me to surrender.

President sat fixed in his chair, glaring at me with eyes and nostrils flaring, waiting and daring me to counter. His defensive attitude seemed rather excessive considering I had yet to verbally offer any rebuttal. What was most disheartening, however, was that as he so vehemently verbalized the pillars of his religious testimony, he had conveniently omitted what should have been the central component: (5) Jesus Christ—the rock, the foundation. In his witness of his religious beliefs, he hadn't testified of Christ once. Akin to my mission president the day before, a declaration of Jesus did not come from his lips, and therefore, the Spirit of God was not revealed in him.

By now, Hansen must have known that I was refusing to display any interest in his pontification. But rather than conclude his fruitless endeavor, he unexpectedly opted to appeal to me in goodwill.

"How do you *feel* about my testimony, Elder Wilder?" he asked with surprising tenderness as he unfolded his arms and smiled.

His question was a tactic we had used as missionaries hundreds of times with potential converts. The manner of solidifying truth in the Church was through feelings—a "burning in the bosom"[113]—by which the Spirit of God would testify truth to the individual. I had learned how dangerous and susceptible to deception this method of testing truth could be, and how contradictory it was to the Word of God, which states that "the heart is deceitful above all things"[114] and "out of the heart come[s]... false witness."[115] Instead of relying on feelings to gauge truth, Scripture tells us in 1 John 4:1, "Beloved, do not believe every spirit, but test the spirits to see whether they are from God, for many false prophets have gone out into the world."

"I respect what you believe, President," I said diplomatically but firmly, "but it didn't impact me, and it doesn't change what I know to be the truth. I'm no longer putting my faith into how I feel. I base everything I believe on the simple gospel of Christ as found in the Bible. What you have witnessed of does not align with God's Word, so I cannot accept it as truth. My testimony is now in Christ alone; I don't need any of those other things. I'll never turn back now that I've found Jesus and His saving grace."

This marked the first time I had verbally witnessed to my parents that I no longer had a testimony in four of the foundational pillars of the Church. Regardless of what suppositions had been communicated to them by my religious leaders, the condemning confession finally came directly from the horse's mouth. I was afraid to see their reactions, so I continued to gaze straight forward at Hansen.

"If you think what you have found is Jesus, son, you are sorely mistaken! You are just like Nehor in Alma 1. This path that you think is the right path is the path of deceit…the path of the devil!" he roared in a burst of anger that sent spit flying from his mouth.

Hansen's accusation finally gave me enough confidence to glance over at my parents to see how they were reacting to his disciplinary speech. They both appeared aghast.

My mother, whose face was beet red, looked like she was now bearing my scarlet letter, and her embarrassment and shame over Hansen's behavior could not be concealed. My father was exhibiting a tic that I knew all too well as an indication of oncoming fury—his eyes were flinching and his head bobbing up and down.

Fearing that my father might lose his composure, I remained silent and calm, which was, unexpectedly, becoming easier and easier. I now knew that Hansen was doing more damage to himself on his own accord than I could have ever tried to explain or reason to my parents. The deed had been done: the leadership had lied to my father and broken their bond. Hansen had put a crack in the armor that I possibly could not, and I prayed God would use that as a catalyst to bring my parents to salvation.

Story of Love

I turned my eyes back to President, seated on his self-imposed throne before me. A leader that I once feared and revered less than twenty-four months ago was now a shadow of his former self. He had gone from a spiritual giant to a diminutive man. My heart broke for him.

"So, who is this young girl that you are going to marry?" he asked, now bringing things to a very personal level. Although trying to appear considerate, his contempt was still clearly detectable.

"Her name is Alicia Devitt. She lives here in Alpine," I answered, wondering why he was bringing my bride-to-be into the conversation. His eyes became large and he nodded and smiled.

"I know the Devitts very well!" he said enthusiastically. "I know Alicia's father. He is in the bishopric of his ward. A very kind and upright man."

Alicia's father no doubt held a respectable position in his congregation and in the community. Not only was he a multigenerational Mormon, but he oversaw many of the duties of the local church. He was a good and reputable man—we were in agreement there.

"I spoke with him a few days ago, Elder Wilder, and he seemed to have some severe concerns about you." Hansen's voice changed, his smile faded, and he no longer maintained his pretense. "Alicia is a very good girl from an upstanding family. Don't take her away from that, Elder Wilder. Her father does not feel good about the path you are leading her on. Frankly, I agree with him. She has *not* made a wise choice in you. You are poisoning her."

At this point it took every ounce of strength I had to sustain my composure. The only outlet I had was my rapidly springing knee. As challenging as it was for me to remain still, I didn't give him the reaction he was pursuing. Regardless of his accusation, I knew that I had done nothing more than lovingly lead Alicia to the truth in God's Word. That assurance alone gave me enough comfort to remain silent, but Hansen wasn't done.

"You are taking her away from Christ, young man! I will not allow you to continue leading this girl on a dangerous path away from this Church. You are lost, but we don't have to lose her too. I fear for both of your souls!" he bellowed. His face was now glistening with the first signs of sweat.

The irony of his indictment was that for the first time in my life I didn't fear for my soul at all. I now had the guarantee of my good standing with God through the offering of His Son. I no longer had to work for my salvation in order to be saved after all I could do; I was now saved because of all that Christ had done! He died for me; He gave His life for mine. And nothing could separate me from the love of God in Christ Jesus.

As I deliberated over Hansen's ignorant allegation, I reflected on the volley of letters that had ping-ponged between Alicia and me over the past two years. At the same time that God had been miraculously healing my heart and revealing His infinite love for me, He was also transforming Alicia's heart; and through me, she was given the same challenge that had forever changed my life and now hers: Read the Bible like a child. Through God's grace, Alicia, too, had come to know the sufficiency of the blood of Jesus to cleanse her of her sins and wash away her guilty conscience, and she was born again to a living hope through the resurrection of Jesus Christ. God's incredible story of love had been written on both of our lives.

> Micah, my love, you have been a true friend to me and the one who has taught me to know of God's amazing love. You have brought me to a place where I have found rest in Christ. You have been the bearer of hope that has shown me where to find Light. Your hope in Christ's love and in our love provides me the greatest source of happiness and joy. And in all this love for you I know—for it consumes me—that Christ's love is all, is eternal, and is everything we need.
>
> Your friend forever, Alicia[116]

Now I could so clearly see the remarkable metamorphosis both of us had undergone as a result of God's love. I decided at this point I had contained myself for long enough, and the cork went flying out of the bottle.

"I am sorry you feel this way, sir. But I am not leading Alicia away from Christ, but *to* Christ. He is our Lord and King, and we will live the rest of our lives for Him, reflecting His love and witnessing of His grace. You are in no place to tell me where God is leading me unless through His Word. I am and will always be focused on Christ alone, and I will tell the world of the true gospel and salvation through Jesus. I am not ashamed of the gospel of my Lord."

By God's grace—and to my astonishment—the words had flown from my mouth with calmness and assurance. I knew that I was walking with Christ and following His gospel. His promises gave me peace, but President Hansen still wouldn't quit until every ounce of respect my parents and I once held for him was purged.

"Your doctrines are confused, Elder. Your mind has been twisted by the devil and you have fallen into the corrupt teachings of being 'saved by grace.' You are deceived, taking the easy way out with your cheap grace. You think all you can do is accept Jesus and that's it?" he asked with sarcasm.

President had touched on an important point. Growing up, I was taught by the Church that Christians believed in a cheap grace. I thought that these self-proclaimed "born-againers" would throw their hands in the air, declare "I'm saved," and then live for sin, indulging in every desire of the flesh without believing that works had any part in the Christian life.

Now that I myself had become born again and received the life-changing love of God, my perspective had changed radically. I now realized how much love transmutes the heart: When I came to know and understand the immeasurable love that God had for me and finally fathom the grace—the unmerited favor—He had shown to me, I didn't see that as a license for me to sin as I pleased. In fact, it had the *opposite* effect. What child, knowing the undeserved love and forgiveness given to them by their father, wants to deliberately take advantage of that love? For me, that love removed my desire to sin against God. I didn't want to sin—I *hated* it. I wanted to live a life that reflected the marvelous love that had transformed me. I wanted to love because He first loved me.

However—as I had learned repeatedly throughout my life—no matter how hard I tried, I struggled with the weakness of my flesh daily and would always fall short of God's glory. As Paul lamented, "Wretched man that I am! Who will deliver me from this body of death?"[117] So what, then, is our hope? Jesus! Paul continues just two verses later, "There is therefore now no condemnation for those who are in Christ Jesus."[118] The beauty of God's grace is that no matter what, if we are in Christ, we are forgiven!

So no, grace is certainly *not* a license to sin as we please. Rather, it is the promise of forgiveness and redemption through the blood of Christ even when we do sin. And no, grace is not cheap. It cost Jesus the ultimate price. But to me, and to all mankind, it has been offered freely to be received by faith. And that grace, once received, is like a heart transplant. It changes us from the inside out, makes us new creations, and gives us an inborn desire to want to love and follow God because we know the depth of His love for us. That's what President Hansen—and the entire Church leadership—didn't understand.

Free

I was weary and determined to bring this charade to an end. This had gone on for long enough. The compulsion to deliver the message I had rehearsed earlier finally hit me, so I rose out of my chair to speak. He observed me suspiciously, almost as if he was expecting me to hit him square in the face.

"President, no longer can you put down my Lord and Savior Jesus. I did not come here to discuss doctrines. If you would like to do that, we can arrange another meeting. I came here to be released, and I'm asking you to release me." I then sat back down and stole a look at my parents, who were paralyzed with disbelief.

President was in a predicament. Without a doubt the last thing he wanted to do was submit to my request, but he had exhausted all other options. None of his methods were effectively shaking my testimony or bringing me to repentance as he must have hoped, and now he was being forced to live up to his original promise to release me.

After a long silence, he dejectedly dropped his shoulders and said, "I release you, Elder Wilder. You are no longer a full-time missionary for the Church."

With a full awareness that it was God's limitless grace that had brought me to this point, my heart was filled with compassion for this man who embodied the bondage that had once enslaved me. As much as I wanted to, I couldn't place self-righteous judgment on President for what I per-ceived to be his wrongdoings. Rather I was called to forgive him as I had been forgiven.

Inconceivably, even after Jesus was spat upon, cursed, reviled, mocked, beaten, and His beard pulled out by the roots, He still petitioned His Father to forgive those who wronged Him. I was equally as guilty as those who had committed such atrocities toward Jesus, and yet God was still willing to forgive me. After all, I was the chief of sinners—even God's very enemy—yet He had so liberally offered me His abiding love and mercy. If God could save me, He could save anybody. I was evidence of the broad reach of His grace. Humbled by God's everlasting kindness, I knew what the core of my ministry had to be moving forward: love.

President Hansen looked defeated. He stood up, his confidence gone, and forcing a counterfeit smile, he said to me, "We would like you to come before the high council tomorrow morning at eight o'clock to report on your missionary service."

This was no insignificant request, but it was indicative as to their plan all along to break their promise and excommunicate me. Although they had already determined my fate, I had no intention of subjecting myself to interrogation by a dozen Church leaders only to be convicted of living the true gospel of Jesus Christ and then being banished. I would run as David did to a new land and a new home.

I nodded, shook his hand, and walked away. My mission was over. Through it all, I kept my promise to my father. I had served with all my heart.

———

Not a word was spoken in the car on the way back to my parents' house. In less than forty-eight hours, everything in my life had changed profoundly. God had solidified a new trajectory for His lowly servant David, and I would never return to the life I had always known. My roots had been ripped out from under me and I was replanted, grounded now in true, abiding love and faith through the Word of God.

Jesus of Nazareth, my great Redeemer and Savior, had traversed the mountainside searching for me, the lost and hopeless sheep who had gone far astray in the wilderness. And in His unfailing grace, He had found me, placed me upon the same shoulders that bore the cross, and carried me to green pastures, to the glory of God in heaven.

I was free.

EPILOGUE

The next morning, I—along with my parents' support—elected not to attend the meeting with the high council. Then, after a short but tumultuous thirty-six hours in Utah, I returned to Florida and made the Edgewater Hotel my permanent home. Three days later, on my twenty-first birthday, Alicia and I went to Disney World and eloped—truly making it the happiest place on Earth. We began our new lives as disciples of Jesus and have been grounded on the rock of Christ ever since. That very week, I began writing my story, and continued to do so—on and off—for the next *fifteen* years. In that time, it was both a labor of love and source of unending frustration. It has only come to fruition by God's grace.

The path moving forward as a young Christian was not always easy. I made many mistakes and learned countless hard lessons along the way. But God's grace was and has always been greater than my foolishness. And even in my weakness and simplicity, God used me to plant seeds in the lives of my loved ones. Although there was some tension in our familial relationships for a time, Mom, Dad, Matt, and Katie all accepted my invitation to read the Bible like a child—perhaps out of a thirst for truth, or out of sheer, morbid curiosity. Either way, seeds were planted, and God began to give growth over time.

At the time, my older brother, Matt, was completing his junior year at BYU as a piano performance major. Matt intensely read the New

Testament over the subsequent months and God miraculously opened his eyes to the glorious gospel of Jesus Christ. Through the Holy Spirit, he was eventually crucified with Christ and raised into newness of life as a follow of Jesus, along with his girlfriend, Nicole. They have been married since 2006 and have a beautiful daughter, Tessa, who was born in 2010.

Shortly after returning to Utah from his LDS mission in June of 2006, Joseph Warren received the free gift of eternal life through faith in Jesus Christ and he, too, was born again. He immediately left the only life he had ever known in Utah and moved to Florida to walk in discipleship of the Lord Jesus.

And so, in the summer of 2006, Erik's proclamation was fulfilled, and I—along with Matt, Joseph, and two other young men recently out of the Mormon Church—founded Adam's Road, a music ministry dedicated to proclaiming the gospel through song and testimony. The five of us new Christians immediately started writing music as a vehicle to share our newfound faith. Over time, that vision focused completely on directly putting Scripture—God's Word—into song.

In April of 2007, Alicia and I welcomed our first child into the world, a beautiful son named Jacob Andrew. A teenager now, Jacob has blossomed into an incredible young man. He is loving, smart, selfless, compassionate, and funny. In August of 2008, we were blessed with our second son, the tenderhearted Benjamin Micah, a passionate and thoughtful kid who shares my propensity for emotion. In February of 2010, God sent us a third boy, the perpetually joyful Timothy Schuyler, whose infectious laugh and smile has been the source of joy for many people. All three boys love the Lord Jesus and strive each day to follow Him in discipleship. What more can I ask for as a father?

In October of 2007, I had the privilege of officiating Katie's wedding. She had been born again through reading the Word of God her senior year of high school. Somehow, my gangly and goofy friend, Joseph, managed to hypnotize my unsuspecting sister and convince her to marry him (I never should have shown him that picture). They remain happily married in Christ to this day, and Katie has been an integral part of the Adam's Road Ministry since—both in the operation of the Edgewater Hotel and in contributing her angelic voice to the band.

My parents' path to eternal life was not without its impediments. My mother and father experienced a long and rather arduous road of reading the Bible and coming to fully know and understand the love of God…and then live out the repercussions of their faith. But, to God's amazing and wondrous grace, they did. In late 2007, after eighteen months of fervently studying God's Word, my mother resigned her tenured position at BYU and she and my father officially left the Church to follow Christ unreservedly. They moved to southwest Florida shortly thereafter and have called the Sunshine State their home ever since. They founded their own ministry, Ex-Mormon Christians United for Jesus, and have travelled the world proclaiming the gospel of Jesus Christ. My mother has detailed her moving testimony in her own book, *Unveiling Grace,* which essentially picks up where my book leaves off and gives her vantage point to the many life-altering events that brought them to grace. Without a doubt, one of the greatest and most fulfilling aspects of my life has been witnessing the salvation of my parents and siblings. To say that God did a miraculous work in my family would be an enormous understatement. Praise God!

Shortly after moving to Florida, I contacted pastor Alan Benson by phone after learning he moved out of state. "Pastor Benson, my name is Elder Wilder. Do you remember me?" I asked. "Oh, I remember you!" he said. I conveyed to him all that God had done in my life and for two hours, we laughed and cried together. During that call he made a powerful statement that I have never forgotten: "I never knew anything I said to you had any impact on your life. In fact, I walked away from that meeting feeling like I had failed." His confession has been a source of hope and encouragement for me, knowing that oftentimes when we share the gospel with lost people, we rarely see the fruit in the moment. It helps to remember that we are called only to lovingly plant and water the seeds—only God can give the growth. Pastor Benson and I finally reunited in person in 2014, and I was given the privilege of sharing my testimony at his (now former) church. We remain close brothers in the Lord and he refers to me as his Timothy—a great and humbling honor.

Pastor Shaw and I reconnected in a way only God could orchestrate (another story for another time). He still lives locally in Central Florida and we continue our deep friendship and love for the Lord. Two of his sons, Dominick and Jonathan, have been regular vocal contributors on Adam's Road albums over the years.

As for Erik, he and I remain great friends. He is currently retired and generously volunteers his time as the official bus driver for Adam's Road.

For nearly a decade and a half, our ministry has continued faithful in our calling to put the Bible to music, proclaim the gospel through our testimonies, and encourage and equip the body of Christ to fulfill its supreme purpose: the Great Commission. We spend four months and nearly 25,000 miles each year living on a bus, travelling throughout North America declaring the good news of Christ. Through the years, we have grown in the knowledge and grace of God. Although our ministry has matured and our membership has changed over time, our mission has not.

In 2013, two of our founding members left the ministry for other pursuits, but Joseph and Matt continue to serve in full-time capacities with Adam's Road. Then, in 2015, God mercifully sent us a young, shy girl—Lila LeBaron—from a polygamous Mormon offshoot community in Mexico to intern with our ministry. Lila has metamorphosed into a powerful and bold witness of the gospel of Jesus Christ and now serves as our lead vocalist.

To this day, the Edgewater Hotel continues to serve as a home and "tent-making" operation for much of our ministry team. As Paul the apostle made tents to supply his own living in order to alleviate that financial burden from the church, we have done the same through our humble bed and breakfast. Through the hotel, God provides all our personal financial needs so that we, too, can offer the gospel free of charge, as inspired by the words of Paul: "What then is my reward? That in my preaching I may present the gospel free of charge, so as not to make full use of my right in the gospel."[119]

We are blessed to have an incredible team of faithful disciples and followers of Christ who work tirelessly to support our ministry through many capacities, with all being unified in heart and mind. In a sense, we all act and live as a modern Acts 2 church: "And all who believed were together and had all things in common" (verse 44). We live and work for a purpose greater than ourselves, holding up high the light of the world, keeping our eyes fixed on Him and not the fading dreams and treasures of this earth.

ec

The day is soon coming when every knee will bow and every tongue confess that Jesus Christ is Lord. My greatest hope and prayer, until that time, is that my life can be a testimony to the vast and wonderful love of God, and that through such a flawed and wretched man like me, others may come to know the Christ and His immeasurable love. Grace and peace.

AFTERWORD

ALAN BENSON

The author of the book of Hebrews wrote, "The word of God is living and active, sharper than any two-edged sword, piercing to the division of soul and of spirit, of joints and of marrow, and discerning the thoughts and intentions of the heart" (Hebrews 4:12). For as long as I have been a pastor, I have not only believed these words to be true, I have claimed them weekly as I would stand to preach. But never have I seen the amazing power of the Word of God at work in a life like I have since the days of my gospel encounter with Micah Wilder. In Micah, the Lord allowed me to meet a young man who had a tremendous zeal for his religion. Years later, Micah and I met again, only this time, his zeal had been redirected toward his Savior. In that initial meeting in my office, I had no idea what the Lord was going to do as a result of our conversations.

While it is always special to meet with a person and share the life-changing gospel of Jesus Christ, add to that the dynamic that the person is a devout follower of another faith, and the encounter takes on an added significance. By God's grace, my meeting with Micah was not marked by angry rhetoric and dismissive attitudes. The Holy Spirit allowed passionate dialogue through which the gospel was made clear. That said, it was not human conversation or argumentative convincing that made an impact in

Micah's life. Rather, as Micah read the Word of God, it gripped his heart and led him to saving faith in Jesus Christ.

This was the beginning of some wonderful relationships. God's Word was not merely a means of introducing Micah to Christ, it was the means of a growing, life-changing relationship with Christ. As Micah "read the Bible as a child," setting aside prior biases or misconceptions, it brought him to faith in Christ. And he has since continued to study the Word of God with fresh eyes, which has led him to a life of faithful service for the Lord.

In Romans 10:13-14, Paul wrote, "'Everyone who calls on the name of the Lord will be saved.' How then will they call on him in whom they have not believed? And how are they to believe in him of whom they have never heard? And how are they to hear without someone preaching?" The global impact that Micah and Adam's Road is having as they take the gospel to their generation has been remarkable—particularly as they reach young adherents to the Church of Jesus Christ of Latter-day Saints with the true gospel of Christ. The apostle Paul wrote in Romans 1:16, "I am not ashamed of the gospel, for it is the power of God for salvation to everyone who believes." *Passport to Heaven* presents Micah's story of being gripped by the grace of the gospel. However, his conversion is just the beginning of a beautiful story of thousands of other people hearing of this gospel through Micah and Adam's Road.

The other wonderful relationship that has grown from that initial encounter in my office is the friendship between Micah and me. Scripture tells us that Barnabas mentored the apostle Paul, whom God transformed and used to change the world. This Paul became an inspiration to Barnabas and his future ministry. While I am blessed to claim Micah as "my son in the faith," his life of faith is a constant challenge to me. His love for Christ, the Word of God, and people is truly an inspiration that rebukes my own apathy and distraction.

Paul asked the believers at Colossae to pray "that God may open to us a door for the word, to declare the mystery of Christ, on account of which I am in prison—that I may make it clear, which is how I ought to speak." In turn, he challenged them to "walk in wisdom toward outsiders, making the best use of the time. Let your speech always be gracious, seasoned with salt, so that you may know how you ought to answer each person" (Colossians 4:3-6).

What a heart for evangelizing the lost Paul displays! We must be looking for gospel opportunities, and when the Lord brings them, we must be prepared to speak kind and careful words that season the conversation. In *Passport to Heaven*, you can see that God had been working behind the scenes, preparing Micah's heart for his encounter with the Bible. What you don't see is that God had also been preparing my heart. Through recent conversations, the need to work through conflicts, and teaching about how to share the gospel with people of other faiths, my approach to having a conversation with zealous Mormon missionaries was very different than what would have been typical for me.

At that time, God had done a humbling work in my life. As a result, I didn't brush off Micah just because he was a Mormon. A humbled belief in the power of the gospel and a ready awareness of my own unworthiness and inability compelled me to give my best because this was an opportunity that the Lord had given. Out of love for the gospel and compassion for Micah, I prayed, prepared, and fully engaged with him, believing that this might be the only opportunity I would have. And God did the rest.

As we continue through life, we need to pray for God to give us opportunities, and we need to be prepared and "prayed up" when they come. When a door opens for us to share the gospel, our role is to point the person to the life-transforming, soul-saving Scriptures, then place that person in God's hands. Passport to Heaven is a testament to the fact that when we are faithful to the simple task of sharing the gospel and connecting people to the Word, God can do incredible things we might never know about until we get to the other side of heaven.

It is my prayer that as a result of reading this story, you will not only come to appreciate one man's personal journey to faith, but that you will be gripped by the power of God's Word and the beauty of the gospel in such a way that you will be inspired with renewed passion to live out your faith and be ever ready to speak as an ambassador for Christ.

Soli Deo gloria!

APPENDIX A:

CHRONOLOGICAL TIMELINE OF EVENTS

Childhood in Indiana: 1989–1999 (Chapter 13)

Teenage years in Utah: 1999–2003 (Chapter 14)

First meet Alicia: September 2002 (Chapter 14)

Missionary Training Center (MTC): February–April 2004
  (Chapters 3–4)

First hear about Erik: April 20, 2004 (Chapter 15)

Meeting Erik at the Edgewater Hotel: June 1, 2004 (Chapter 16)

Encounter with Pastor Shaw: June 4, 2004 (Chapter 6)

Visiting Calvary Baptist Church: June 27, 2004 (Chapter 8)

Meeting with Pastor Benson: June 29, 2004 (Chapters 9–11)

Hurricane Charley: August 12, 2004 (Chapters 17–18)

Hurricane Frances: September 5, 2004 (Chapter 19)

Hurricane Jeanne: September 26, 2004 (Chapter 20)

Schuyler's passing: August 8, 2005 (Chapter 22)

Love elders zone meeting: October 11, 2005 (Chapter 23)

Hurricane Wilma: October 24, 2005 (Chapter 24)

Zone leader conference: October 27, 2005 (Chapter 25)

Demotion and transfer to Beverly Hills: October 31, 2005 (Chapter 26)

Born-again experience: January 15-16, 2006 (Chapter 27)

Final zone conference testimony: January 18, 2006 (Chapter 30)

Meeting with President Sorensen: January 20, 2006 (Chapters 5, 7, 12, 21, 28, 29)

Reading Erik's letter: January 20, 2006 (Chapter 31)

Bingham's betrayal: January 20, 2006 (Chapter 32)

Meeting Sorensen at hotel: January 20, 2006 (Chapter 33)

Returning to Utah: January 21, 2006 (Chapter 34)

Meeting with President Hansen: January 21, 2006 (Chapter 35)

Moving back to Florida: January 23, 2006 (Epilogue)

Eloping with Alicia at Disney World: January 26, 2006 (Epilogue)

Founding of Adam's Road: July 2006 (Epilogue)

PHOTOS

I'm a spitting image of my father (1970)

The quintessential Mormon family (1985)

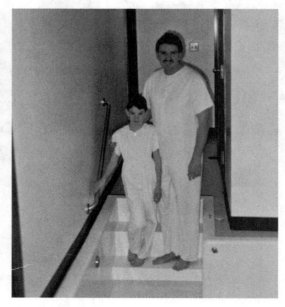

My Mormon baptism at age 8 (1993)

Me, Schuyler, and Ryan in Indiana (1999)

The Wilder family in Zion (2000)

Alicia and me at the Salt Lake Temple my senior year of high school (2002)

Opening my mission letter (2003)

Saying goodbye to my parents at the MTC (2004)

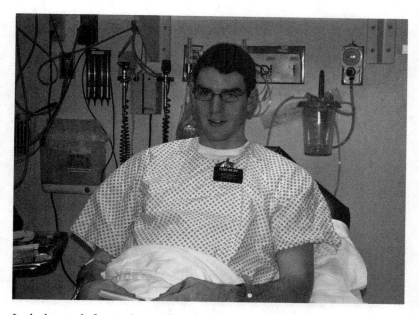

In the hospital after my lung collapsed, zealously studying (2004)

Arriving in Florida, ready to make converts! (2004)

Meeting the baby-faced Elder Joseph Warren (2004)

The resplendent Lake Apopka (2004)

The Edgewater Hotel

Ready for Hurricane Charley (2004)

The infamous water pipe disaster (2004)

At the Red Cross shelter with Elder Gaertner during Hurricane Frances (2004)

Alicia and me eloping at Disney World (2006)

Dad and Mom getting baptized in Israel (2011)

Jacob, Alicia, and Ben on the banks of the White River (2014)

Reuniting with Pastor Benson for the first time since my mission (2014)

The Wilder Family: Matt, Dad, Katie, Mom, Josh, and me (2015)

Nothing but smiles with Pastor Shaw (2019)

Baptizing my oldest son, Jacob, as a follower of Jesus (2019)

Jacob, Alicia, Timothy, and Benjamin: my gifts from God (2020)

Adam's Road Ministry: Joseph, me, Lila, and Matt (2020)

NOTES

1. A mission president is a spiritual overseer who presides over the missionaries serving in a geographic area known as a mission.

2. A stake center is a regional LDS (Latter-day Saint, or Mormon) church building.

3. Email from Erik (January 17, 2006), from the author's personal files.

4. Luke 21:12-13

5. Luke 21:14-16

6. Matthew 16:24-26

7. Matthew 19:29

8. Excerpt from author's personal journal entry (March 21, 2004).

9. Excerpt from author's personal journal entry (January 12, 2006).

10. My father was married at the time that he joined the LDS Church and was therefore not permitted to go on a full-time mission, which is reserved for unmarried young men and women.

11. The Prophet is the highest spiritual leader and President of the entire LDS Church.

12. Excerpts from author's official LDS mission call (November 4, 2003).

13. The "Brethren" is a nickname for the upper echelon of Church leadership, usually referring to the fifteen highest leaders—the Prophet, his two counselors, and the Twelve Apostles.

14. See Luke 14:28

15. The Word of Wisdom is a set of dietary restrictions, in which hot drinks, such as coffee and tea, are forbidden (see Doctrine and Covenants 89).

16. See Doctrine and Covenants 1:38

17. See Luke 10:25-37

18. See 2 Timothy 2:24-25

19. See Luke 22:14-23

20. See Ephesians 2:19-22

21. A ward is a local LDS congregation, defined by geographical boundaries.

22. The Standard Works are the four books of official scriptural canon in the Church: the Book of Mormon, the Bible, the Doctrine and Covenants, and the Pearl of Great Price.

23. James 1:5 (KJV)

24. Amos 3:7 (KJV)

25. See Book of Mormon, Moroni 10:4

26. 1 Corinthians 15:3-4

27. John 1:12

28. 1 Timothy 2:5

29. Romans 12:4-5

30. Matthew 24:35

31. Matthew 16:18

32. Romans 10:4

33. Galatians 2:16

34. See Book of Mormon, 2 Nephi 25:23

35. Ephesians 2:8-9

36. See James 2:26

37. John 8:31-32

38. Book of Mormon, 2 Nephi 33:10-11,14

39. Matthew 1:1

40. In LDS theology, a man and woman must be married in the temple to receive eternal life in the highest (celestial) kingdom of heaven.

41. 1 Corinthians 2:9

42. In Mormon theology, an individual cannot sin—and subsequently be held accountable for that sin—until they are eight years of age.

43. See Romans 4:4-8

44. "Like Saul he [David] was guilty of grave crimes; but unlike Saul, he was capable of true contrition and was therefore able to find forgiveness, except in the murder of Uriah. As a consequence David is still unforgiven…Because of his transgressions, he has fallen from his exaltation…But he paid, and is paying, a heavy price for his disobedience to the commandments of God." See at https://www.churchofjesuschrist.org/study/scriptures/bd/david?lang=eng

45. See Doctrine and Covenants 82:7: "…but that soul who sinneth shall the former sins return, saith the Lord your God."

46. The Aaronic Priesthood is the lesser of two special priesthood authorities in the LDS Church, given to qualifying young men beginning at the age of twelve, allowing them to perform certain tasks such as administering the sacrament (communion).

47. See Matthew 23:27-28

48. "Happy Valley" is the nickname for Utah County.

49. The patriarch is specifically set apart and endowed with the gift of communicating God's plan and will for individual lives of Church members by direct revelation from God.

50. The First Presidency consists of the three highest leaders of the LDS Church—the President (Prophet) and his two counselors.

51. The Quorum of the Twelve Apostles is the second-highest group of Church leaders, comprising twelve men deemed to be Apostles.

52. An investigator is a non-Mormon individual who is investigating the Church for prospective baptism.

53. A zone leader is a missionary who oversees a geographic region within the mission boundaries, usually comprising sixteen to twenty-two missionaries.

54. A bishop is the overseer of a local congregation, akin to a pastor.

55. John 6:28-29,33-34

56. John 6:35,39

57. John 6:47-48,51

58. Iced tea is forbidden according to the LDS Church's dietary restrictions in the Word of Wisdom.

59. See Acts 17:11

60. Mark 16:15

61. See 1 Corinthians 11:28

62. See Luke 21:14-15

63. Author's personal email (August 8, 2005).

64. Excerpts of letter by Schuyler, from author's personal files.

65. Luke 23:42

66. "There are three kingdoms of glory: the celestial kingdom, the terrestrial kingdom, and the telestial kingdom. The glory we inherit will depend on the depth of our conversion, expressed by our obedience to the Lord's commandments." See at https://www.churchofjesuschrist.org/study/manual/gospel-topics/kingdoms-of-glory?lang=eng.

67. See Luke 18:13

68. See Matthew 20:1-16

69. See Luke 15

70. 1 John 4:9,11

71. "Hurricane Wilma was the most intense tropical cyclone ever recorded in the Atlantic basin, and the second-most intense tropical cyclone recorded in the Western Hemisphere." See at https://en.wikipedia.org/wiki/Hurricane_Wilma.

72. The Improvement Era, June 1945, Ward Teaching Message. Concept repeated here: "When the Prophet speaks...the debate is over" (*Ensign*, Nov. 1978, 108), see at https://www.churchofjesuschrist.org/study/ensign/1979/08/the-debate-is-over?lang=eng.

73. Matthew 6:2,19-20

74. See Luke 14:7-11

75. See Revelation 1:9

76. Hebrews 7:22,24-25,27-28

77. Hebrews 8:6,13

78. Hebrews 9:9,14,24,26

79. Hebrews 10:1,9,14,19-22

80. Matthew 25:35,40

81. Romans 7:18-19,24

82. See Matthew 9:17

83. Psalm 22:1

84. 1 Timothy 1:13-15

85. Psalm 22:8

86. Psalm 22:24

87. John 17:17

88. John 14:6

89. See Romans 12:1

90. Isaiah 55:1,3

91. Luke 21:12-15

92. Psalm 23:4

93. 1 Timothy 2:5

94. Galatians 1:8

95. "I told the brethren that the Book of Mormon was the most correct of any book on earth, and the keystone of our religion, and a man would get nearer to God by abiding by its precepts, than by any other book." See at https://www.churchofjesuschrist.org/study/scriptures/bofm/introduction?lang=eng.

96. John 8:32

97. A stake president is a regional overseer of a stake, which is comprised of multiple wards (congregations).

98. Luke 21:16

99. 1 John 4:7-8

100. Doctrine and Covenants 1:30

101. John 3:16

102. Romans 5:8

103. Matthew 10:27

104. Psalm 23:1-2,6

105. Excerpts from letter by Erik, from author's personal files.

106. 1 Samuel 19:2

107. See 1 Corinthians 1:18

108. Luke 21:16

109. See John 3:30

110. "More Than You'll Ever Know," by Watermark

111. John 7:37

112. Luke 21:14-15

113. See Doctrine and Covenants 9:8

114. Jeremiah 17:9

115. Matthew 15:19

116. Excerpts from handwritten letter by Alicia, from author's personal files.

117. Romans 7:24

118. Romans 8:1

119. 1 Corinthians 9:18

MINISTRY CONTACT INFORMATION

Adam's Road Ministry
99 W Plant St
Winter Garden, FL 34787
(407) 656-0885
info@adamsroadministry.com
www.adamsroadministry.com

JESUS IS ENOUGH storehouse
99 W Plant St STE 312
Winter Garden, FL 34787
contact@jesusisenoughstorehouse.com
www.jesusisenoughstorehouse.com

Adam's Road Piano
info@adamsroadpiano.com
www.adamsroadpiano.com

Ex-Mormon Christians United For Jesus
(239) 989-7102
lynn@unveilingmormonism.com
www.unveilingmormonism.com

LIBRARY OF CONGRESS
CATALOGING-IN-PUBLICATION DATA

Names: Wilder, Micah, author.
Title: Passport to heaven : the true story of a zealous Mormon missionary
who discovers the Jesus he never knew / Micah Wilder.
Description: Eugene, Oregon : Harvest House Publishers, [2021] | Summary:
"In Passport to Heaven, Micah shares his gripping journey from living as
a devoted member of the Church of Jesus Christ of Latter-day Saints to
embracing the mercy and freedom that can only be found in Jesus
Christ"-- Provided by publisher.
Identifiers: LCCN 2020050321 (print) | LCCN 2020050322 (ebook) | ISBN
9780736982870 (trade paperback) | ISBN 9780736982887 (ebook)
Subjects: LCSH: Wilder, Micah, 1985- | Church of Jesus Christ of Latter-day
Saints--Controversial literature. | Mormon
missionaries--Florida--Biography. | Ex-church members--Church of Jesus
Christ of Latter-day Saints--Biography. | Protestant
converts--Biography. | LCGFT: Autobiographies.
Classification: LCC BX8695.W54435 A3 2021 (print) | LCC BX8695.W54435
(ebook) | DDC 289.3092 [B]--dc23
LC record available at https://lccn.loc.gov/2020050321
LC ebook record available at https://lccn.loc.gov/2020050322

To learn more about Harvest House books and
to read sample chapters, visit our website:

www.harvesthousepublishers.com

HARVEST HOUSE PUBLISHERS
EUGENE, OREGON